D0500666

12-

WOMAN THE HUNTER

Woman the Hunter

MARY ZEISS STANGE

BEACON PRESS
Boston

Beacon Press
25 Beacon Street
Boston, Massachusetts 02108-2892

Beacon Press books
are published under the auspices of
the Unitarian Universalist Association of Congregations.

02   01   00   99   98   97   8   7   6   5   4   3   2   1

Text design by [sic]
Composition by Wilsted & Taylor Publishing Services

Credits and Library of Congress Cataloging-in-Publication Data
can be found on page 249.

FOR MY PARENTS —
HER STRENGTH OF SPIRIT,
HIS LOVE OF LITERATURE —
IN MEMORY.

Contents

Acknowledgments

Eight years ago I wrote a short essay titled "The Woman Who Hunts," which I presented as a work-in-progress at the Rocky Mountain/Great Plains regional meeting of the American Academy of Religion. I never found a publisher for it, though I received several very complimentary rejection letters from editors, and ample encouragement from colleagues who urged me to continue the line of inquiry initiated in that modest paper. *Woman the Hunter* is the result, and I am deeply grateful to the numerous individuals whose insights and suggestions over the ensuing years have helped this book take shape.

Skidmore College has provided me with a fertile environment for thinking and writing. I owe special thanks to my colleagues in the Department of Philosophy and Religion for our ongoing conversations, as well as for the two departmental colloquia devoted to portions of chapters 2 and 5; I particularly thank Joel Smith and Austin Lewis for agreeing to disagree with me, with such sustained verve and commitment. Colleagues in other departments have been invaluable resources for my interdisciplinary work. I especially thank Susan Bender for important suggestions about where I should be looking in the anthropological literature, Leslie Mechem for consulting about "the slings and arrows of outrageous Artemis," Penelope Ploughman for several pointed and constructive conversations about women and firearms, and John Thomas for explaining what exactly it takes to make a Grand Canyon. Several sister-scholars in the Women's Studies Program read and critiqued the manuscript or parts of it; my thanks especially to Pat Ferraioli, Charlotte Goodman, Mary C. Lynn, and Patricia Rubio. My profound gratitude, too, to Terence Diggory for his very special kind of intellectual support during the past year.

The Skidmore College Faculty Development Committee facilitated my travel to four "Becoming an Outdoors-Woman" workshops, and Phyllis Roth, dean of the faculty, provided supplemental funding that allowed me to stretch a semester's sabbatical leave into the full year that afforded me time to write the bulk of the manuscript. My hearty thanks for this material support. Thanks also to our departmental secretary, Mona Clear, for negotiating my numerous long-distance requests for research assistance during my leave year, and to my student assistants Lisa Rowe for chasing down references and constructing the bibliography, and Kristin DeCou for her help with the index. Finally, I must thank the students I have had the privilege of working with over the past six years at Skidmore, in my feminist theory seminar and in courses on women, religion, and spirituality. This book is immeasurably richer for their insights.

Among colleagues in the field of women's studies in religion, Christine Downing has been and continues to be an inspiration. Words cannot adequately express my appreciation for her sensitive reading of an early version of the manuscript, as well as for twenty years of intellectual, and often emotional, support. In addition, I am indebted to the members of the Women and Religion section of the Pacific/Northwest region of the American Academy of Religion—particularly Joanne Carlson Brown, Karen Barta, Nancy Howell, and the late Winnie Thomm—for their enthusiasm about, and hardheaded critiques of, various phases of this project over the last several years.

I am especially grateful, as well, to Stephen Bodio (who rejected "The Woman Who Hunts" but urged me to take a crack at writing what turned out to be my first hunting story), and to Ted Kerasote, for encouraging my efforts at outdoor writing. Thanks also, in this regard, to the editors at *Sports Afield* magazine. My perceptions of, and writing about, hunting would be far poorer were it not for lively exchanges with sister-outdoorswomen Kitty Beuchert, Barbara Bosworth, Brandy Church, Maggie Hachmeister, Rosemary Laird, Diane Lueck, Linda Poole, Christine Thomas, Lori Wagner, and Berdette Zastrow. Thanks, too, to Cressida Wilde and the late Jorinda Springer, for their lessons by example in female hunting prowess.

Don B. Kates, Jr. and David Kopel have been extraordinarily helpful over the years on the subject of women, guns, and aggression. David Greenberg provided much-needed technical assistance to this computer neophyte, and Helene Schneider helped me collect resources about animal activism.

Two women have been extremely important midwives when it came to the final birthing of this book. My literary agent, Cassandra Leoncini, a careful and critical reader, believed in *Woman the Hunter* at times when I myself was having doubts about what I was up to; her infectious enthusiasm and many good suggestions helped me bring the text into focus. And my editor at Beacon, Marya Van't Hul, wielded a subtle and astute editorial pen in a velvet glove. My deepest gratitude to her for her blend of probing insight and plain good sense, and for her refusal to take no for an answer on a couple of key questions regarding content and structure.

Finally, most ardently, I thank Douglas Stange, my most perceptive reader and my hunting and life partner, for all things gentle and tender, pure and natural.

WOMAN THE HUNTER

Introduction

Roughly one in ten American hunters is female, and hunting's popularity among women is growing. In the past decade, owing no doubt to some extent to the women's and environmental movements in this country, the number of women who hunt has doubled, from one to well over two million. Women are more likely than men to have taken up hunting as adults than as children. More often than not they have to overcome substantial barriers of male sexism and negative peer pressure from other women to become adept at what might be, in the popular mind, the most male-identified cultural pursuit.

Why women hunters, and why now? Is this merely another instance, in the afterwash of second-wave feminism, of women "entering into a previously male-dominated field"? Or does this shift in the composition of the so-called hunting fraternity signal something of deeper social and cultural import? After all, the "field" in question in this case is literally millennia old. Might these women be taking back something that began to be denied us all, roughly ten thousand years ago, in the shift from hunter-gatherer to agrarian cultures that spelled the dawn of patriarchy? This book had its genesis in questions such as these.

The story of Man the Hunter is by now a familiar one. In light of his evolution, a generation and more of scholars—some feminist, some not—have understood and interpreted the host of dualities that have shaped the Western experience of being human. A series of dichotomies characterize Western thinking about human culture and nonhuman nature: male/female, mind/body, civilization/wilderness, domestic/wild, aggressive/passive, dominator/victim. Historically these dualisms have determined the "natural" scheme of things in which women and men have occupied their relative places. "Man" has conventionally been more closely identified with those forces that work to overcome and manipulate nature, "woman" has been more closely identified

1

with that nonhuman natural realm. Whether one looks at the tradition of patriarchal scholarship or at recent ecofeminist critiques thereof, the story is essentially the same. Men, alienated from nature, buy culture and control at the price of violent aggression. Women bring into play values of nurturance and nonviolence, but at the cost of being, like the nonhuman natural world, victimized by male domination.

To the extent that hunting has served both patriarchy and feminism as a root metaphor for men's activity in the world, Woman the Hunter is a necessarily disruptive figure. She upsets the equilibrium of the conventional interpretations on both sides. This no doubt helps to account for the virtual invisibility of women hunters, both in most popular literature (positive and negative) about hunting and in the various strains of feminist discourse. Regarding the former, the facts that some women in some cultures have always hunted, and that more women in Western cultures are hunting than perhaps ever before, are understandably unsettling to macho-traditionalists who want hunting to remain a rite of initiation into masculine culture and an occasion for "male bonding." Yet these same facts certainly ought to be of interest to feminist interpreters, and especially to those who engage in what has come to be called ecofeminist analysis, that is, who focus on the relation of women to nature. The erasure of the fact of women's hunting from feminist discourse is therefore more than a little puzzling.

That women's hunting has not appeared within the purview of feminist analysis owes, I demonstrate in what follows, to the fact that American ecofeminism often unwittingly, but nonetheless deliberately, accepts and perpetuates traditional gender stereotypes about femaleness and femininity, and about women's identity with nature—their "innate" passivity and nonviolence—against men's inborn aggressiveness and alienation from the nonhuman world. Woman the Hunter is—on both the literal and metaphorical levels—a direct challenge to these stereotypes. She affords a vital perspective that has to date been lacking in feminist discussions about women and men, nature and violence.

The rhythms of life and death in the natural world appear differently, I suggest, when sensed with a hunter's heart and seen through a hunter's eyes. I am, of course, far from the first to suggest this. In *A Sand County Almanac,* Aldo Leopold remarks at one point (in the gender-exclusive language of the 1940s) that there are "four categories of outdoors men." These categories, he observes, "have nothing to do with sex or age, or accoutrements: they represent four diverse habits of the human eye." By Leopold's classification, we are respectively deer hunters, duck hunters, bird hunters, or nonhunters. And what we are by inclination affects how we perceive and behave in the natural world:

> The deer hunter habitually watches the next bend; the duck hunter watches the skyline; the bird hunter watches the dog; the non-hunter does not watch.
>
> When the deer hunter sits down he sits where he can see ahead, and with his back to something. The duck hunter sits where he can see overhead, and behind something. The non-hunter sits where he is comfortable.[1]

Leopold was not, I think, talking merely about alternate methods of nature appreciation. Habits of eye are also habits of mind. The way one engages one's natural surroundings is also the way one engages ideas. The hunter's habit of mind has more to do with a mode of awareness, a discreet style of engagement, than with pulling a trigger or drawing a bowstring.

Following a line of thinking is much like treading a game trail. The way is often less linear than it first appears, especially if one diverges from the main path. I am primarily a deer hunter. This means that I keep my attention at ground level, focusing on the tracks and signs of concrete reality, with an eye toward the next curve in a trail, attentive to the possibilities that hide beyond, that might leap out at any moment. It also means that I am used to being uncomfortable. Indeed, like all who share a hunting habit of mind, I believe some measure of intellectual discomfort is a very good—in fact, a necessary—thing.

It was chiefly this fact, perhaps, that drew me to the radical feminist critique of patriarchy when I began college teaching in the late 1970s. Radical feminism occupied the cutting edge in a quite literal sense, slicing through the Western intellectual tradition in such a way that none of the conventional wisdom about femaleness/femininity and maleness/masculinity could be comfortable again. A generation of feminist scholars and activists developed various strategies for intellectual and political change, but it was radical feminism that went farther and deeper than any other approach. It provided the template for gender analysis. Contemporary women's scholarship is arguably unthinkable without that radical foundation.

Yet somewhere along the line, radical feminism ceased to be radical, in the best sense of that term. It had begun in outrage at the uncovering of the roots of male dominance and female subordination, laying bare the social and biological facts so as to demolish inherited stereotypes about the "essential" differences between women and men. Some would argue that it is still engaged in this work. But over the last ten years or so, a widely remarked essentialist strand has woven its way into radical feminist discourse about women, men, and their relations both to each other and to the natural world. In idealizing female biology and psychology (and, too often, demonizing the male), radical feminism today reinforces precisely those gender dualisms it originally sought to dismantle.

This is perhaps nowhere clearer than in discussions of women's relation to violence and their capacity to do as well as to suffer harm. In establishing women as essentially "biophilic" (that is, "life-loving") and nurturing, radical feminism stresses women's incapacity for violent aggression, aside from isolated cases of self-defense against batterers, or of "male-identified" women who are really dupes of patriarchy. The charge that this insistence upon women's fundamental innocence amounts to "victim feminism," while too facile, is not entirely unjustified. Yet the fact that this argument has most frequently been made by antifeminists like Camille Paglia and Christina Hoff Sommers has allowed radical feminism to remain (too) comfortably perched on its moral high ground. This is especially true with regard to those distinctly American strains of ecofeminism inspired by radical feminism.

Women and animals, in this view, are necessarily the prey, men the predators.

The testimony of women hunters, however, confounds this interpretation. Take, for example, the following narrative by a seventeen-year-old deer hunter about shooting her first turkey:

> The bird was less than thirty yards away and I had never been that close before. So when it let out a gobble from that range it sounded so loud and so deep, like it came from the pit of its soul, I wanted to run! But I didn't, I just watched as it walked behind a large tree. He went into a full strut, and I had a chance to put my gun up. I was doing everything just as I was taught. I waited. I had the bead from the Model 37 Ithaca 12 gauge right on his head, but I waited. Then it happened, the bird stretched up his neck and pulled in his fanned tailfeathers. He was beautiful and he was going to be dead. I gently squeezed the trigger, never feeling the recoil.[2]

Or this remark by a middle-aged Texas housewife and college student, who had been deer-hunting for years with her husband but had just experienced her first women-only outdoor skills-training workshop: "With men, you have to be one-dimensional. Here, you can be multifaceted. You can decompartmentalize your life. You can talk about babies and bullets in the same conversation!"[3] Or this reflection by a Montana nature writer, on why she decided to actively take up hunting:

> Walking behind a man with a rifle used to make me feel like the original natural woman. Male and female, single file: The hunter and the helpmate. Sometimes movie soundtracks would play in my head since I wasn't using it for much else. Then I got religion— moon religion. This rebirth came not in a vision in the night but in a figurine of indeterminate yellowish-white material that may have come from a garage sale for all I know, I never asked the man on whose windowsill she sat. Artemis: Greek moon goddess, huntress. Flowing up from the bare back of a fluid steed, she surged forward with her pack of hounds, wild, elusive, needful of nothing, capable of anything, open-eyed knower of nature. Helpmate to her own damn self. *This*, I suddenly knew, was a *real* woman.[4]

Statements such as these suggest an intricacy of perspective far subtler than radical feminism—or any them-versus-us perspective—can comfortably comprehend. These women, and millions of others like them, do not appear to be hapless pawns of patriarchy. They do not seem to want to be, or to act like, men. They may or may not identify themselves as feminists, but whether or not they do, they have in common the fact that in taking up weapons for the explicit purpose of killing, they are shattering one of Western culture's oldest and most firmly entrenched taboos. The image of a woman "armed and dangerous" is obviously profoundly unsettling to the Western cultural psyche. Hence its rejection, with approximately equal hostility, if for somewhat different reasons, by both macho males and radical feminists.

If ecofeminism is right—and I believe that in many ways it is—that the treatment of nonhuman nature in Western cultures mirrors the patriarchal domination of women by men through recorded history, then the relation of women to hunting surely warrants a much closer look. In hunting, such apparently opposed functions as killing and nurturing, aggression and attraction, and power and vulnerability are paradoxically united. Convenient distinctions like that between "nature" and "culture," for example, evaporate in the face of the fact that from the vantage point of the hunter and the hunted, the only distinction that matters, and is compellingly real, is the one between life and death.

My immediate concern is the way certain kinds of feminist faith-statements prop up and perpetuate patriarchal biases about how women and men relate to nature and to violence. Hence at many points I focus on specific variations on the feminist theme: radical feminism, radical ecofeminism, goddess spirituality. But these variations, all of them distinctly American, are in turn rooted in two far broader cultural matrices: the history of American naturalism on one hand, and contemporary popular environmentalism on the other. American feminism has too often tended to pick up and amplify some of the worst tendencies of both, in romanticizing and idealizing the nonhuman world and in oversimplifying human interactions with the nature of which we are, in fact, very much a part. And so my topic, ultimately, has implications far broader than an argument within feminism. It has to do with the way we as a society tend to evade some social and enviromental issues that make us distinctly uncomfortable.

We live today in a world of deceptively easy choices. The "ethical vegetarian" who persists in ignoring the consequences of large-scale agriculture, and the meat-eater who would rather not think about how a steer becomes a Big Mac, are in this regard equally self-deluded. But as poet/environmentalist Gary Snyder has remarked, "Innumerable little seeds are sacrifices to the food-chain. A parsnip in the ground is a marvel of living chemistry, making sugars and flavors from earth, air, water. And if we do eat meat, it is the life, the bounce, the swish, of a great alert being with keen ears and lovely eyes, with foursquare feet and a huge beating heart that we eat, let us not deceive ourselves."[5] It is in this light that meat, as environmental philosopher Paul Shepard remarks, can be "the best of foods," in that it embodies the encounter of life and death.[6] However, this can only happen to the extent that a society perceives, and celebrates, the literal and symbolic value of the hunt.

The unthinking exploitation of nonhuman animals—and increasingly, of human ones—in contemporary American society would appear to foreclose the possibility of such valuation. But it is a deceptively easy evasion to argue that since we cannot adopt traditional or archaic lifeways, we ought no longer to value the symbolism of that world view. We (or the vast majority of us) cannot "go primitive" literally, of course, and most of us would not want to. But we can, in one way or another, "stray back into the woods."[7] Not only can we, but at the present historical juncture our very lives and souls may depend on it. The key question, then, is how we go about doing it.

In order to do it honestly, we need first of all to disabuse ourselves of the widespread fiction that there is such a thing as "nonconsumptive use" of nature. The distinction between "consumptive use" of nature and wildlife (hunting, trapping, fishing, and so on) and "nonconsumptive use" (hiking, camping, birdwatching, nature photography, and the like) originated in the field of wildlife management. The language has subsequently been appropriated by animal-rights activists and others opposed, for various reasons, to so-called blood sports. This is unfortunate, since these oppositional categories are not only imprecise, they are down-right misleading.[8] No matter how lightly one treads the earth, one leaves one's mark in myriad ways, not all of them intended or even immediately evident. The popular fiction that it is possible to just "let nature be nature" is, as novelist Margaret Atwood re-marks in a different (but not entirely unrelated) context, in fact, "a lie which was always more disastrous than the truth would have been."[9] It is in this regard that, as Shepard put it in an important early article on "A Theory of the Value of Hunting," the hunter can serve as an "agent of awareness" for culture at large:

> What does the hunt actually do for the hunter? It confirms his con-tinuity with the dynamic life of animal populations, his role in the complicated cycle of elements . . . and in the patterns of the flow of energy. . . . Aldo Leopold postulated a "split rail value" for hunt-ing, a reinactment of past conditions when our contact with the natural environment and the virtues of this contact were less ob-scured by the conditions of modern urban life. . . . Regardless of technological advance, man remains part of and dependent on na-ture. The necessity of signifying and recognizing this relationship remains. The hunter is our agent of awareness.[10]

Hunters take to the field now, for the same inner reasons they always have: for food, of course, but also for connection, and for knowledge about what it means to be human in our complex and increasingly fragile world. It is not simply that, as Clarissa Pinkola Estes has remarked, the shadow that trots behind us is four-footed.[11] "The world," in Snyder's well-turned phrasing, "is our consciousness, and it surrounds us. . . . The depths of the mind, the unconscious, are our inner wilderness areas, and that is where a bobcat is *right now.*"[12] It is against this backdrop that descriptions of hunting as a "wildlife management tool" tend to ring, if not exactly false, at least fundamentally incomplete. So, too, do depictions of hunting as a nostalgic reminder of our pre-industrial past.[13] It is surely more than that. It trivializes the complexity of human hunting and all it can represent socially and symbolically, to relegate it to the realm of nostalgia, or for that matter of the pleasure-seeking implied in the word "sport." People hunt for various reasons, but fundamentally—as the literature about hunting widely attests—they hunt for meaning.[14]

Today a growing percentage of American hunters are female. Like their male counterparts, these women hunt for meaning, to express themselves as members of the human race and of the wider animal community. But, given the millennia of women's literal and figurative disempowerment under patriarchy, theirs is necessarily hunting with a difference. And, I suggest, it is in their wildness that we might now more fruitfully seek clues about the preservation of our world.[15]

This does not mean that I think every woman should hunt. (I do not think every man should, either.) Hunting, like childbearing, involves commitment, skill, training, and dedication. For most of human history and in most places, it has been respected and valued for these reasons. But like childbirth, hunting can function symbolically for those who do not experience it literally. It is in this sense, I think, that the hunter functions as an "agent of awareness" for culture at large. Woman the Hunter can be that for feminism as well.

I remarked above that the rhythms of life and death in the natural world appear differently when seen through hunters' eyes. This work might be regarded as an extended meditation on that theme, and on what it means, more especially, when the eyes are those of a woman. I approach this discussion as a feminist, with a conviction that Woman the Hunter is a figure contemporary feminism needs to seriously reckon with. In grounding a discussion of hunting in female experience, however, I hope less to accomplish something new than to imagine a sense of possibilities that were lost ages ago but that finally—now, at what might be the end of women's prehistory[16]—are once more recoverable.

A few general remarks about what follows:

Writing as a feminist, I believe it is crucial to situate my scholarly work in relation to my lived experience. Given my subject, I cannot but incorporate some of my own experiences during the dozen years that I have been hunting. However, because I intend to project neither an apologetic nor a prophetic stance, I determined early on in this project to keep my personal reflections on hunting as clearly distinct as possible from the scholarly analysis. Each chapter is preceded, therefore, by a narrative prologue. The prologues bear a (sometimes direct, sometimes rather oblique) relationship to the academic discussions that follow them; in each instance, they suggest questions—some of them excruciatingly poignant—relating to the ethical and philosophical dimensions of hunting. These narratives are autobiographical. I trust they help to illustrate the complex value of a woman's hunting in ways a mere scholarly discussion cannot.

Hunting has become a highly charged issue of late, in some circles. Readers who steadfastly believe that all hunting is wrong in any circumstances probably need read no further. I do not imagine I will change their minds. However, neither do I intend to defend all hunting in all circumstances. There are some activities that go by the name of hunting that should not. And, as in every other sphere of human action, there are hunters who are irresponsible or unethical. There are also, however, hunters who possess not only deeper knowledge and more comprehensive appreciation of the workings of the natural environment than most nonhunters do, but also more sharply honed ethical and aesthetic senses about the world of nonhuman nature. They are my subject. And I believe a higher percentage of female, than of male, hunters fall into this latter category.

Two final notes about the language and argumentative method I employ. I consistently use gender-inclusive language—"humanity" or "human beings"—when I mean all of us, and "man" or "men" with reference to the male of our species. I do not, of course, alter the language of quotations. In those few cases where (as above) the "inclusive male" sneaks into a quotation with which I obviously otherwise agree, I ask the reader to be tolerant of the phrasing—it grates on my nerves, too.

As to method: A friend who read an early version of this manuscript described its argumentative style as "hunterlike," which of course I took to be a compliment. What she was getting at, and what the reader will discover, is that the inquiry that follows is deliberate, stealthy, and seldom moves in a straight line. Its logic is the logic of game trails and riverbanks. I invite the reader to explore with me.

1

Tracks

It was that time of year, late October, when the days suddenly cease to drift lazily into evenings. That time of year, the sun when it sets seems to plummet, abruptly calling an end to daylight and stealing its fire away to smaller, cozier skies. Or so it would have seemed to, had thick clouds and a light, steadily falling snow not masked the precise moment of its descent behind the peaks of the Bitterroot Range to our west.

We were antelope hunting, my husband, Doug, and I—or rather, he was hunting, in the active sense of stalking, armed, with the intention of killing, and I was along for the trip. This had been our habit for somewhat more than a year, since shortly after we married and I moved with him to Montana. Before then, Doug had been, customarily, a solitary hunter. When I expressed a desire to accompany him, he initially resisted the idea. "You're the satin-sheets type, Mary. You wouldn't like it." But I persisted. Hunting was so much, and so deeply, central to the identity of this man I loved that a part of me felt I would not truly know him until I shared something of this experience. Besides, I enjoyed the outdoors, was in good physical shape, and craved the exercise. All this was easy enough to explain to him, and to myself.

Less simple to articulate was an intimation that what he did in the field bore some immediate relation to what I did in our vegetable garden. Many years of growing fruits and vegetables had convinced me of the importance—much of it symbolic, to be sure—of being involved with my food, having some sort of (for want of a better word) personal relationship with it.

12

It had begun to occur to me that unless I participated in some way, at the very least imaginatively, in procuring meat, I would feel impelled to give up eating it. I could not always let the blood be on somebody else's hands, the dirt under someone else's fingernails.

So, horribly underequipped when it came to clothes and other outdoor gear, I shared with him drizzly mornings crouched in reeds awaiting flights of ducks and geese, and sunswept afternoons walking the edges of stubble fields flushing grouse and pheasants. In spring we hunted turkey in eastern Montana national forest land, and hiked into high wilderness in the western part of the state looking for bear. In early fall we scouted elk in that same steep country. "You're a good sport, Mare," he would cheer me, when I had flopped waist-deep in an irrigation ditch I was trying to ford, or had developed blisters on my blisters from miles of trekking in ill-fitting boots, or had gone more days than I like to remember without shower or shampoo. For my part, I relished the experiences. Most of them, at any rate.

Antelope hunting, Doug had assured me, tended to be especially fine in Montana, what with the October nights merely on the chilly side and the days brilliant and generally balmy. Before the season opened we scouted some public land in the southwestern part of the state, not far from the Centennial Peaks that mark the Idaho border. It was broad, rolling, high sage country nestled among rugged hillsides. One area, a bowl-shaped valley tucked between a steeply rising slope on the north and a wide saddle to the south, looked especially promising. Several times we sighted there what appeared to be a resident herd of about two dozen pronghorns, including at least three bucks.

It was to this spot that we returned a few weeks later, under leaden skies and a shower of fluffy, early-season snow. As we made our way along a two-track road to our campsite, dusk was rapidly overtaking the scant remaining afternoon light. We parked and set out on foot. Visibility was too poor to see anything more than a few yards away. We walked a broad circle, getting reacquainted with the lay of the land, and as we were heading back to our truck, Doug noticed tracks. Nothing distinct, just the merest suggestion, snow that had been kicked aside here and there by several sets of hooves. It was too late for stalking now. It would have to be enough, overnight, to know the antelope were still there.

Lacking a camper, we slept in the back of our Toyota pickup. As the snow tapered off and the night sky cleared, the temperature must have plunged below zero. In the morning, even our toothpaste was frozen solid. Doug set about melting some water on the camp stove. "Nothing like these balmy October hunts," I mumbled through chattering teeth as I wrestled, in the back of the pickup, to draw on as many layers of clothes as I could muster. "You're a good sport, Mare," Doug grinned as he handed me a steaming mug of tea.

"I'm pretty sure they'll be right over that ridge, where we saw the tracks last night," he gestured as we set out. Two or three inches of snow had fallen. We made our way up and over the wide saddle we'd walked several hours earlier, expecting the pronghorns to be in the valley on the other side. They weren't . . . but they had been recently. We quickly discovered their now unmistakable prints in the snow, but leading in a direction roughly opposite to what Doug had predicted. Pronghorns often move in circles, and it was likely they would work a sweeping arc through higher country then descend back toward the valley. But rather than try to second-guess them, Doug suggested (at this point in our hunting career together, his role was to "suggest" and mine to "agree") we simply follow the spoor. This seemed logical enough to me. It would be my first bona fide experience tracking game, and at least would be a good way to get warm. As I later realized, it would also change me in a decisive, if barely discernable and perhaps not altogether logical, way.

I had always imagined animal tracks as rather like an Ariadne's thread, leading unerringly to the heart of some mystery. Yet had Ariadne's thread been so tangled as the trail we were following now, Theseus might never have found his way out of that maze. Time and again the trail dead-ended, doubled back on itself, zigzagged up and down hillsides and along ridges. Doug would lose it, then I would pick it up again, or vice versa. Sometimes it would fork and each of us would follow a branch, to be reunited in due course. As the morning wore on, we began to retrace our own tracks, which led to some momentary uncertainty: Were those pronghorns amusing themselves at our expense, or had we begun traveling in circles, having lost the antelope completely? No, that was impossible.

The tempo of pursuit quickened with every turn, every surprise in the trail. My pulse racing, I was gulping rarefied high-country air by the quart, alive in every sense. By midmorning, though we had yet to sight the herd, their tantalizing realness and presence in those tracks convinced me I would see them, I must see them, soon.

We found a fresh lead in the trail where the herd had, as it were, spun out of its orbit, angling off down and around an expansively curving hillside. Doug took off in this new direction, back toward the valley after all. I followed several yards behind. Working his way along the hillside, he suddenly dropped down on all fours: "They're right . . . over . . . there!" he whispered hoarsely, and I knew from his body language that meant they were close indeed. Ready to explode with anticipation, I crouched down as well and carefully worked my way toward him. He was just out of my sight now, a few yards around the slope to my right. I knew he was positioning himself to shoot.

All of a sudden a rifle blast split the air, followed almost instantly by a second crack. I felt oddly disoriented. I was already familiar with the way mountain air can distort the snap of a rifle, but these shots seemed to come from the next hillside over, a couple of hundred yards to my left. Doug jumped up, waving his arms frantically. "Hey! What the hell do you think you're doing?" he roared in that direction.

"Whaa—?" came the bemused response. Then I saw them: two men in red plaid jackets, their only "hunter orange" on their caps. (We both, on the

other hand, wore enough blaze orange to be easily visible a mile off.) That
they had just done something incredibly irresponsible—shooting toward a
rocky hillside where there were other people—was undeniable. Bullets do
crazy things when they ricochet, and Doug was at that moment more alive
than I to the precise amount of danger we had been in.

I, however, was simply furious that these interlopers had taken shots at
the antelope herd we had spent all morning tracking. I knew better than
to think of the antelope, or of any wild things, as "ours," exactly. But we
certainly had a stronger claim to them—or a stronger relationship with
them—than those others to whom our wrath seemed utterly incomprehen-
sible. The pronghorns took off across the valley, racing up the precipitous
hill bounding its northern end. The men in plaid followed. We sat and
watched for several minutes as they huffed and puffed up the steep incline.
It was a futile chase.

Doug hunted the rest of that day, I following along somewhat half-
heartedly, on the downside of the morning's adrenaline rush. We saw nothing further of the herd, and we heard no more shooting. Toward nightfall,
as we were making our way back to the pickup and discussing the next day's
strategy—should we stay here, or go elsewhere?—the antelope herd burst
into view ahead of us, running straight across our path, hugging the same
ridge where our hunting day had begun. For some reason, probably because
they spied our truck not too far off, they slowed to a stroll. I froze in my
tracks, and Doug shouldered his rifle. Firing offhand, he missed, and the
herd again broke into a run. He fired again, another clear miss, and they
were out of sight. That was all right. It had been, aside from the men in plaid,
a good day.

As it turned out, we would not have any antelope in our freezer that winter. But the fruits of days afield are measured in different ways. That was, I
would realize somewhat later, the day I realized I could no longer merely
follow along. I had read a message in those tracks. I must be a hunter.

❧

People become actively involved in hunting in various ways. Some like to start small, shooting birds or small game, working up to larger prey. The idea of thus easing oneself into killing troubles me. It implies a hierarchy of values that makes the death of a rabbit or squirrel somehow less significant than that of an elk or a bear. I cannot watch the death-arrested flight of a duck or a pheasant without an inner pang. Should the day come when I could, I would never shoulder a shotgun again.

My first kill was a mule deer buck. It had seemed a long time coming. Because it would be a year or two before I had a rifle of my own, Doug and I shared a gun—his Browning semi-auto .30/06—between us. Throughout antelope season, he would pass me the rifle when a good shot—nothing too long or too fancy—presented itself. Twice I missed excellent opportunities. The first time I couldn't manage to get the rifle's safety off in time. The second time I neglected to chamber a cartridge before firing. Ever conscious that I'd never intentionally killed anything bigger than a spider, I had clutched.

"You've just got to do it," Doug said matter-of-factly. In part, I understood that he meant I simply had to get this over with: Subsequent deaths would never be easy, but the first one is indeed hard. Yet I also understood that if the year's worth of thought, feeling, and practice that followed my first antelope hunt meant anything, then I just had to do it. Otherwise I should stay home. Let the blood be on somebody else's hands.

I shot my first deer in the Finger Buttes of southeastern Montana: a rugged area of badlands and knobby outcroppings that look rather as if they might be more at home in the desert southwest. It is terrific mule deer country. There were several inches of snow already on the ground, but this mid-November day was fine: sunny, clear, and just cold enough to make several miles' hiking in rough terrain pleasurable.

The rut was in its early stages. We stalked a particular buck and doe for the entire morning. It seemed they were always far enough ahead of us to be just out of reasonable range. Finally, as they were cresting a ridge, the buck stopped and stood in profile, as mule deer often do. He was about two hundred yards away. Resting the rifle on a boulder, I tried to calm my breathing, pretty much succeeded, and squeezed the trigger. The safety was still on. The buck ambled over the ridge and out of sight.

I sat down on the ground and cried out of sheer frustration. I should perhaps point out that the safety on a Browning rifle is easy to operate and virtually foolproof. I could not blame the gun, or even my novice's reflexes, for my failure to shoot. I had the hunting equivalent of writer's block. The spirit and the flesh were both willing, but something held me back. "Maybe I should just go home and forget it, maybe I'm really not up to this," I whimpered. I almost thought I meant it.

"OK, look, we'll just go to the top of that next rise, and see whether we can see where those deer went. Then we'll turn back," Doug said. "I doubt you're going to get another shot like that one, though. They're too skittish now."

I collected myself and, resigned to failure, trudged toward the top of the rise. We stood there, glassing the area, seeing no movement anywhere. Then Doug, who was standing nearer the edge than I, eased back and wordlessly pointed straight down. I crept up and peered over the rock ledge. There, fifty or so yards directly below, were a buck and a doe. They may or may not have been the ones we had been stalking. They were completely unaware of us.

It was an awkward shot, but the close range improved my chances of making it. Sitting cross-legged at the edge of the rock wall, I aimed straight down. The buck was looking away; I placed the crosshair of the scope on his back. With an inward prayer part petition, part apology, I pulled the trigger. The buck staggered a few yards, and collapsed. The doe lingered briefly, then ran away.

The tears that rushed to my eyes issued from a collision of remorse and release. The former, because the killing hurt; the latter, because it was done well. I bore, I realized, a profound responsibility, and always would.

I made my way down to my buck. He was beautiful. I was elated. By the time we had field-dressed him, the shadows were growing long. We had walked about three miles into the buttes on our stalk: too far to drag a large deer with such a late start. We decided to leave him at the foot of an unmistakable landmark—a tall, steeple-shaped rock formation—and retrieve him the next day. And so I enjoyed an unencumbered sunset hike back to the truck, and then home to a celebratory pizza and a dreamless sleep.

The next day dawned frigid and foggy. As we drove back to the Finger Buttes, Doug remarked cheerily that one great thing about Montana weather is that fog never lasts long. Well, it nearly never does. Our steeple landmark was enshrouded in murk somewhere out there, and although we could tease our way through the badlands with a compass, the exercise was pointless without that signpost to orient us.

By midmorning it became clear that the only way we would find my buck would be to follow our own tracks of the day before. Since that meant retracing a lengthy stalk, it also meant going considerably out of our way, but it seemed the only reasonable solution. So we began to track ourselves, the first snow trail I had followed since that antelope hunt more than a year earlier.

It's an odd sensation, following one's own tracks. The way was at once familiar and strange, yesterday's dazzling wide-open vistas and looming rock prominences equally concealed now behind an impenetrable grey curtain. Since our destination was itself something of a secret now, it felt much like tracking an animal, yielding a kindred sense of mystery about the eventual outcome of the pursuit.

We soon discovered we were not the first to have traced our snow trail. Our boot prints bore the fresh imprint of deer hooves at many points along our meandering way. The deer, of course, had not been tracking us. They had merely taken advantage of the path we had cut in the snow, in much the same way one treads an established game trail through the woods. Still, this presented a neat inversion of hunter and quarry. What, I wondered, drifts through a doe's consciousness as she traces this alien trail of mine? Does she ponder my presence as I do hers?

We followed our trail to the rock ledge, then down to where my buck had fallen. Just as we arrived, the fog parted precisely enough so we could finally see our steeple landmark. This made it possible to set compass bearings for a more direct way back out. And a good thing, too, for the thick snow that was now beginning to fall would quickly erase our trail.

It was nightfall by the time we made it back to the pickup. By morning, all trace of our tracks had disappeared. Only a few deer, and coyotes, and magpies knew we had passed their way.

Either of these stories might have been titled, "The Day I Became a Hunter." In the first instance, the title might be true in emotional terms; the second perhaps more literally. Yet in neither case does the title feel right to me. Recollecting these experiences now, in the broader context of my life and memory, I find myself hard-pressed to discern a time when I was not a hunter. Such is the process of self-discovery. We spend a lifetime learning to become what we in some sense have already, always, been.

How is it that tracks—those most ephemeral of realities, quite literally here today and gone tomorrow—can claim so much attention? What is it we recognize in them? Perhaps our animal selves, or our animal past. I do not know as much as I would like to about those tracks—human and nonhuman—I retrace now in memory. But I do know that they lead me to myself.

I also know that they are very, very old.

Plants Stand Still, But Animals Move:

The Hunting Hypothesis Revisited

The trail this inquiry traces begins with the so-called hunting hypothesis of human origins. Man the Hunter and his helpmate, Woman the Gatherer, achieved near-mythic status in the archaeological and ethnographic literature of the last generation. Yet these figures are clearly less harkings-back to the dawn of human prehistory than they are recapitulations of key Western gender stereotypes about men and women in relation to each other and to nonhuman nature. The assumptions at work in both the hunting hypothesis itself and in subsequent feminist critiques of it are distinctly rooted in late twentieth-century Western sensibilities and concerns: the alienation of the human from nonhuman nature, the universality of male hunting and female nonaggression, the idea of male questing versus female nesting, the problematic impact of human technological advance on the natural environment. Therein lies the power of Man the Hunter and Woman the Gatherer: Their story is our own, masquerading as a reconstruction of the past, that is, of the essentially human. The various "just-so" stories involving these figures present more or less comfortable variations on some fairly nettlesome themes having to do with the complexity of human societies and psychologies.

We want to know about how we began, to gain some understanding of (or make excuses for?) what we are now, and perhaps what we can be: In our beginning is our end. Stories of origins are so consistently compelling precisely because the past is an ideal screen onto which to project present realities. It is therefore essential to bear in mind that any theory about the way we were is, more or less self-consciously, a hypothesis about the way we are. Of course, as we shall see, it depends very much on who is telling the story.

JUST-SO STORIES

Imagine a group of people walking beside a lake in East Africa two million years ago: five thin, wiry men who carry spears for throwing at game or enemies walk rapidly away from the group. These hunters will search for bushbuck and may be gone for several days while the women and children stay behind. The women move slowly; they are pregnant, carrying toddlers, and besides they are not going anywhere that day. They will stay close to the edge of the lake, cooking the remnants of the meat the men brought several days before, maybe looking for snails or gathering some squalid roots from the rather sparse vegetation. They will wait patiently until their men return with meat. Each woman was chosen by her husband, so the legend goes, on the basis of her loveliness, especially her prominent breasts and buttocks. Her father or brother gave her to her husband on the basis of his hunting skills and fierceness. Other men will not seduce her because they fear her husband's anger.[1]

Thus anthropologist Frances Dahlberg has characterized the "just-so" story that, until fairly recently, dominated theorizing about human biological and social evolution. The story of Man the Hunter and Woman the Gatherer begins with the impact of Darwin's evolutionary theory, and a few early fossil discoveries, on a budding anthropological imagination. They suggested a developmental scheme that, by the middle of the twentieth century, would be summed up in any high school biology text via a simple illustration. A series of figures, it begins with a familiar enough simian, say a baboon, loping along in profile. Next in the sequence, a hairy Australopithecine, vaguely suggesting a "missing link," slouches toward bipedalism. Next comes a slope-foreheaded Neanderthal, fully erect and clutching a stone axe, but obviously too dim-witted to survive in a complex world. Finally—tall, handsome, and gripping a flint-tipped spear—*Homo sapiens sapiens* strides confidently off the page.

That we evolved from, or at least alongside, our fellow primates was abundantly clear. But how? What had caused the decisive adaptations that marked the beginnings of humanity? This was a puzzle to scientists, until they hit upon what came to be known as the hunting hypothesis of human origins. Relying on two sources of data—observations of primate behavior on one hand, and of modern hunter-gatherer societies on the other—anthropologists and ethologists of the mid-twentieth century constructed a story of disarmingly elegant simplicity. In their reading, once our hominid ancestors had decided to come down out of the trees, they had to accomplish a series of developmental tasks quite evidently beyond the ken of your average simian. In summarizing the evolutionary agenda that had confronted the so-called Killer Ape, Desmond Morris stated the essential elements of the hunting hypothesis as follows: "First, he had to hunt if he was to survive. Second, he had to have a better brain to make up for his poor hunting body. Third, he had to have a longer childhood to grow the bigger brain and to educate it. Fourth, the females had to stay put and mind the babies while the males went hunting. Fifth, the males had to cooperate with one another on the hunt. Sixth, they had to stand up straight and use weapons for the hunt to succeed."[2]

"First, he had to hunt . . ." The sequence is deliberate, and telling, for in this view, hunting was the linchpin of human evolution: Had ape never determined to turn killer, those adaptations which mark the human animal would never have burst upon the evolutionary scene. Hunting spurred the development of those characteristics that make us human: intelligence, erect posture (bipedalism), language, the spirit of cooperation, the construction of tools with which to interact with the environment, and—perhaps most importantly—the sexual division of labor.

Man, according to proponents of the hunting hypothesis, needed intelligence to recognize and remember good hunting areas, to anticipate animal behavior, and to effectively stalk his quarry. He needed to walk erect to see above tall grass and to free his hands for spear-throwing, and he needed language to com-

municate with fellow members of his hunting band. He needed
to learn to cooperate, not only during the hunt but after, when it
came time to share meat with the rest of the group. Above all,
he needed tools—specifically weapons—to successfully bring
down large game. Over time, the theory went, these same tools
also came in handy for the purpose of defending his family group
against outside invaders. Hence the act of hunting also yielded
the human characteristic of courage—as Robert Ardrey described it, "a bundle of qualities in itself: willingness to dare,
to persevere, to respond to challenge by attack rather than escape." [3]

Early man would never have been able to manage all this hard
work had he not been able to count on early woman to "stay put
and mind the babies." The hunting way of life, some anthropologists argued, was thus also responsible for the development of the
nuclear family structure and the very idea of a home. Because
family and home needed to be defended against invasion, men
drew on their weapons, and their courage, to develop the art of
war. Women, meanwhile, kept the home fires burning, took an interest in the plants they gathered near the homesite, and eventually originated horticulture. [4]

The sexual division of labor was, thus, crucial to the hunting
hypothesis. This is one of the central arguments of Sherwood
Washburn and C. S. Lancaster's "The Evolution of Hunting"—a
massively influential essay that quickly achieved a sort of canoni-
cal status in the literature about Man the Hunter. In their view,
human hunting was to be distinguished from predation by other
mammals precisely because the "hunting way of life" depended
for its success on leaving the major work of evolution to the males.
Humans never would have evolved at all if they had hunted like
other species—wolves, say—in which both males and females
are active hunters. For them, the notion of a social pattern based
on women's sharing in the hunt was patently absurd:

> Human females do not go out and hunt and then regurgitate to
> their young when they return. Human young do not stay in dens
> but are carried by their mothers. Male wolves do not kill with

tools, butcher, and share with females who have been gathering. In an evolutionary sense the whole human pattern is new, and it is the success of this particularly human way that dominated human evolution and determined the relation of biology and culture for thousands of years.[5]

The developers of the hunting hypothesis rather grudgingly recognized that another thing that sets humans apart from wolves is the fact that in virtually all contemporary hunter-gatherer cultures, hunting accounts for a relatively small proportion of the total food supply. Vegetable foods, fish and shellfish, and small game—the products of women's gathering—generally represent between sixty and eighty percent of the diet of contemporary hunter-gatherers.[6] They also recognized that prehistoric peoples enjoyed a much lower population density, and richer and more varied vegetable resources, than any contemporary hunter-gatherer cultures. Nevertheless their observation of these cultures led them to conclude that "hunting is so universal and is so consistently a male activity that it must have been a basic part of the early cultural adaptation, even if it provided a modest proportion of the food supplies."[7]

And besides, anatomy was destiny. Males were physically better suited for hunting, being larger, faster, and stronger than females. They could afford to range farther from home, since unlike the females they were not hampered by pregnancy and child-rearing. It just so happened that in the activity of hunting, the males' minds were stretched and challenged in crucial ways that, fortunately for us all, propelled the entire course of human evolution.

Questions remained, of course: Why would the men have gone hunting when, strictly speaking, they did not need to? And why would only men hunt? Some anthropologists reasoned that even if hunting was in some ways "unproductive," it at least gave the men a distinct social role and status.[8] As if sensing that explanation to be a bit too lame, others observed that hunting and gathering are activities that simply cannot be carried out in the same area simultaneously. Gatherers rummaging about for roots and berries would disrupt the hunters' stalking and spook the game animals. This naturally led hunters to wander farther afield. Since only men could afford to wander far from home, logically men became hunters and women became gatherers.[9]

Some proponents of the hunting hypothesis also discerned psychological reasons why men—innately active and curious— were better suited to hunting than women, who were by nature more passive and reflective. To quote Washburn and Lancaster:

> Men enjoy hunting and killing, and these activities are continued as sports even when they are no longer economically necessary. . . . Part of the motivation for hunting is the immediate pleasure it gives the hunter, and the human killer can no more afford to be sorry for the game than a cat can for its intended victim. Evolution builds a relation between biology, psychology, and behavior, and, therefore, the evolutionary success of hunting exerted a profound effect on human psychology. Perhaps this is most easily shown by the extent of the efforts devoted to maintain killing as a sport. . . . And until recently war was viewed in much the same way as hunting. Other human beings were simply the most dangerous game. War has been far too important in human history for it to be other than pleasurable for the males involved.[10]

Washburn and Lancaster were eager to exempt females from the pleasure of killing. To do otherwise would raise some obvious, and troublesome, questions about women's "innate" capacity for violent aggression. They therefore argued that socially constructed gender roles are the logical outcomes of biological predispositions: Anyone who observes children at play will notice that it is the boys who are enthusiastic about "hunting, fishing, fighting, and games of war," while the girls would rather play house.[11]

The programming of children for their adult roles, through appropriate play activities that exploit their "natural" psychological inclinations, would have massive implications. William S. Laughlin showed, for example, how the games played by Aleut boys, under the guidance of adult males, are actually exercises designed to cultivate the upper-body strength and flexibility required to hunt

with a spear from a kayak. Boys who are not properly so programmed, from a very early age, will not be able to "perform normally" as adult hunters.[12] Needless to say, women who had not received such training would not be able to perform as hunters at
all.

Another element of the division of labor had to do with the
manufacture of weapons. It was acknowledged that women in
contemporary hunter-gatherer cultures were occasionally
known to join in communal hunts, and that hunting of small animals by women "is not a rare phenomenon." But in no society was
"individualistic" hunting of large animals a recognized female
prerogative. The main reason for this, according to one inter-
preter, was that "women have no weapons of their own which are
specially made to hunt animals." Weapons were always manufactured by males. Left to their own female devices, women might
fashion "some provisional weapons such as sticks." Otherwise,
they could at best try (and most often fail) to borrow men's tech-
nologically superior tools.[13]

But women spent most of their time using their primitive tools
to gather plant resources. Such activity was in any event more
suited to their limited conceptual abilities, since it afforded a
"lack of challenge or psychological stimulation. . . . Plants do not
run away nor do they turn and attack. They can be approached at
any time from any direction, and they do not need to be trapped,
speared, clubbed, or pursued on foot until they are exhausted."[14]

Or, as Hitoshi Watanabe summed it up, "Plants stand still, but
animals move."[15] Women were better suited to a "sedentary" lifestyle of gathering near the settlement.[16] Meanwhile, the serious
business of evolving was left to the men. Hunting provided, in
Laughlin's phrase, the "master behavior pattern of the human
species," inasmuch as males became programmed for thinking,
communicating, and cooperating.[17]

What, exactly, *was* woman supposed to have been doing in the
meantime? As archaeologist Margaret Ehrenberg has—with
well-placed sarcasm—inquired, "Was she sitting at home, twid-
dling her thumbs, waiting for 'man' to feed her and increase his
brain capacity and abilities until he became '*Homo sapiens sapi-*

ens'?" [18] Obviously women had more to do over all those eons
than digging roots, picking berries, and evolving wider pelvises
to accommodate the larger braincases of their male-hunter off-
spring. Yet Lee and DeVore had, in their introductory chapter to
Man the Hunter, been content simply to acknowledge, with
sweeping understatement, that it was "likely that early woman
would not have remained idle during the Pleistocene." [19]

This is putting it mildly, to say the least. The framers of
the hunting hypothesis understood, after all, that women were
hardly the original leisure class. From the Upper Paleolithic forward, they had apparently provided not only the bulk of the food
supply, but also the lion's share of the labor when it came to breaking, moving, and reestablishing camp. At one point Laughlin
blithely noted that "women and dogs have been the principal
beasts of burden since Paleolithic times." [20]

The picture of women's role in prehistory that emerges in the
hunting hypothesis is illogical enough that, were other evidence
lacking, reason alone should call it into question. Take this example from a standard introductory text, in which the author
claimed that, despite her inferior strength and stamina, "Woman
is at no disadvantage . . . in lighter tasks which can be performed
in or near the home, e.g., the gathering of vegetable products,
the fetching of water, the preparation of food, and the manufacture of clothing and utensils." [21] Who, precisely, defines a task
as "light"? Are the ones enumerated here "lighter" because they
are less strenuous, or because they are women's work? Fetching
water is by no stretch of the imagination easy work, as anyone
knows who has camped in a modern "primitive" campground. [22]
Nor is child-rearing—curiously missing from this list of women's
tasks—without rigor.

Feminist anthropologists Patty Jo Watson and Mary Kennedy
have pointed out that archaeologists of prehistory have conventionally operated under one of two schemes for explaining the
sexual division of labor. One is "based upon the assumption that
women are seriously encumbered and disadvantaged by their reproductive responsibilities and that men are unencumbered by
theirs." It yields the pattern:

MEN > HUNT > ANIMALS > ACTIVE

WOMEN > GATHER > PLANTS > PASSIVE

This scheme assumes that psychological differences between the sexes are innate and universal, and were as present at the dawn of human prehistory as they are today. In this view, "women cannot be responsible for culture change because they are not men."

In the second scheme, the question of innate differences is laid aside, but the assumption remains that since contemporary hunter-gatherers divide labor along gender lines, it is therefore likely that prehistoric ones did, too. So the pattern remains:

MEN > HUNT > ANIMALS

WOMEN > GATHER > PLANTS[23]

The first scheme depends on an essentialist bias about gender differences, the second on the idea that gender roles are socially constructed.[24] But either way, the men and animals move, and the women and plants stand still.

Women's activity is thus effectively restricted to the domestic sphere, and such culture-advancing activities as are assigned to them include those that seem compatible with a sedentary lifestyle: horticulture, pottery production, weaving, and so on. Another reason these activities are assigned to women, of course, is that they are what are left over when hunting is factored out of the equation. But this tendency to assign to women all these elements of material production that are not outcomes of hunting creates a wildly distorted picture of the division of labor.[25]

Another problem with the hunting hypothesis was that most of the tasks it assigned to women require far more intelligence than could be assumed for the sedentary plant gatherer who lacked the mental stimulation supposedly only hunting could provide. As sociobiologist Sarah Hrdy has observed, "Curiously, few anthropologists have asked why intelligence never became sex-linked or why—if intelligence evolved among males to help them hunt—Nature should have squandered it on a sex that never hunted."[26]

Such obvious theoretical shortcomings of the hunting hypothesis led a group of women anthropologists in the 1970s to propose what came to be called the "gathering hypothesis." Intended as a balancing corrective to the hunting theory of human evolution, their alternative interpretation took the dubious question of women's sedentary lifestyle as its starting point. Adrienne Zihlman and Nancy Tanner, key framers of the hypothesis, set about demonstrating that the hunting hypothesis was founded upon a bizarre tendency to overlook the obvious: If the products of gathering accounted for as much as 80 percent of the prehistoric human diet, and if women and children account for roughly 75 percent of the total human population, *and* if foraging preceded hunting in the evolutionary history of hominids, then it was only logical to assume that those key adaptations that marked the beginnings of humanity were to be sought in the women's work of gathering, rather than in men's hunting.

Proponents of the gathering hypothesis[27] appealed to the same "checklist" of adaptations as had those of the Man-the-Hunter school: bipedalism, tool use, communication, and cooperation. Erect posture was important, they held, to free the hands for picking, digging, sorting, and carrying. Tools of various kinds were of course necessary. The earliest may well have been digging sticks (primate studies had by the seventies shown that such primitive tools were in fact regularly used by chimpanzees). But the crucial tools to develop out of gathering were two kinds of containers: slings for carrying infants, to free their mothers' hands for work, and various sorts of containers for transporting and cooking the fruits of foraging. Cooperation—in such forms as sharing the tasks of child care and food preservation, and working together to most effectively exploit the resources at their disposal—was surely as necessary to efficient gathering as to big-game hunting. So was communication: sharing information about what plants were good and which ones were toxic, about where to look for particular delicacies, and so on. Mothers foraging with their children, and spending time around the home settlement, would have had the time, as well as the practical impetus, to develop language. Human society as we would come to know it was, in this view, far more firmly rooted in the home site than in the hunting camp.

Studies of contemporary hunter-gatherer cultures leant some weight to the argument. These studies had shown that while in most cases hunting tended to be restricted mostly or totally to males, gathering was generally something that both sexes engaged in at least some of the time. In this light, it seemed far more reasonable to infer that hunting was itself a relatively late adaptation, made possible by the evolutionary advances already secured by gathering. The digging stick could be seen as the prototype of the spear, and the idea of pursuing prey that could move about as a logical outgrowth of the process of stalking the wild asparagus (or its Pleistocene equivalent).

The gathering hypothesis cast an entirely new light on the question of the sexual division of labor. The mental skills that might have developed out of gathering were, essentially, the same as those requisite to hunting. And contrary to the man-the-hunter theory, ethnological evidence had borne out that in hunter-gatherer cultures there were, in fact, cases in which women either joined men in large-game hunting bands, or even hunted big game by themselves.[28] If these cases were not anomalies, exceptions that proved the rule of gender-divided labor, then why *did* hunting develop as a "universally" male activity in the first place?

The obvious solution was that it made good practical and economic sense for the men to hunt and the women to gather. Those women who were most likely to be in the kind of physical condition needed for the hazardous business of large-game hunting would have also been of child-bearing age. Those were the women whose loss to the community would have been most keenly felt.[29] Furthermore, women's mobility would be restricted in the later stages of pregnancy, or by an infant carried in a sling. Also, silence is crucial to effective stalking, and babies are notoriously noisy at the least convenient moments.

It may simply have been more efficient, therefore, to divide labor along gender lines. This argument was not entirely foreign to adherents of the Man-the-Hunter school of thought. Those who advanced the gathering hypothesis, however, read the evidence in a crucially different way. For them, the gendered division of labor must have come about as a matter of conscious choice, rather than because of any innate physical or psychological differences between women and men. The sexual division of labor was most likely a relatively late development in evolutionary history, and probably far less "universal" in prehistoric times than in modern hunter-gatherer groups. As the "anomalous" modern societies show, those women who are not hampered by pregnancy or child care (this includes those who can get babysitters) and who are good at hunting can and do hunt as effectively as men. Among the Philippine Agta, for example, "Hunters, both female and male, begin hunting when their stamina and ability make it worthwhile and cease when they lose strength. Hunters who enjoy hunting will hunt frequently; those who do not will hunt rarely. Each hunter uses techniques that work for her or him; hunting techniques are not sex-typed."[30] There is no logical reason, proponents of the gathering hypothesis quite reasonably argued, why this situation would have looked much different fifty thousand years ago.

The anthropologists who developed the gathering hypothesis were at pains to insist that their theory was a complement to, rather than a refutation of, the hunting hypothesis. Zihlman and her colleagues stressed that the species-defining advances that spawned humanity were surely effected by women and men gathering and evolving together. However, in practice, because it opted to work from the same evolutionary checklist, the gathering hypothesis tended to set *woman* the gatherer against *man* the hunter when it came to those key adaptations of language, cooperation, and tool use. As Sarah Hrdy observed, "It is different wine in the same bottle: now woman is the toolmaker. From this perspective, male 'superiority' is simply an impression conveyed by biases in data collection and analysis."[31]

In short, while in some ways it represents a clear advance beyond the hunting hypothesis, the scheme at work in the gatherer hypothesis is still:

MEN > HUNT > ANIMALS

WOMEN > GATHER > PLANTS

And the hidden assumption at work is still that one way of going about the business of living is fundamentally better, and certainly more productive, than the other.

JUST SO MANY JUST-SO STORIES?

Both hypotheses ultimately suffer from the same theoretical short-sightedness: a tendency to see things in the light of either/or logic, to reduce complex problems to overly simple—and single—solutions. Granted that foraging played a crucial role in human evolution, it remains difficult to account not only for why hunting would have developed in the first place, but also why it would still play a prominent role in certain cultures. As paleoanthropologist Donald Johanson (of "Lucy" fame) has remarked, not much is gained, theoretically, by replacing the male killer ape with "a clutch of resourceful she-hominids," nor by reducing the male role in human evolution from "Mighty Hunter" to "Idle Sportsman."[32]

The problem with the gathering hypothesis is that, suggestive as it was in terms of providing a corrective to the Man-the-Hunter ideal, it wound up echoing the male biases it was designed to oppose. Indeed, especially as time went on, it even reinforced those biases. In her essay "The Use and Abuse of Anthropology," the late Michelle Rosaldo judiciously criticized the gathering ideal: "If anything, Woman the Gatherer seems a being who is content unto herself; absorbed in what in fact appear as relatively domestic chores, she frees her male associates to engage in risky hunts, forge wider bonds, and so, again, she allows Man the upper hand, permitting him to make the social whole."[33]

This is new wine in the same old bottle (or skin) indeed. And it produces much the same old hangover: an evolutionary picture in which the male of the species holds the center of the action, the female passively playing a supporting role. As feminist historian

Gerda Lerner has observed, the history of human events is like a stage play, populated in relatively equal numbers by male and female players, but in which men traditionally have conceived and directed the action and given themselves all the juiciest parts. "It takes considerable time," Lerner wisely remarks, "for the women to understand that getting 'equal' parts will not make them equal, as long as the script, the props, the stage setting, and the direction are firmly held by men."[34]

Lerner's theatrical analogy is helpful. The real question is are we all watching the same play? That is, are we sure we know what the "action" is, when it comes to the gendered division of labor and its theoretical and social implications? Toward providing a more truly balanced picture of the division of labor, British anthropologist Tim Ingold has pinpointed a too-often-overlooked problem inherent in the debate over the relative importance of hunting and gathering in human evolution and social economy. Citing Lee and DeVore's pronouncement that "Cultural Man has been on earth for some 2,000,000 years; for over 99 percent of this period he has lived as a hunter-gatherer," Ingold remarks that "these opening words of the celebrated symposium on *Man the Hunter* conceal, with a flourish of confident rhetoric, a yawning uncertainty about what a life of hunting and gathering actually entails."[35]

Where, to begin with, does gathering leave off and hunting begin? Ingold emphasizes that "hunting and gathering refer, in the first place, to what people do rather than to what they eat; that is, to patterns of conduct rather than nutrition."[36] But what, exactly, *is* it that people do? Literature on the subject has produced a veritable rat's nest of terminology: hunter-gatherer, hunter-forager, predator-forager, gatherer-predator.[37] Conventionally, gathering includes the procurement not only of vegetable resources, but also of other protein sources such as small animals, insects, eggs, and shellfish—things, in other words, that pretty much "stand still" as plants do, and are there for the taking in one way or another. Nets and clubs are as much gathering tools as are baskets and digging sticks. Hunting, on the other hand, refers to the stalking and killing of large land and sea mammals, through the use of implements as various as spears, bows and arrows, boomerangs, and harpoons. Gathering involves *collecting*, whereas hunting involves *pursuit*, and this "behavioural opposition" is the basis of the distinction between the two activities.[38]

So far so good. But where, then, does fishing fit into the scheme? Or trapping? Or fowling? Recalling archaeology's just-so stories of human beginnings, Ingold remarks that it is one thing "to imagine man the hunter, fleet of foot and armed with club, spear or bow and arrow, as lovingly depicted in countless 'artist's impressions' of our ancient ancestors, setting off in hot pursuit of mobile big game," but quite another to imagine the mighty hunter in pursuit of grubs or snails, which (albeit they are animal protein sources) more properly are gathered.[39]

Ingold concludes that it is the sexual division of labor that creates a largely artificial distinction between hunting and gathering as human activities: "The same arguments that were developed to set humans above and apart from their primate ancestors were also invoked to set men above and apart from women." Noting that, as even the champions of the hunting hypothesis recognized, women frequently engage in the active pursuit of mobile small game, Ingold suggests—with manifest good sense—that the precise extent of women's involvement in such activity "has been obscured by a systematic observers' bias towards regarding such pursuit, which would usually be classed as 'hunting' if performed by men, as mere 'gathering' or 'collecting' if performed by women."[40] That is, the hunter-gatherer dichotomy is sustained by designating as gathering "much of what would count as predation by non-human primates," and thus obscuring "the substantial contribution of human females in this field of activity."[41]

The questions of tool use, and of scavenging, further challenge the ready dichotomy between male hunting and female gathering. The activities of hominids are in part reconstructed from the tools they left behind. This originally leant more apparent weight to the hunting hypothesis, because stone and fossilized bone tools last over time, whereas digging-sticks and carrying-skins decay and leave no trace. However, the argument that because butchering an animal can involve stone scrapers and choppers,

and that these are among the earliest stone tools found so therefore hunting provided the earliest instance of tool-use, is maddeningly circular. No one knows the precise function of these
early tools: A chopper might well be used to extract marrow from
bones, and it might just as easily be a nutcracker.[42]

Stone tools bear no mark of the sex of their manufacturers.
That it does not take a human male to fashion a stone tool is evi-
denced by animal studies on one hand, and ethnography on the
other. Chimpanzees use rocks to crack open nuts, and—somewhat reversing the process—some birds of prey are known to
drop eggs or turtles onto rocks in order to get at the goods inside.
Among the Australian Tiwi aborigines, the men fish and hunt
food from the sea, while the women gather and hunt for food on
land. Prior to the introduction of steel implements, these women
fashioned their own stone tools—axes that bore a strong resemblance to those of prehistoric Europe, and which the women
used both for stripping bark for baskets and delivering death
blows to prey animals.[43]

Even when stone tools are recovered at sites where fossilized
animal remnants strongly suggest the tools were used to process
meat, the question remains open as to whether the meat resulted
from hunting or scavenging. Indeed, it was over this question that
anthropologists seeking a way out of the apparent impasse of man
the hunter/woman the gatherer floated two further theories of
human evolution.

One, articulated by Glynn Isaac, stressed the sharing of food
over the means of its procurement. Whether meat was hunted or
scavenged—and scavenging, a form of foraging, most certainly
preceded hunting in human evolution—was in Isaac's view
largely immaterial. The important thing was that the meat,
along with the products of gathering, was shared among the
members of the group. "Home base" was where sharing happened. Language developed out of the sharing of information
about food resources, and food-sharing also led to a system of
reciprocal responsibility that provided the foundation of human
social arrangements. Isaac assumed the sexual division of labor
was part of this scheme.[44]

Meanwhile, Lewis Binford read the evidence of proto-human scavenging in another way. Nurturing a thoroughgoing sense of skepticism about anything smacking of a just-so story of human origins, especially those founded in too-facile comparisons with modern hunter-gatherer groups, he reconstructed the beginnings of human evolution in something of an anti-just-so story.[45] In Binford's view, our prehuman ancestors were at best opportunists who were lucky enough to stumble upon a carcass from time to time, and were just bright enough to figure out how to use a chunk of rock to crack open a bone for its marrow. In Binford's analysis, protohuman hominids were far less intelligent—less *human*, in fact—than previous theories had made them out to be. How exactly they got along, and what propelled the evolutionary process forward, remain mysterious and will continue to, he argued, until we learn to ask better questions about the data: questions less obviously rooted in the experience and behavior of modern humans.[46]

In response to Binford's radical skepticism, some supporters of Isaac's food-sharing hypothesis highlighted the positive side of foraging for meat, and man the scavenger was born. Like hunting, they pointed out, scavenging involved "coordinated group activity" and "repeated participation in dangerous subsistence pursuits."[47] However, while they ventured suggestions as to how scavenging might have led to bipedalism (for essentially the same reasons gathering might have), they were harder pressed to account for how scavenging would necessitate sharing, or the establishment of a "home base," or the development of more sophisticated tools.[48]

THE IMAGE OF OURSELVES UNDRESSED

What all of these theories have in common is the unspoken assumption that we can look at fossil evidence, using modern hunter-gatherer cultures as convenient points of comparison, and see—to borrow Michelle Rosaldo's insightful phrase—"the image of ourselves undressed."[49] In each case, the criteria that ostensibly make humans different from other animals, and espe-

cially from our ape-like ancestors—tool use, cooperation, language, bipedalism—are interpreted in the light of contemporary
experience. But, as Johanson cautions, "Only when we strip early
humans of their future can we begin to understand the secrets of
our past."[50]

Besides, the more data archaeologists and ethologists accumulate, the clearer it appears that all of these theories of human
origins are wide of the mark. The more we learn about our fellow
primates, and about animals in general, the more obvious it becomes that human beings are far less "distinct" than we liked to
think we were. Tool use has been documented among a variety of
species, as have cooperative hunting and the sharing of food back
at someplace very like "home base." Chimpanzees and gorillas
obviously possess some capacity for symbolic communication. As
for bipedalism, it is widely recognized to be among the least efficient of adaptations for getting around. That the sexual division
of labor is the *only* adaptation that consistently remains as a "distinctly human" trait says less about its role in human evolution
than it says about theories about evolution and the social matrices
from which those theories arise.

The hunting hypothesis posits long-term monogamy, the male
as dominant food-provider, and the channeling of "normal" masculine aggression through hunting as universal patterns. In fact,
not only are none of these patterns universal, they are least likely
to be found in those contemporary hunter-gatherer societies
whose lifestyles would presumably bear the closest resemblence
to early human groups.[51] Yet in anthropological reconstructions,
prehistoric and contemporary hunter-gatherer societies are collapsed in a weirdly distorted picture, constructed to serve the re-
quirements of the just-so story.[52]

Johanson remarks the curious timeliness of each proposed
theory of human origins: "the killer ape of the [post–World War
II] fifties, the imperial, space-exploring *machismo* of the sixties'
mighty hunter, so quickly superseded by a vignette of human
beginnings as soft around the edges as a John Denver lyric."[53]
It took the women's liberation movement to breathe life into

Woman the Gatherer, and a post-hippy culture of newly sensitive males to spawn early-human groups of Sharers. Man the Scavenger may, for that matter, be an oddly appropriate mascot for the Reagan years.

The hunting hypothesis took the academic establishment virtually by storm in the 1950s and 1960s in part because, as historian of science Donna Haraway has elaborately argued in her *Primate Visions*, it represented a not entirely unselfconscious move to establish "United Nations post–World War II universal man" as the prototype for all of humanity in all places and times.[54] In the face of the political pressures of the Cold War and the complex economic realities of the emerging Third World, Man the Hunter—who accomplished, by becoming a hunter, that evolutionary leap that separated us from our apelike forebears—just happened to emerge as the Western nuclear family man par excellence, whose proper sphere was the wider world, just as his woman's "natural" realm was that of home and hearth. Under the guise of erasing potentially strife-inducing racial and ethnic differences in the name of defining the essentially human, "man" just happened to look a lot like middle-class capitalistic anticommunist Judeo-Christian Caucasian man.[55]

But why was *hunting* so important as the linchpin of this family-values-laden post-war ideal? In the face of mounting evidence that, as we have seen, the first tools developed were no doubt for use in foraging,[56] and that other animals use simple tools for food collection besides, proponents of the hunting hypothesis clung tenaciously to the notion that the first *real*, that is, distinctly *human*, tools were weapons for killing large game, and subsequently for use in warfare.[57] Hunting and warfare—the provision of food and of protection for the family group, that is, the women and children at home—were obviously masculine prerogatives.[58] Hence by extension it was as natural for the modern male to venture forth into the asphalt jungle to bring home the bacon for the wife and kids, as it had been for his ancestor in the Upper Paleolithic to join a hunting band in search of some prime rib of mammoth to complement the greens and tubers gathered close to home by the little woman.[59] Similarly, when he went to war it was now, as it had been then, for the sake of protecting his women and children.

The centrality of warfare to the hunting hypothesis is far from accidental. Euro-American history in the first half of the twentieth century had begun with the war-to-end-all-wars, only to be followed within a generation by a global conflict that included the Holocaust and culminated in the dropping of atomic bombs on Hiroshima and Nagasaki. That the fifties were dubbed the Cold War era suggests that warfare had come to be the root metaphor for the human (or at least the Western) condition. In this context, the idea of Man the Killer Ape, while not new, became peculiarly attractive.

A BLOOD BESPATTERED ARCHIVE

The Killer Ape hypothesis had actually been the brainchild of Raymond Dart, an anatomist who in 1922 discovered the fossil skull of the "Taung Child" (*Australopithecus africanus*) in South Africa. That discovery is commonly regarded as the beginning of modern paleoanthropology. Dart, a Darwinian at a time when Darwin's theory was under heated popular attack (this was the decade of the Scopes "monkey trial"), assumed that he had stumbled upon the missing link. When his discovery failed to receive the notice he felt it merited, a disillusioned Dart abandoned paleontology. It was not until a generation later, when Louis and Mary Leakey made their first significant finds at Olduvai Gorge in Tanzania, that Darwin's hypothesis of African origins began to gain favor and Dart's earlier work was vindicated. He returned to the field.[60]

Walking the earth about three million years ago, *A. africanus* was not exactly a missing link in the chain of human evolution, but he was definitely a relation. One of the things he had in common with the earliest humans (*Homo habilis* and *Homo erectus*) was his use of tools. It was abundantly clear to Dart that these tools were used for killing. Indeed, killing was *A. africanus*'s evolutionary claim to fame. In a 1953 essay, "The Predatory Transition from Ape to Man," Dart characterized these early "ape-men" as "confirmed killers: carnivorous creatures, that seized living quarries by violence, battered them to death, tore apart their broken bodies, dismembered them limb from limb, slaking their ravenous thirst with the hot blood of victims and greedily devouring livid writhing flesh." Not only did the killer ape feed on prey species; he "ruthlessly" killed and fed on his own kind.[61]

Reflecting upon the "blood-bespattered, slaughter-gutted archives of human history," Dart drew a direct connection between the primordial ape-man's murderous ways and the brutalities of far more recent times, arguing that "the most recent atrocities of the Second World War accord with early universal cannibalism."[62] His florid pessimism captured the attention of playwright Robert Ardrey, who went on to popularize the idea of Man the Killer Ape in a series of articles for *Life* magazine, and in several widely read books.[63] Ardrey summed up the hunting hypothesis succinctly: *"Man is man, and not a chimpanzee, because for millions upon millions of evolving years we killed for a living."*[64]

Ardrey agreed with Dart that killing "for a living" marked the key transitional leap from ape to human. In a scene oddly reminiscent of the opening sequence in Stanley Kubrick's *2001: A Space Odyssey* (1968), he presented a window, as it were, on evolutionary process in action. The actors were several chimpanzees in captivity, held "in a large quarry with walls high enough to prevent escape." Their keeper had scattered a number of sticks, of various sizes up to that of a clothes pole, about their enclosure.

> Then, at the top of the wall where visitors usually came to watch, he exhibited a tame leopard. At the sight of their natural enemy the chimpanzees rose, significantly, to bipedal posture. Also significantly, they did not flee but charged. And as they charged they picked up the poles on their way, hurling them like spears against the wall. Their aim was poor, their charge futile, but the armed attack told much about a chimpanzee potential that is difficult to explain.[65]

It takes a pretty powerful bias to convert an empirically observed behavior into an enactment of "potential." Claiming (erroneously) that such behavior was never observed of chimpanzees in the wild, Ardrey went on to account for his vignette of apes haplessly struggling to evolve into hunter-aggressors by suggesting that "in the forest the chimpanzee has degenerated, but . . . our common ancestor behaved more like men."[66] That is, he came down out of the trees, lost his claws, struggled toward erect stature, began fashioning weapons, and developed a taste for meat long before it was a "survival necessity." He learned to kill for a living. Significantly, Ardrey titles the chapter in which he recounts this evolutionary tale "Paradise Lost."

At the same time Ardrey the armchair anthropologist had been working all this out, professional scientists were also preoccupied with the darker theoretical implications of innate male aggression as a motive behind human evolution. As we saw earlier, Washburn and Lancaster posited a link between hunting and warfare, based in the fact that "men enjoy hunting and killing." Rene Dubos had similarly seen in the "hunting urge" an instinctual drive so essential that "its persistence can be recognized even in the most urbanized city dweller."[67]

Yet it appeared that if the instinctual drive to hunt and kill unites us with other animals, its peculiarly human variation also distinguishes us from the rest of the animal kingdom. Washburn and Lancaster had pointed out (also erroneously) that alone among carnivores, humans have a penchant for killing members of their own species.[68] "Whatever the origin of this behavior," they asserted, "it has had profound effects on human evolution, and almost every human society has regarded killing members of certain other human societies as desirable."[69]

"Almost" is an important word here. Curiously enough, hunter-gatherer cultures tend to be among those few human societies in which warfare does not appear to play an especially prominent role.[70] Washburn and Lancaster's neglect of this fact would be baffling were it not for the obvious inference that the warring human societies they were really concerned about were much closer to home in time and space: those same "blood-bespattered" cultures that had produced the atrocities of World

War II. Operating from the assumption that violent aggression is a normal component of male psychology, it was easy to argue that because men like to kill, they like to hunt (to provide sustenance for their families) and to wage war (for the sake of the women and children).[71] It is important to note that in this model, killing and weapons-use only provide incidental links between hunting and warfare; the real connection is the masculine proclivity for violent aggression. In the case of warfare, or so the theory goes, this accounts for men's alienation from one another, while in the case of hunting, it accounts for their alienation from all of nature.

For not only was the hunting adaptation deeply bound up with intraspecies human violence, according to this line of thinking it also signalled the estrangement of human beings from the rest of the animal kingdom.[72] Washburn and Lancaster present a vignette that in some ways is the flip side of Ardrey's chimpanzee episode. They tell of anthropologist James Woodburn having taken a Hadza hunter on a visit to Nairobi Park. "The Hadza was amazed and excited, because although he had hunted all his life, he had never seen such a quantity and variety of animals close at hand. His previous view of animals was the result of his having been their enemy, and they had reacted to him as the most destructive carnivore. In the park the Hadza hunter saw for the first time the peace of the herbivorous world." This leads them to reflect upon how with the hunting adaptation men somehow fell from grace. The relation of humans to the rest of the natural world was irrevocably altered, and we became enemies to our hitherto friends. In their version of "Paradise Lost," the "world of flight and fear is the result of the efficiency of hunters."[73]

Of course, they do not take into account the fact that animals that have become habituated to seeing tourists trundle through their environment in Land Rovers are not "wild" in quite the same sense as the Hadza's customary prey.[74] The fact that they choose a refuge where human hunting is prohibited, to exemplify primordial nature, indeed reflects a deep sense of estrangement from nature. It is, however, a sense far more characteristic of twentieth-century Euro-American than of traditional hunter-gatherer cultures. It also suggests a simpler, more idyllic view of the workings of the natural world than any hunter-gatherer would likely entertain.

JUST WHOSE PARADISE WAS LOST?

In point of fact, a traditional hunter-gatherer is far less likely to see himself or herself as an entity distinct from or in opposition to the natural environment. Ingold has suggested that for these groups, relating to their surroundings is not a matter of "territoriality" (which in the hunting hypothesis is one way to account for the development of warfare between hunting bands), but of "tenure." Humans do not possess or manipulate a landscape; rather, they inhabit it, and it to a certain extent embodies them. "In holding sites or paths, hunters and gatherers do not divide up the world among themselves, each group taking its own portion and looking after it exclusively. It would be more true to say that each takes hold of one aspect of the world, or one part of the creative essence that underwrites its total constitution. And in tending that essence, every group makes a vital, albeit partial contribution to the maintenance of the whole."[75] There are various ways to "take hold of" aspects of one's world. Agriculturalists and city planners do it two-dimensionally, marking off fields, roads, and boundary lines. Hunter-gatherers, on the other hand, move about in landscapes not markedly altered by their human presence. Some of the time, they move about, as do other carnivores and omnivores, as predators.

To tread a path through the hunter-gatherer landscape is to follow the ways laid down by the other, nonhuman inhabitants of that landscape. It is, in a sense, to "act naturally," as predator in search of prey. Yet human hunting is not mere predation. It is also a social action—as Ingold phrases it, "directed *on* the physical world rather than going on *within* it. . . . As a hunter, man confronts nature *in person*." Because of the level of self-awareness humans possess about their interactions with nonhuman nature, hunting is an extension of human social life. It therefore, in some senses, "pertains to the human history of nature rather than the natural history of man."[76]

For the adherents of the hunting hypothesis, a crucial component of the "human history of nature" was the alienation of man from nonhuman nature—hence Washburn and Lancaster's references to "enmity" between hunter and hunted.[77] They depicted the hunter as the warrior who confronted and conquered those other natural forces that might just as readily feed on him were it not for his superior cunning and prowess. For this reason his esteem within his social group might far exceed the protein his meat contributed to their collective diet. This was reflected not only in tribal social structures, but also in the symbolism of myth and ritual.[78]

What this portrayal of the opposition of man to nature tended to overlook, however, was the way traditional hunters understand their quarry. This is reflected in those same social structures, myths, and rituals. The symbolic and social weight attributed to hunting, and to the meat that hunting provides, indeed far exceed those attributed to other protein resources, like fish, in hunter-gatherer and hunter-horticulturalist societies. This no doubt is due, in part, to the fact that while gathering and small-scale horticulture are more reliable sources of food, the meat derived from hunting is more costly in terms of risk to the hunter, and thus is more symbolically freighted.[79]

But there appears to be an additional factor at work in the higher symbolic valuation of hunting and its products. Relying upon extensive cross-cultural data about hunter-gatherer and hunter-horticulturalist societies, anthropologist Susan Kent notes that "in these types of societies animals are classified as intellectual beings. They are placed in the same macro-category as humans, whereas plants and fish are not."[80] Cross-cultural studies have, in fact, demonstrated that "the human-nonhuman animal dichotomy so sharp in Western civilization is not at all as clear or even present in all societies. Hunter-gatherers and small-scale farmers who hunt do not differentiate between humans and nonhumans in the same way as do Europeans/Euroamericans. Nonhuman animals are seen as having intellectual capabilities

that are similar to or sometimes even surpass those of humans."[81]
Hence it is in mythologies based in a hunter-gatherer worldview
that one encounters brainy nonhuman figures like Trickster Coyote, Raven, and Spider Woman. Elsewhere, one still detects their
mythic remnants, as in a serpent debating the limits of human
knowledge with the first woman.[82]

It is only when larger-scale agriculture enters the scene, and
with it the differentiation between "wild" and "domesticated"
animals, that people begin to make meaningfully sharp distinctions between the intellectual capacities of human and nonhuman animals. Here, too, hunting apparently plays a key role. For
in societies in which people hunt regularly and also raise domestic animals, only the latter are denied status as intelligent beings
over against intelligent human and nonhuman wild animals. And
only in a society like our own, in which hunting plays no prominent role while the domestication of animals does, are nonhuman
animals both domestic *and* wild stripped of their status as intellectual entities.[83]

It was with the development of agriculture, beginning about
twelve thousand years ago, that several decisive shifts occurred in
the shape of human society, and in the relationship of humans to
the world of nature. Washburn and Lancaster had intimated that
in the Upper Paleolithic, hunting itself was responsible for the
series of complex adaptations that led to horticulture, the domestication of animals, and the development of an agrarian lifestyle.[84] This of course was a good thing, in their view, inasmuch as
it laid the evolutionary groundwork for their own highly developed culture, in which—as one corporate slogan of the sixties
had it—"Progress is our most important product."

Yet not all partisans of the hunting hypothesis saw the evolution of agrarianism in so inevitable, or so favorable, a light. Environmental philosopher Paul Shepard, for whom Eden was less a
garden than a happy hunting ground, saw in animal domestication the beginning of the devolution not only of the human species, but indeed of the human spirit as well. In *The Tender Carnivore and the Sacred Game,* he wrote: "What must surely have
preceded farming was a shift in style and in man's sense of his

place in the world; a shift whereby man would presume to own the world and wild organisms would be screened for those having a certain infantile, trusting placidity that could be nurtured and increased in captivity."[85] Elsewhere, Shepard observed that "in the ideology of farming, wild things are enemies of the tame; the wild Other is not the context but the opponent of 'my' domain."[86] In a similar vein, science writer Boyce Rensberger described the farming lifestyle as a war against the natural world: "the fact is that a farmer's success depends on his winning battles against pests and predators and even against nature's efforts to recolonize his fields with 'weeds.'"[87]

It is the farmer, *not* the hunter, who approaches the world of nature as something over which he must seize control: marking off fields and pastures, churning up the soil and changing patterns of vegetation, damming and diverting streams, confining small animals and birds to yards and pens, bringing large animals under the yoke, and through selective breeding manipulating their physical and psychological characteristics. It is also in the context of farming that nature begins to be experienced as an unpredictable, capricious, and often inimical, force. Hunter-gatherers, by contrast, do not need to work as hard as farmers for their food, and even in bad years, they very seldom go hungry.[88]

With a settled agrarian lifestyle, property and possessions take on significance quite inconceivable to the relatively unencumbered hunter-gatherer. So, too, does the need to defend one's territory against attack, one's goods and animals against plunder.[89]

Because farming is labor-intensive, agrarianism requires more workers. We have seen that the gendered division of labor makes a certain amount of practical sense in hunter-gatherer contexts; however, it does not necessarily entail the dominance of one sex over the other. Quite to the contrary, ethnographic studies have shown that hunter-gatherer societies tend to display relatively more egalitarianism than do agrarian or industrialized societies.[90]

In agrarian societies, women's reproductive role is all-important: Women provide the labor (in more ways than one) to run the farm. Wives (or more strictly speaking, their procreative

abilities) are thereby among the farmer's most important possessions, and daughters—along with herd animals—among his
most lucrative mediums of exchange. Ironically, at the same time
their reproductive abilities are valued, the inability of women to
do heavy tasks during pregnancy and the distractions of continual childcare devalue their worth as farm workers.

There is considerable historical irony in the fact that women
are commonly believed to have originated horticulture only
to have the farming lifestyle eventually turn against them. Of
course, in evolutionary theory nothing happens overnight or
owing to a single cause. The slow historical march toward the
establishment of patriarchal cultures, with their hierarchical
social structures and their sharp differentiation between "man"
and "nature," was obviously the product of multifarious factors, including the rise of various technologies, the development
of specialized crafts and trade, and the elaboration of religious
structures that supported the idea of social class and gender stratification.

It seems clear, however, that for upwards of two million years
humans lived in remarkably stable—and probably fairly egalitarian—hunter-gatherer cultures. Beginning about fifty thousand years ago, and owing largely to the environmental pressures
of the last Ice Age, the "hunting way of life" seems to have un-
dergone some decisive changes: Human encampments ("home
bases") gradually achieved more permanence, gender-divided labor allowed the women more time to devote to horticulture and
crafts,[91] and the men began to work out the domestication of animals. *Homo sapiens* had been producing art for thirty thousand
years, but now at the close of the Old Stone Age was poised to become civilized. Farms, then villages, began to appear. The human population grew exponentially.

The first clear archaeological evidence of social or class strati-
fications does not occur until the sixth millennium B.C.E., in
Neolithic ("New Stone Age") Mesopotamian farming villages.
Evidence supporting gender stratification has been recovered
from Bronze Age burial sites in Scandinavia dating to about the
fourth millennium.[92] Social and sexual hierarchies, far from
being "natural" aspects of human evolution, really appear to be

quite recent developments. Such hierarchies are only possible insofar as one group can perceive another as "other," inferior, and worthy of subordination. Rather than hunting—in which animals are viewed as equal or superior to humans—the domestication of animals and the agricultural "taming" of wild nature clearly played the decisive role in the rise of the idea of human superiority over the nonhuman. But what initially gave men the idea that they could also subordinate other humans, as slaves or as servants?

The startling, and indeed troubling, consensus among a number of scholars is that human domestic relations, entailing the husband's dominance over wife (or wives) and daughters, provided the original pattern for all other forms of human dominance, including slavery.[93] At least one scholar also sees human domestic arrangements as setting the pattern for the domestication of animals.[94]

Civilization "as we know it"—the actual, though camouflaged, subject of the hunting and gathering hypotheses—thus results from a cruel historical irony. The sexual division of labor, which most probably entered the human scene for purely practical reasons, had nonetheless set the context for the differential valuation of the tasks performed by men and women (men's hunting being valued more highly), and eventually for the differential valuation of the men and women themselves. The devaluation of women and of women's work is an old story. But the pace of its telling clearly accelerated with the development of agriculture. And the capstone of the tale is the twentieth century myth of Man the Hunter.

Among partisans of the hunting hypothesis, whether paradise was lost with the development of hunting or of agriculture would depend, as we saw above, upon whom you ask. In point of fact, human society was never a paradise in the first place, but the myth of idyllic beginnings is a strong one just the same.[95] What is indisputable is that in our evolutionary "fall" women had the most to lose.

What if it all had happened differently? After millions of years of biological and several thousand of social evolution, this might

seem the ultimate preposterous question. Then again, since all
our theories about the past are at best educated guesses based in
our experience of the present, it may be the only kind of question
really worth asking. What if women had continued to hunt? What
if nonhuman animals continued to be viewed as intelligent
equals, even superiors, of human beings? What if the world of nature were not experienced as opposite to, or other than, human
culture? Might such teasing questions about the past help us to
imagine a saner and more livable future?

In the last twenty years anthropological theory has moved well
beyond the hunting hypothesis of human origins—and indeed
beyond any "single cause" explanation of how we got to be the
way we got to be. At the same time, feminist scholarship has demonstrated that patriarchal structures of dominance and subordination, grounded in a series of assumptions about man, woman,
and nature, are to a far greater extent products of history than of
biology.[96] Yet in both the popular and the academic imaginations,
Man the Hunter and Woman the Gatherer are curiously alive
and well, and still exerting a powerful mythic influence. It is to
that influence that we must presently turn.

2

In the Snow Queen's Palace

The walls of the palace were formed of drifted snow, and
the windows and doors of the cutting winds. There were
more than a hundred rooms in it, all as if they had been
formed with snow blown together. The largest of them extended for several miles; they were all lighted up by the
vivid light of the aurora, and they were so large and empty,
so icy-cold and glittering! There were no amusements here
. . . no pleasant games. . . . Empty, vast and cold were the
halls of the Snow Queen.

HANS CHRISTIAN ANDERSEN,
"THE SNOW QUEEN"

The ancient Norsemen called her Skadi, "the Dark One," Goddess of Winter and Mother of the North. Only she could love the tundra expanse where,
in her element, she danced snowstorms into being. Huge, furry white
hounds pulling her ice-crystal sled across the drifted plains and through
snow-canopied forests, Skadi aimed her icicle arrows with skill and preci-
sion. Huntswoman extraordinaire, she chose her quarry carefully, with an
eye to the tender young ones. One chilling shot to the heart was all it took to
make them hers forever.

Yet the Norse did not regard Skadi with fear or loathing, awesome as her
power was in its glacial finality. No doubt they recognized that some darkness is the inevitable cost of human existence—as inevitable, indeed, as the
blizzards of northern winters, as certain as death itself.

It takes a southern imagination, one trained in the seasonless sameness
of the Mediterranean, to concoct a heaven of sweetness and light, an unnat-

ural realm where death has no dominion. And so, early Christian missionaries turned Skadi, the benevolent rescuer of those too young or too weak to suffer the rigors of winter, into the malevolent Snow Queen. It was she, they said, who tempted children away from home, captivated them, turned their tender little hearts to ice.

The stuff of fairy tales, you say? Twentieth-century rationality would have it so. Yet a primal imagination still flickers in the heart of the modern-day hunter. There is wisdom in the ancient legend of the winter goddess. It is a wisdom born of hunting in northern climes, where extremities shape experience, where nothing comes easily except, perhaps, the drawing of a last breath.

The winter of 1985–86 brought record-breaking cold to the Northern Plains. Beginning early in November, an unremitting flow of arctic air swept down from Alberta into the Dakotas and eastern Montana, bringing early snow cover and daily high temperatures around ten below zero, when the sun was shining. At night the thermometer regularly plunged to thirty, forty, fifty below. On still days, the air itself felt frozen. When the wind blew, the congealed air shattered into myriad invisible particles, minuscule projectiles that pierced through layers of clothing and found their way through the tiniest cracks.

Skadi's arrows, a settler from an earlier time might have mused. The first Europeans who tried to make a living off this land were, after all, well-acquainted with the ways of the Snow Queen. Winters are typically harsh in this country. Today, long-abandoned homesteads dot the countryside, bearing mute testimony to the cold, dark, and often despairing wintertimes their inhabitants must have endured.

This landscape is scarcely more forgiving now than a century ago. Driving the gravel highway in the southeastern corner of Montana, one passes a reminder of the tenuousness of living in these parts. Before a cluster of now-vacant buildings that once formed a settlement with town hall, school, and post office hangs a large and carefully crafted wooden sign. It reads simply, "Albion: 1914–1964." Had Albion's demise had something to do with the winters here?

So I would have believed in November 1985, though the extreme chill of that season seemed oddly appropriate to me. My mother had died horribly the preceding spring after a long struggle with cancer. In the fall my thirteen-year-old cat also developed cancer; I'd had him put to sleep in October. I was overworked and underpaid, doing a one-year stint teaching English at a state college in western South Dakota. My husband, Doug, meanwhile, was between teaching jobs and frustrated about it. We were as near to a subsistence economy as we had ever been, or hope to be again, living close to the bone. Hunting had never been mere sport to me, but in these circumstances it took on a special urgency, not only because we needed the meat (we hunted for that every year), but because it leant some degree of normalcy, or sanity, to a world otherwise gone askew.

So the weather, brutal as it was, could not keep us indoors as the end of deer season drew near. It may have been a matter of not giving in when the conventional wisdom would have been to settle down by a cozy fire with a brandy and a good book. But the wisdom of hunters is in any case unconventional. Better to risk frostbite and endure what could only promise to be, in physical terms, an utterly miserable experience than to let deer season slip by for a year. With subzero temperatures the day-to-day norm, it seemed more reasonable to be out braving the same elements as the deer than to be shut up, unnaturally, indoors. There has to be, between hunter and hunted, more than a fair-weather kinship.

On the day before Thanksgiving we set out for a spot not far from Albion, some public land along the Little Missouri River where we had frequently seen mule deer in the trees hugging the shallow river bank. We drove, mostly in silence, in the pre-dawn darkness, our breath frosting the windshield. As we neared our destination, the day gradually came on, sunrise in the form of a soft shimmering of light through the crystalline air. It would be an overcast day, and bitingly cold.

We were hunting antlerless deer, having both filled our "A-tags" earlier in the season. Since this was a hunt for meat, and since safety dictated limiting our outdoor exposure, this outing had a no-nonsense feel about it. Doug brought the pickup to a stop and cut the ignition. Staring ahead through the windshield, on which our suffused breath was laying a fresh veneer of frost, he sighed after a moment or two, "Come on, let's get this over with." Roused from the fairly comfortable reverie into which I'd slipped in the relative warmth of the cab, I reluctantly opened my door and, though I had known it was coming, was nonetheless stunned by the assault of numbing cold on my face.

As the daylight increased, so did the wind. We would need to walk a broad arc across wide-open pasture land to get downwind of the deer we felt reasonably sure would be lingering along the creek that feeds the river there. Even with the wind at our backs, the cold was excruciating. Doug remarked that he thought the tears in his eyes must be freezing; my eyelids, too, scraped when I blinked. Breathing was difficult, virtually impossible when facing into the wind. The sun, a translucent disk, was retreating into the frigid sky. Snow would be falling before long.

After several hundred yards of crunching through ice-encrusted grass, we sprinted along a fenceline toward the creek bed. Skidding down an embankment where the fence dipped toward the creek bottom, we were suddenly brought up short by what lay ahead: a little fawn, curled as if asleep, snugly nestled in the snow drifted against a fencepost. The tiny deer was frozen solid. It might have died days, or mere hours, ago. Doug knelt and stroked the fawn affectionately, as one might a cat or dog found napping by the woodstove. We kept a few moments' quiet vigil: A little death like this could not go unmarked, unmourned. Then we continued down toward the creek.

It was a relief to descend into a prairie cut, between the sheltering walls of the creek. Ordinarily, one of us would have walked the meandering creek bottom while the other walked the rim, on the alert for deer jumping ahead. But today was a day to err on the side of prudence, so we stayed together, the wind whirling overhead.

With miles of uninterrupted rangeland extending east and west of the Little Missouri, this waterway is a major deer-run, providing not only shelter, but also an escape route from danger. Yet there were surprisingly few tracks or other deer-sign here. We worked our way slowly, quietly, along. I became aware that, aside from the dead fawn, a couple of shivering magpies were the only wildlife I had seen.

At one point, where the creek doubles back on itself, there is a small grove of ash and poplar. Rounding a curve in the creek, we came within sight of this stand of thicker cover, and there we spotted four deer—a small buck, a rather large doe, and two fawns. They knew we were there, scarcely a hundred yards off, but they remained motionless, looking in our direction. We continued to weave cautiously through the creek bed toward them. When we were within fifty yards of them, we eased our way up the bank and into the open. Still, the deer stood as if frozen in space and time.

Stressed to the limits of endurance by so much cold so early in winter, the deer were conserving every bit of energy they could. This helped account for the absence of deer-sign in the creek; this little group probably never strayed from these trees if they could possibly avoid it.

We stopped perhaps twenty-five yards from them. The deer began edging away, clearly reluctant to expend the precious energy they would need to flee. They were, in effect, trapped by their instinct to survive. In such a situation, shooting was impossible. We stood as motionless as the deer.

Then, exchanging a quick glance and a wordless nod, we turned away and tracked across the snowswept pasture in their full view, without looking back.

Circling back to the creek bed, we followed a different branch now. It was midmorning, and our own energy reserves were ebbing. Taking a shortcut back to our pickup, we started across a stubble-field toward the fenceline we had walked along earlier. Almost immediately, we spotted some deer at the far end of the field, several hundred yards off. No more than indistinct shapes, they appeared and disappeared, phantoms in the now thinly falling snow. With the wind in our favor, and the snow as much camouflage for us as for them, we proceeded along the fence until we were perhaps two hundred yards away. Steadying my .30/06 on a fencepost, I focused the scope on a doe, another doe, a fawn, another fawn.

Teeth chattering and my right hand burning with cold (I had to remove my deerskin mitten to shoot), I thought quickly about the fawn we had seen curled peacefully in the snow, about those deer paralyzed for sheer survival in the trees. "I'm taking the one farthest to the left," I whispered to Doug, who was also aiming his rifle. I placed the crosshairs for a heart shot, and fired. His shot came an instant later.

We had killed the two fawns.

Too Good a Heart
to Be a Killer?
The Continuing Adventures of Man the
Hunter and Woman the Gatherer

That the stories of Man the Hunter and Woman the Gatherer
amount to little more than useful (if inaccurate) generalizations
about human realities led anthropologists to abandon the hunting hypothesis years ago. Yet its hero and heroine remain curiously alive and well in the popular and scholarly minds. In this
chapter I explore the implications of their subsequent careers, in
hunting literature on the one hand, and ecofeminism on the
other. What seems to be centrally at stake in both cases is the
question of women's special relationship to the nature from
which men are held to be essentially alienated, and against which
they vent their frustration. The exclusion of women from hunting
turns out to be a necessary counterpart to their social and psychological subordination to men. It all comes down to the issue of
power, both literal and symbolic, and to American culture's deep-
rooted ambivalence about power in female hands.

HUNTERS, WILD MEN,
AND MOTHER NATURE

Man the Hunter muses about life, death and love:

> Now, looking out the tunnel of trees over the ravine at the sky with
> white clouds moving across in the wind, I loved the country so that
> I was happy as you are after you have been with a woman that you
> really love, when, empty, you feel it welling up again and there it

57

is, now, you can have, and you want more and more, to have, and
be, and live in, to possess now again for always, for that long,
sudden-ended always; making time stand still, sometimes so very
still that afterwards you wait to hear it move, and it is slow in starting. But you are not alone, because if you have ever really loved her
happy and untragic, she loves you always; no matter whom she
loves nor where she goes she loves you more. So if you have loved
some woman and some country you are very fortunate and, if you
die afterwards it makes no difference.[1]

This passage, from Ernest Hemingway's hunting memoir
Green Hills of Africa, is an excellent example of what literary
critic Annette Kolodny has termed the "pastoral impulse" in
American life and letters, "a yearning to know and respond to the
landscape as feminine."[2] The envisioning of the land as wife, or
mother, or mistress (or some combination thereof) is a literary
convention nearly as old as those green hills that, designating
them "nature," the masculine imagination has long perceived to
be in some irreducible sense other than itself. Indeed, just as the
sexual division of labor forms the basis of the story of Man the
Hunter, the close identification of women with nonhuman nature is the foundation of Euro-American culture, a theme that
has predominated its religious and cultural mythology since the
advent of agrarianism.[3] "Nature," like "Woman," can be roman-
tically envisioned as a kind mother or a willing mistress. But
experience teaches that she is just as likely, and just as unpre-
dictably, cruel, heartless, and destructive. She therefore needs
to be possessed, tamed, and controlled, lest her power over-
whelm "Man."[4] Reversing the terms, one might say a woman un-
leashed is the exact equivalent of a natural disaster.
    Kolodny suggests that the idea of land-as-woman achieved a
particular poignancy in the American cultural imagination because of the sheer vastness and untamed wildness of this "New
Eden." She asks, "Was there perhaps a *need* to experience the
land as a nurturing breast because of the threatening, alien, and
potentially emasculating terror of the unknown? Beautiful, indeed, that wilderness appeared—but also dark, uncharted, and

prowled by howling beasts. In a sense, to make the new continent Woman was already to civilize it a bit, casting the stamp of human relations upon what was otherwise unknown and untamed."[5] The key phrase here is "civilize it *a bit*," since from the patriarchal point of view there is something fundamentally (and necessarily) *un*civilized about woman, except insofar as she has been shaped, molded, defined by a masculine imagination.

This, of course, was something at which Papa Hemingway was quite adept. His reflections on loving a country/loving a woman are especially interesting, and revealing, when compared with what he says about the flesh-and-blood women in his life. In *Green Hills of Africa,* he describes his second wife, Pauline (or "P.O.M." for "Poor Old Mama"), in nonhuman terms: "[A]lways lovely to look at asleep . . . close curled like an animal," to him she is like a "little terrier." Pauline apparently felt herself to be on the losing end of this simile: "P.O.M. disliked intensely being compared to a little terrier. If she must be like any dog, and she did not wish to be, she would prefer a wolfhound, something lean, racy, long-legged and ornamental."[6] No mere "ornament" around the hunting camp, however, Pauline was an accomplished hunter in her own right. While she gets her share of apparently sincere (if hardly unstinting) praise from Papa on this account, she receives even more of his approbation on those occasions when she defers to his necessarily superior skill—claiming, for example, to miss shots she had actually made so the credit would be his. One gets the decided impression in this narrative that Papa loved his nature wild but his wives domesticated.

This becomes even clearer in what he writes of his later wife, Mary, on a subsequent Safari recounted in his *African Journals.* Mary, he says, had "too good a heart to be a killer." She nevertheless hunted at his side. In the celebrated story "Miss Mary's Lion," Hemingway writes, "In six months of daily hunting she had learned to love it, shameful though it is basically, and unshameful as it is if done cleanly, but there was something too good in her that worked subconsciously and made her pull off the target. I loved her for it in the same way that I could not love a woman who could work in the stockyards, or put dogs or cats out of their suffering, or destroy horses who had broken their legs at a race-course."[7] Might one also suspect that he loved it because it rendered Mary less threatening to his carefully guarded masculinity? In the macho scheme of things, any woman is in principle a potential danger. When a woman becomes *actually* dangerous, she also becomes the "human correlative" to the dark, thick, beast-filled forest where the unwary adventurer may lose not only his way, but his life.[8]

Such a dangerous woman married the hapless hero of one of Hemingway's most famous stories, "The Short Happy Life of Francis Macomber." Lest we entertain any doubts about the sort of creature she is, Wilson, the British white hunter in the story, describes her. She is, he says, typical of American women in general. He knows the type; they are "the hardest in the world: the hardest, the cruelest, the most predatory and the most attractive and their men have softened or gone to pieces nervously as they have hardened. Or is it that they pick men they can handle?" When, at story's end, Mrs. Macomber shoots and kills her unfortunate spouse, Wilson reflects that she has dispatched one of "the great American boy-men."[9] The professional hunter knows that type, too: they are the tender-minded ones who let themselves be seduced, only to be destroyed, by the call of the wild.

Hemingway's ambivalence about female power in these narratives is not a matter of mere metaphor. "The Short Happy Life of Francis Macomber" was inspired by an actual incident, in which a woman who was widely regarded as a better hunter than her husband had apparently killed him in an "accident" that was patently a case of murder.[10] Hemingway leaves the ending more ambiguous in his fictional rendering of the incident, as did the subsequent Hollywood film adaptation of the story.[11] Here, as in his descriptions of his wives, the goodness of a woman's heart seems to relate directly, and inversely, to the accuracy of her shooting. The mere notion that a woman could handle a gun—that obvious symbol of male potency—as efficiently as could a man, and for the same approximate reasons and toward the same apparent ends, is just too unsettling to patriarchally constructed masculinity.

This calls to mind a question posed by Donna Haraway, who not insignificantly cites Hemingway's *Green Hills of Africa* as one of the signal texts elucidating the "crisis of white manhood" in the twentieth century. She asks: "Does society fall apart if men lose their equipment?"[12] Or, we might venture, if women have that same equipment? (Fear of emasculation cuts both ways, after all.) As already stated, patterns of tool manufacture and use among early humans are far from clear, but studies show that modern hunter-gatherer groups display a marked tendency to define tools that can be used as weapons as men's tools, and to keep them out of women's hands.[13] Among those same groups, manhood is something that must be proved, generally through a display of hunting prowess. Indeed, the need for males to prove their masculinity—usually through demonstrations of aggressive behavior—appears to be a universal phenomenon. "Manhood" cannot be inferred from mere anatomical maleness.[14] Yet to achieve it one has to possess the right biological and psychological "equipment." In this light, Paul Shepard has written, "the male of the species is genetically programmed to pursue, attack, and kill for food. To the extent that men do not do so they are not fully human."[15] More to the point— as Hemingway surely would have agreed—they are not fully *men*.

Along similar lines, some interpreters have suggested that men are anxious about masculinity because evolutionary pressures have "predisposed" them to be anxious about it. When we were all hunter-gatherers, the reasoning goes, our success and group survival depended upon men's developing genetically determined "masculine" traits, especially tendencies toward aggression and male bonding. As we saw in the first chapter, this argument actually explains more about modern western male self-consciousness than about anything else, prehistoric or otherwise.

Perhaps for this reason, sociologist David Gilmore judges it to be "useful in certain cases . . . most notably in the violent patriarchies."[16] Relying on post-Freudian theory, Gilmore suggests that males are driven to sharply distinguish the men from the boys by a primal fear of the power women can exert against them:

"The principal danger to the boy is not a unidimensional fear of the punishing father but a more ambivalent fantasy-fear about the mother."[17] The fear is of self-annihilation—symbolized, of course, by castration.

Gilmore's analysis is helpful here. Indeed, one need not be an adherent of post-Freudian, nor indeed of any psychoanalytic, explanations of human behavior to see that many men in modern American society fear annihilation—or at the least, very serious damage—at the hands of women. The John and Lorena Bobbitt case in 1993 had men nationwide fretting about an outbreak of female violence directed at their "equipment," and the neoconservative argument for "white male rights" equates any feminist challenge to male dominance with "man-bashing." Perhaps even more telling than the general atmosphere of antifeminist backlash is the concerted effort on the part of the mainline media, the medical and legal establishments, to keep weapons—most specifically firearms—out of the hands of women.[18]

Whereas men have to achieve "masculinity," women in western societies have "femininity" thrust upon us. We do not have to prove ourselves, we have simply to be what we are: "caring nurturers." From early childhood forward, we learn not only that it is unfeminine to want to play with boys' weapon-like toys and join in their rough-and-tumble activities, we also (and more importantly) learn that although males can use aggression to get what they want, the same tactic will not work for us.[19] Aggressive power, like that symbolized by a loaded gun, is seen as dangerously counterproductive in female hands. A good woman has "too good a heart to be a killer." Females are "by nature" weaker, more passive and emotional, and more dependent, and the men in charge want to keep us that way.

Obviously, the hunting hypothesis comes in extremely handy here, and this helps to account for why it continues to exert a powerful influence over the popular imagination, even as it has been abandoned by professional anthropologists. Indeed, unfettered by the constraints of logic or fact, the myth of man-the-hunter has enjoyed something of a renascence in the last few years. "Wild Men" seek to reconnect with their hunter-warrior selves, to recapture the masculine identities that powerful women (their mothers, their wives) have robbed them of. "Men's movement" gatherings are replete with the trappings of idealized hunter-gatherer life: masks, drums, sweat lodges, loincloths, dances, and chants around the camp fire. The rituals at Wild Man retreats are necessarily free form, as one practitioner puts it, because "nobody knows what a postprimitive ritual should be, now that we don't live in the woods anymore." This does not preclude men "who ordinarily might not know which end of an ax to grasp" from living out "a fantasy of aboriginal frolic."[20] The hunting at these gatherings is, of course, strictly metaphorical.[21]

This is a source of some annoyance to those "real men" in our midst who neither eat quiche nor snake-dance by firelight. Speaking on their behalf, outdoor writer George Reiger wrote an article, "Instinct and Reality," for the September 1991 issue of *Field and Stream*, in which he observed that "Most of my male friends smile at what the media claim to be a growing male identity crisis." Remarking that a recent cover of *Newsweek* had proclaimed the men's movement to be the social reform movement of the nineties, Reiger complained: "Few of the middle-aged men I know . . . fit into this category. As boys, most went to summer camp or had fathers who took them on hunting and fishing trips. Most also served in the military. In other words, they all passed through traditional rites of passage as young men and consequently today don't have to beat tom-toms in woodsy group-therapy sessions to compensate for the lack of those experiences."[22] Hunting, Reiger goes on to explain in what might serve as a primer of the main points of the hunting hypothesis, "enables a boy to seek and find manhood without the attendant guilt of killing other humans." With a nod to Joseph Campbell (whom he apparently does not recognize to be a mentor for Wild Men), Reiger further explains that questing—venturing forth into the great wide world—is an essential need for men, and is in fact "uniquely masculine." Men "are forever drawn to frontiers, to the unknown."[23]

Women, meanwhile, "prefer returning to places where they've been secure and happy." While they might sometimes participate

in men's "expeditions of self-discovery," for women such exploration is more an "option" than a "need." Reiger seems aware that
this observation might draw the charge of sexism. And so he explains:

> This does not belittle women. Indeed, it acknowledges their cru-
> cial role as the custodians of our species' reproductive and cultural
> potential. But it also acknowledges that men and women often are
> motivated by different instincts. Few women see much advantage
> in the cold, wet realm in which ducks, dogs, and certain males
> seem to thrive—unless, by sharing a blind, a girl might make her
> father proud, or a young lady might find a husband like her own
> duck-hunting dad.
>
> Ever since our species evolved the capacity for contemplating
> the meaning of life in the face of inevitable death, boys have intu-
> itively sought passage into manhood through enduring some ritual
> of hardship or suffering. . . . Our canine companions link us to na-
> ture and our misty origins in the Pleistocene.[24]

Meanwhile, "our women" presumably would rather be home
planting petunias.

Significantly, Reiger's meditation on the inner cave man is
linked to a discussion of different philosophies of wildlife management, in this age of ever-more-limited opportunities for the
kind of initiatory outdoor experience it takes, so he would argue,
to make boys into men. The more problematic men's relation to
the wild world becomes, the more seductive is the myth of Man
the Hunter. And the more tangled his relation to women in the
afterwash of second-wave feminism, the more attractive nonag-
gressive, stay-at-home Woman the Gatherer appears. The world
of nature (itself a woman, a mother) affords a retreat where men
can still be men, whether "Wild Men" or hunters.

THE CLOSING OF THE FRONTIER

Masculine discourse about Man the Hunter and his relation to
women and nature cannot take quite the same form now, of
course, as it could before the feminist revolution of the 1970s.

The pressure that second-wave feminism exerted on proponents of the hunting hypothesis is reflected in the writings, from that period, of Paul Shepard. In important works of environmental philosophy like *Man in the Landscape* (1967), and *The Tender Carnivore and the Sacred Game* (1973), Shepard argued that the course of human social evolution went badly off track ten thousand years ago, when more egalitarian hunter-gatherer cultures began to be overtaken by agrarian, and later urban, societies. Key products of this supposed cultural advance were the development of private property (with women and children reckoned among a man's major possessions) and the institution of slavery. A pernicious side-effect of agrarianism was the process of environmental depredation that would eventuate, ten millennia later, in today's global ecological crisis. In *Nature and Madness* (1982), Shepard further argued that our supposed evolutionary progress has in fact yielded something like a mass neurosis, which technological man is acting out in violent behaviors that are destructive of both self and environment.

Shepard urged that the way to regain our sanity, and to save our fragile planet, would be to effect a return to something like a hunter-gatherer cultural and religious mindset, which he termed "techno-cynegetic."[25] In the reformed society he envisioned, animals would no longer be domesticated, and food would be produced in laboratories (microbially) and small home gardens, allowing the land outside human settlement to revert to wilderness. Children's education would focus on an intimate knowledge of the workings of the natural world. Boys would be initiated to manhood through hunting, and as adults would spend a designated part of each year-cycle engaging in that activity. Girls and women would not hunt large animals, but would engage in gathering and gardening; women would also perform most of the administrative and educational tasks within the human community. "It is time to confront the division between man and the rest of nature," Shepard declared, "between ourselves as animals and as humans, not by the destruction of nature or by a return to some dream of the past, but by creating a new civilization."[26] In Shepard's view, he and his urban contemporaries were poised at the ideal historical moment for such a project, because of similarities between postindustrial and hunter-gatherer men laid down by human evolution.[27]

Yet, as with the hunting hypothesis that so clearly inspired Shepard's visionary writing, this perceived kinship between the civilized and the tribal *is* in fact grounded in "a dream of the past." This was especially clear with regard to women's natural and social roles, which were also, in his view, predetermined by the forces of evolution. Men came to hunt and women to gather, he ventured, because "Women in some measure share with the apes a pre-hunting perception and psychology, even a musculature, from which men are excluded: a world of frugivorousness and pensiveness, at once more intensely social and more tranquil than that to which man's symbolic carnivorousness led."[28]

Shepard was writing this in 1973, as the second wave of American feminism was beginning to crest. Thus he had to take into account questions about gender difference, whose answers Papa Hemingway, and his hunter colleagues and forebears, could pretty much assume as givens. Sensitive to the emergent feminist critique of sex-role inequalities, Shepard therefore tried to distinguish his belief in essential gender differences—psychological as well as biological—from cruder forms of sexism. Immediately following the passage about women and apes quoted above, he remarked:

> In a time of increasing confusion over gender differences, the evolutionary past provides a meaningful perspective. Admittedly the line between specialization of role and arbitrary social oppression as seen today is not easy to determine. . . . The reality of innate temperamental differences does not justify any social-status distinctions. Male chauvinism based on evolutionary determinism is reprehensible. But it is futile to pronounce, at the end of fifteen million years of hominid evolution, that men and women are alike.[29]

There are some obvious, and egregious, flaws in Shepard's reasoning. As Adrienne Rich was remarking at about the same time he was writing *The Tender Carnivore*, under patriarchy women are forced "to learn, often through painful self-discipline and self-cauterization, those qualities which are supposed to be 'innate' in us."[30] Social oppression, "as seen today," is anything but "arbitrary." It is grounded precisely in those differences that are called innate, but that amount for the most part to learned behaviors related, for ideological reasons, to accidents of anatomy.

Shepard's evident failure to see the ideological agenda at work in his own analysis would not be especially noteworthy, given the traditions of patriarchal scholarship, were it not for the fact that in so many other ways his analysis of contemporary culture is congruent with the best feminist scholarship.[31] What accounts for the fact that a thinker as perceptive and as sensitive as he, despite evidence before his eyes, could yet cling so tenaciously to the fundamental gender ideals of Man the Hunter and Woman the Gatherer? Perhaps, in the face of massive environmental degradation and social upheaval, he sensed the only way forward to be the way back. The frontier is closing, he seems to be saying, and we must live to learn within these boundaries.

The idea of the closing of the frontier is particularly apt in this case because for Shepard, as for Hemingway (and for Reiger), Man the Hunter is defined by, indeed he is a hunter by virtue of, his unique relationship to the frontier, the wide open spaces. This brings us back to the question of the land as female.

Annette Kolodny suggests that Frederick Jackson Turner's 1893 declaration of the significance of the closing of the American frontier, reflected "the final frustration" of the pastoral impulse. The loss of a frontier upon which to imprint the masculine urge for exploration and domination was analogous to the infant's loss of its exclusive access to the mother. It constituted a threatening disillusionment, and—as in the inarticulate rage of the disappointed child—it generated a violent response. Kolodny summarizes:

> As with all frustrations that cannot be either mediated or resolved, the frustration of the pastoral impulse was finally expressed through anger—anger at the land that had seemed to promise and

then defeat men's longings for an ambiance of total gratification. It is an anger that did not end with the nineteenth century. What appears today as the single-minded destruction and pollution of the continent is just one of the ways we have continued to express that anger.[32]

What appears even clearer today than it was in the 1970s is that frustration at the closing of the patriarchal frontier is at the root of epidemic violence not only against the earth, but against women as well. This is indeed a central insight of that branch of feminism known as "ecofeminism." Drawing on connections between male domination of women and of nonhuman animals and nature, ecofeminists have singled out Man the Hunter for radical reproach. It is, therefore, doubly ironic that he and his mate, Woman the Gatherer, are not only alive and well in ecofeminist critiques of hunting, but appear to be the driving forces behind them.

"THE ROARING INSIDE HER"

The direct parallel between the rape of women and the rape of nonhuman nature in patriarchal culture is a familiar theme in feminist discourse. In *Woman and Nature: The Roaring Inside Her*, one of the signal texts of second-wave feminism, Susan Griffin develops the connection with explicit reference to hunting:

> She has captured his heart. She has overcome him. He cannot tear his eyes away. He is burning with passion. He cannot live without her. He pursues her. She makes him pursue her. The faster she runs, the stronger his desire. He will overtake her. He will make her his own. He will have her. (The boy chases the doe and her yearling for nearly two hours. She keeps running despite her wounds. He pursues her through pastures, over fences, groves of trees, crossing the road, up hills, volleys of rifle shots sounding, until perhaps twenty bullets are embedded in her body.)[33]

Griffin juxtaposes images of rapacious sexual pursuit with violent hunting vignettes (the killing of deer, hare, elephants, wolves, whales) under the heading: "HIS POWER: He Tames What Is Wild." In implicitly connecting male violence against animals and against women, Griffin was one of the first to sound the note of what would come to be referred to as ecofeminism.[34]

Ecofeminism comes in several forms and variations.[35] Of particular interest in the present context is a distinctly American variation on the ecofeminist theme, one which stresses, on one hand, the connection between women, animals, and the earth; and on the other, the links between hunting, warfare, and rape as the predominant ways men relate to women, animals, and earth.[36] Generally referred to as "radical ecofeminism," this line of thinking draws its inspiration from radical feminist theory and goddess spirituality, and from the philosophy of animal rights or liberation. Many consider it to be on the cutting edge of feminist theory.[37]

In the introduction to her book *Rape of the Wild: Man's Violence Against Animals and the Earth*, the late Andrée Collard summed up the central premise of radical ecofeminism in her declaration "that it is a fact that no woman will be free until all animals are free and nature is released from man's ruthless domination."[38] The male domination of women is, in this view, inextricably linked to the mastery of nonhuman animals; sexism and "speciesism" are thus parallel forms of oppression. However, women share with men the spurious privilege of species. It is therefore incumbent upon feminists to speak for those who cannot. As Ingrid Newkirk, national director of People for the Ethical Treatment of Animals (PETA) and a board member of Feminists for Animal Rights (FAR) states the case, "Most oppressed groups of human beings can speak for themselves; but until we learn to understand the languages of other-than-humans, we must 'speak for the animals.'"[39] That this point of view is determinedly naive, regarding the structure and dynamics of human social oppression, is obvious; such human groups as "crack babies," the homeless, adolescent runaways, illegal aliens, and victims of chronic domestic abuse are, in realistic terms, no more able to "speak for themselves" than are nonhuman animals. But from the radical ecofeminist point of view, to point this out and by implication to prioritize human interests over those of nonhuman animals, is to be guilty of the sin of speciesism.[40]

Pressing the argument still further, Carol Adams posits meat-eating and the abuse of women as "fused forms of oppression."[41] Vegetarianism (or, more properly, *veganism*, the eschewing of all animal products) is, thus, a sine qua non for radical ecofeminism, and indeed from this perspective a touchstone for any true feminism.[42] It is small wonder, therefore, that hunting serves here as a root metaphor for patriarchal man's rape of nature. Indeed, from this vantage point hunting and rape are virtually interchangeable.[43]

Man the Hunter and Woman the Gatherer are not only alive, but indeed thriving, in radical ecofeminist theory. In *Rape of the Wild*, published postumously in 1988, Collard presents the by-then-abandoned hunting hypothesis as "current anthropological theory." She then proceeds to develop a critique of that theory which oddly enough accepts all its basic premises: that men originated hunting and that it is an "activity that commonly has been attributed to males only"; that warfare evolved directly out of hunting, and that the invention of weapons resulted from men's inborn aggressiveness and superior physical strength; and that women, by virtue of their close natural connection to hearth and home, are physically and temperamentally unsuited to the ways of hunting and war.[44]

Though Collard recognizes the hunting hypothesis as a product of patriarchal scientific imagination, she nonetheless allows it to shape her own theory of the rise of patriarchy. Citing Washburn and Lancaster's claim that men originated hunting and warfare because they find killing enjoyable, she posits a primitive hoard of "hunter-kings" who "spread their value systems through the violence of wars, destroying nature, killing animals, raping women and in general abusing those they enslaved. It is in this context that human intellect, interests, emotions, and basic social life evolved in patriarchy."[45] Hunting in this analysis is thus not only the cause of, but the primary metaphor for, all forms of male domination. Collard's vitriol against hunters knows no bounds; they are, quite simply, "insane."[46]

Simultaneously, Collard exempts women from any form of intentional violence against animals or the earth, because of their "physical and spiritual connections" with nonhuman nature. Indeed, she goes so far as to argue that when, in certain subsistence situations, women have been involved in killing animals for food, that process in those circumstances is "misname[d] hunting (an inappropriate word when used to refer to the occasional capture of an animal to ensure survival)."[47] This equivocation recalls Tim Ingold's observation that there is a tendency to regard the taking of animal life as hunting when men or nonhuman predators do it, but as something else when women do it. Ingold, as we saw earlier, roots this tendency in a male-dominant imagination that wishes to keep women subordinated. But for Collard and her ecofeminist colleagues, women's essential nonviolence is an important article of feminist faith.

Collard regards Woman the Gatherer as the originator of true humanity. She posits the mother-child bond as the foundation of human society, and grounds language and culture in the female-defined home, which exists in opposition to the wider world of male hunters' savagery. As in other instances of the gathering hypothesis, if one sets ideological nuances aside, her picture (Men> Hunt>Animals/Women>Gather>Plants) comes out looking remarkably like the position she is ostensibly refuting. Her acceptance of the essential differences between women and men is grounded, however unwittingly, in precisely those categories feminism at large seeks to overturn.[48]

This is a common characteristic of radical ecofeminist argumentation. Woman the Gatherer is at work in the insistence that vegetarianism is the only appropriate dietary choice for true feminists. "Gathering," in their lexicon, refers strictly (and mistakenly) only to the procurement of nonanimal plant resources. In *The Sexual Politics of Meat*, Adams rehearses the gathering hypothesis, and sums up the egalitarian nature of "plant-based economies" in feminist-utopian terms:

Plant-based economies are more likely to be egalitarian. This is
because women are and have been the gatherers of vegetable
foods, and these are invaluable resources for a culture that is
plant-based. In these cultures, men as well as women were dependent on women's activities. . . . Yet, where women gather vegetable food and the diet is vegetarian, women do not discriminate as
a consequence of distributing the staple. By providing a large proportion of the protein food of a society, women gain an essential
economic and social role without abusing it.[49]

There is clearly more of fantasy than of fact in Adams's depiction of "plant-based" societies. Working from a broad array of
documented sources, anthropologist Paola Tabet has clearly
shown, for example, that 1) the term "egalitarian" is itself quite
slippery in anthropological literature, and often is used to imply
that women's and men's gender-divided activities are in some
fashion "complementary" or "reciprocal," although men's hunting activity is still more highly valued; 2) the more responsibility
women bear for food production, the more likely it is they will
be overworked and deprived of rest, in comparison with men
who enjoy leisure time when they are not hunting; 3) women's
work is more arduous because their tools are inferior, and it is
more monotonous as well; 4) "the fact that subsistence depends
in great part on the labor of women does not prevent men from
dominating"; and 5) not only does gathering involve the procurement of animal as well as plant resources, these animal
resources are themselves highly valued. Tabet notes several
studies which show that "the stress in the literature on women
as gatherers of vegetable food has . . . been grossly overdone, and
the importance of small protein sources [such] as eggs, birds,
lizards, burrowing animals and grubs has been greatly under-
estimated. [For example] . . . [w]omen in the Eastern Western
Desert [of Australia] saw themselves as going out primarily for
meat."[50]

A key element of Adams's analysis, however, is that meat is a
symbol of male violence, while vegetables symbolize the pacifis-

tic, female life force. Adams therefore also insists that meat is man's food not merely symbolically, but literally, whereas women really prefer to cook and eat fruits and vegetables. That more women do not spontaneously adopt a vegetarian diet owes, in her view, to their fear of violent male reprisals.[51]

Adams's thesis comes out sounding oddly like Paul Shepard's observations about the natural "frugivorousness" of females. Indeed, aside from radical ecofeminism, it is probably only among latter-day adherents of the hunting hypothesis that the opposition of male carnivorousness to female frugivorousness (symbolic or otherwise) is taken all that seriously.[52] The same is true of the contentions of Adams, Collard, Daly, and others that female consciousness has a close affinity with that of nonhuman animals, leading women to be able to communicate with and understand nonhuman animals in ways men cannot.[53]

The general agreement among radical ecofeminists, about women's innate nonviolence and their aversion to weapons and hunting, seems to derive in equal parts from the influences of animal rights philosophy on one hand, and radical feminist theory on the other. With regard to the former, it is certainly of no small importance that by its own reckoning the animal rights movement is between 75 and 80 percent female in its grassroots constituency.[54] To radical ecofeminists, this is symptomatic of the intimate identification women experience between their own and nonhuman animals' suffering in patriarchal culture. Griffin's identification of women with the male hunter's quarry arises from just such a logic of victimization.

Women, according to this logic, can only remain morally and culturally superior to men, to the extent that they are exempt from the male proclivity for violence and aggression.[55] Not all ecofeminists accept such idealizing of women and women's experience; indeed, some (those especially who tend to identify themselves as "social ecofeminists") have openly criticized the radical perspective. Ynestra King, for example, has remarked the problematic romanticization underlying the opposition of "good" women to "dastardly" men. "The problem," she asserts, "is that history, power, women and nature are all a lot more complicated than that."[56] Similarly, historian Vera Norwood has observed that this "utopian strain" of ecofeminist thinking fails to address the extent to which women themselves are implicated in the current environmental crisis.[57] Carolyn Merchant has argued that "in emphasizing the female, body, and nature components of the dualities male/female, mind/body, and culture/nature, radical ecofeminism runs the risk of perpetuating the very hierarchies it seeks to overthrow. Critics point to the problem of women's own reinforcement of their identification with a nature that Western culture degrades."[58]

All the above criticisms are certainly apt, but they do not go far enough. That gender-essentialism amounts to a form of reverse sexism has perhaps been a too-obvious—even if appropriate— ground on which to criticize it. What deserves more serious attention is the way ecofeminist essentialism (and it is not confined to radical writers) not only mirrors, but thereby grants validity to, the patriarchal understanding it claims it wants to dismantle. Nowhere is this clearer, than with regard to Man the Hunter. Just when he was beginning to question his dominant role in the scheme of things, along comes Woman the Gatherer and lets him off the hook. The social consequences of such validation of age-old gender stereotypes warrant far closer scrutiny than any ecofeminist critic has yet ventured.

By far the broadest, and most important, similarity between the seemingly opposed points of view of the hunting hypothesis and radical ecofeminism is their tendency to perceive a close connection beween women and the landscape.[59] Radical ecofeminist Linda Vance vigorously defends this connection, in the name of "empathy":

> Giving nature a female identity reinforces my sense of solidarity with the nonhuman world. . . . For many of us, empathy toward the nonhuman world is the heart of our political stance. We are not persuaded to be vegetarians only because someone argues that animals have inherent rights too, but also by freeing an intuitive kinship with them, or with the land. . . . Identification

and empathy may be dismissed by rationalists as sentimental—
as feminine—but passionate convictions, beliefs from the heart,
can always get us through the hard times when reason and argument fail.[60]

Such a perspective not only reinforces familiar stereotypes of
women as creatures of emotion, rather than reason, it also estab-
lishes for women an essentially privileged relation to nature and
animals. Men in this framework are necessarily cast in the role of
alienated outsiders, which of course renders highly problematic
their ability to imagine new, nonpatriarchal ways of relating to
the environment *or* to women. Given the ways in which this ecofeminism can recapitulate inherited stereotypes about the essential differences between women and men, it sanctions the per-
petuation of macho attitudes and behaviors on the part of men
who are at this point in history more than a little nervous about
the closing of their frontiers. Just when they thought they might
have to become more sensitive and compassionate, and maybe
even go off with their tom-toms into the woods, "cutting edge"
feminists give them a reprieve! And, more significantly, just when
those same men have begun to wonder about the implications of
sharing their power with women, these same feminists assure
them that women really do not want it.

Macho hunters and radical feminists certainly agree on one basic principle. It is summed up in Hemingway's suggestion that
women—the ones worth loving, at least, as "some country" is
worth loving—are distinguished by having "too good a heart to
be a killer." To the patriarchal imagination, such a woman is the
one who pulls off target, deferring to male authority/superiority.
To the radical feminist imagination, she is the woman who es-
chews male carnivorousness and aggression, preferring biophilic
identification with animals and the earth, those other long-time
victims of male aggression.

But what about the woman who lacks such purity of heart?
The woman, that is, who knows how to, and does, shoot straight?
The conventional feminist argument against women's arming
themselves—whether for hunting or for self-defense—derives

from an assumption that women are, either by nature or by social conditioning, less prone to aggression than men are, and further, that to resort to the use of any male-identified instrument of power—a firearm being the chief example—is to capitulate to patriarchy.[61] What seems really to be at work in the literal and metaphorical disarming of women, however, is a deep ambivalence about destructive power in female hands. Far from rejecting patriarchal definitions of female passivity and dependence, feminism tacitly reinforces those definitions when it comes to the question of the relationship of women to weapons and violence.[62]

In the radical feminist vision, the mere involvement of any woman in such male-identified activities as hunting and shooting is enough to qualify her as a creature of the patriarchal system: part of the problem, not the solution. Yet—and here is a crucial irony that calls into question all such facile bifurcations of social reality—women who assert themselves as equal in skill and power to men, who take men's equipment into their own hands for their own use, are perceived by patriarchy's "boy-men" as intensely troubling, divergent and threatening . . . indeed, as feminists![63]

This should tell us something. As long as aggressive power is defined as male, and passivity as female, the two halves of the human species are going to be conceptually at odds not only with each other, but also (though in different ways) with the dynamic realm of nonhuman nature. Feminism's manifest uneasiness about the implications of women's capacity for physical aggression can only be sustained by maintaining a determinedly ingenuous perspective on how the world of nature actually works. Macho males understand this well enough to perceive the advantage of keeping women out of the field. Perish the thought that women might take up arms, become skilled in their use, and become thereby simultaneously able to defend themselves *and* to fend for themselves! Woman the Hunter—as macho men grasp perhaps more readily than most feminists have to date—is a profoundly unsettling figure, her wildness a force to be reckoned with.

Obviously, if women and nature are conjoined in the patriarchal imagination to such an extent that the treatment of the one patterns that of the other,[64] then before we can begin to understand wild women, we must assess our notions of wildness itself. It is to this subject we shall presently turn, the next bend in the path of this inquiry.

3

Peaceable Kingdom

A hillside, just past dawn. Backlit by amber-rose shafts of daybreak, scattered tufts of tall grass and clumps of prickly pear cast long, transparent shadows. The wind is calm, the air clear and fragrant with early autumn. Kissed by the barest trace of dew, things shimmer in the rising sunlight. A small group of mule deer, all does, are browsing below the crest of the hill. They are joined by three pronghorns, two does and a buck. These also are breakfasting, on sage. A hawk lazily coasts the air currents above, riding the cerulean sky.

We are observing this early morning idyll from the cover of a shallow creekbank, perhaps a hundred fifty yards away. I inch up the bank, to get a better view. My movement sets a pebble slide in motion, a tiny disturbance at best in this morning's palpable tranquillity, but nevertheless enough to attract some attention. Up pop two coyotes from behind a dense cluster of brush at the base of the hill. They amble several yards uphill, pause to look around, sniffing the air for trouble. The deer and the antelope leave off their grazing, straighten to alert posture, begin to edge somewhat nearer to one another. Something—possibly the glint of sunlight off of our binoculars—spooks the now wary animals, and they simultaneously freeze in place, gazing our way. Thus is formed a striking tableau of predators and prey, with the deer to the left and pronghorns to the right, the coyotes a mere few paces below them.

"Damn," Doug whispers softly. "I wish we had a camera with us."

78

"So do I," I reply. "This scene could be 'October' on a Sierra Club calendar."

We watch for a few moments longer, holding a pose nearly as still as the others'. Then we stir to our feet to move on. This precipitates an explosion of action on the hillside. The mule deer stott up over the hill, the antelope wheel around and out of sight, the coyotes manage instantly to disappear.

The landscape and the morning, thus rearranged, are ours to explore.

We knew, of course, that the hillside vignette we had just witnessed would only have looked like a picture postcard from the peaceable kingdom to one ignorant of its context. Prey and predator had been briefly united in attentiveness, alive to the presence of a shared potential danger. It was really quite remarkable, we agreed as we strolled over toward that hillside, the extent to which the antelope and deer exhibited greater concern about us than about the coyotes, who for their part seemed oblivious to animals they would customarily regard as potential meals. A neat parable, this seemed, about the impact of human incursions upon nonhuman nature.

We discovered, however, when we reached the hillside, that we had not gotten the picture exactly right. The coyotes had been breakfasting, too; the remains of an antelope lay in the thicket from which they had emerged. No doubt they were already there when the deer and pronghorns had arrived, unsuspecting, on the scene. Indeed, they may well have been readying themselves to attack one of these unwary newcomers; there wasn't much left of the kill they had been feeding on. We very likely interrupted their stalk, and saved a life in the process. Ironic, to say the least, since we were there to do some killing ourselves.

We had been, that morning and the entire day before, scouting the region in preparation for antelope season, which would open the following day. While we had hunted deer in this region of northern Montana before,

we were new to this particular locale. Our first day's scouting had been discouraging, to say the least. All we saw were a lot of other hunters driving
around and glassing the plains, looking generally as frustrated as we were
beginning to feel. Over six thousand licenses were issued for this region,
based upon strong antelope numbers: There had to be pronghorns somewhere. But these animals are prairie phantoms; they can manage to dissolve
into the landscape. Late in the afternoon, we by chance ran into a game warden, who—after checking our licenses to be sure they were in order—suggested we try an out-of-the-way spot along something called Bluff Creek.

We arrived there shortly before sunset and found a good place to set up
camp near the creek, which turned out to be a fairly substantial stream for
this semiarid area. It was a pretty place, and the evening was lovely. As we
ate our supper, a pair of green-winged teal landed in the creek and paddled
about, unruffled by our being there. A muskrat swam by. The last red rays of
the sun caught the silhouette of a mule deer buck atop a nearby ridge.

Ducks—a few mallards had arrived by then—were still placidly swim-
ming next to our camp at dawn. The place had a distinctly special feel about
it, in light of which that early-morning hillside tableau somehow made per-
fect sense. As we spent the rest of the day roaming the area, a good-sized
chunk of public land that, amazingly, we appeared to have entirely to ourselves, it became almost impossible *not* to see wildlife. There were antelope
here, yes; it should be a good opening day. But even more impressive was
the density of the mule deer population; deer were jumping out of virtually
every draw, every bend of a creekbed. We had, it seemed, stumbled upon a
veritable nature park. Unaccustomed to getting such a terrific tip from a
game warden, I began to wonder whether he had not in fact been some sort
of guardian angel. This place was pretty close to a hunter's paradise.

Opening day provided excellent hunting indeed. We did not see any antelope for a while, though again there were deer all over the place. But
around nine o'clock or so, we rounded a hill and literally stumbled upon a

fairly large herd with several bucks in it. Doug shot the largest. After he had field-dressed and tagged it, we headed in the direction the herd had fled. They hadn't traveled far, in this undulating country. I shot my buck perhaps three hundred yards from where his had fallen. Simultaneously, Doug—who also was carrying a doe/fawn tag—shot a good-sized doe. All three were good, quick kills from a closer range than antelope hunting typically affords.

It took much of the rest of the day to drag our pronghorns the two miles or so back to the pickup. The weather had turned warm, so we decided to break camp and make the several hours' homeward drive that night, in order to get our meat in the freezer as quickly as possible. Since our camping gear took up the back of our Toyota, we secured one buck and the doe to a rack on top of the cab, the other buck to the tailgate.

We were on the road the hour before dusk, that other "golden hour" that, along with the dawn, sees the most vigorous hunter activity. We passed numerous pickups and RV's, their drivers and passengers in blaze orange. None of the vehicles we passed bore a single antelope, either buck or doe. And here we were with *three*. I seriously began to think of that warden as a fairy godfather. When we stopped for dinner at a cafe in Malta, and then later for gas in Roundup, we tried not to grin too broadly, to bask too obviously in our good fortune. Hunting has to do with pure luck, among other things; we had happened to be where the antelope were that day. A number of other hunters, dusty and weary but undaunted, admired our day's work. No doubt they went back to their camps or motels to scan their maps and dream about the next day's hunts. One hunter's good fortune often rubs off on another, and hunters thrive on hope.

A few weeks later, about halfway into deer season, we returned to our congenial campsite on Bluff Creek. Our hunterly hope had been sparked by all the mule deer we had seen there, and fueled by a month's anticipation. We projected a thoroughly satisfying sequel to our antelope hunt. Once again, we turned out to be the only hunters there.

Winter slides down from Saskatchewan into this part of northern Montana by early November, and while there was no snow cover yet, the air had turned sharply colder and more blustery. The ducks had long since migrated southward, and the muskrat set up winter housekeeping. Cattails, dry and brittle, rasped against the ice that had formed in the shallows on either side of the creek. The remaining wisps of vegetation had by now either died back, or dried up in a succession of hard overnight freezes. The landscape presented a rather limited spectrum of browns.

All of this was to be expected. The high plains get pretty austere pretty fast that time of year. You might say the effect, overall, is of a vastly clarified countryside, one in which things are thrown into sometimes surprisingly sharper relief, their rough edges laid bare. Mule deer—especially the bigger, mature bucks—are notoriously drawn to just this kind of terrain. Small wonder we had seen so many deer here a month before.

We did not see a single deer now, though. In two days of hard hunting, not a one. We turned over the possible logical explanations for this. The lack of snow cover made it more difficult to spot deer, but certainly not impossible. A more compelling argument was that by the third weekend in Montana's deer season, a sort of lull sets in. The first wave of hunters have been through the area, killing some deer and dispersing others. With relatively low mid-season hunting pressure, the deer typically don't move around much again until the height of the rut, which usually occurs toward the end of deer season, around Thanksgiving. Our timing was obviously off. We decided we might as well go home.

Driving the same county roads we had a month earlier, we passed several vehicles with deer strapped to them. It quickly became evident that it was less our timing that was off, than the story we'd been telling ourselves this last month. Every hunter knows better than to bank on a sure thing when it comes to predicting the outcome of a hunt. We had nonetheless indulged the mutual fantasy of returning, buck and doe tags in hand, to our exclusive deer preserve. Our peaceable little kingdom had gotten the better of us.

"You know," Doug smiled broadly, as we turned onto the interstate. "If there are any deer in there, they're smiling tonight."

"Smiling?" I thought, dreamily. Yes, they probably were, at that. I closed my eyes, and drifted. The next thing I knew, we were home.

The Call of the Wild:

American Eden and the
Domestication of Nature

We want what remains of the wild animals and their wilderness to stay the way we like to think of them . . .[1]

Insofar as women are identified with nonhuman nature, the question of female power connects with the problematic notion of wildness. A brief review of the history of American attitudes toward wild and domesticated nature, and of changing attitudes toward the value of wilderness, displays considerable ambivalence about the human confrontation with nature "red in tooth and claw." The facts of nonhuman predation and other forms of violence in nature have discomfiting implications for humans wrestling with the questions of their relationship to the natural world, as well as to each other.

The radical ecofeminist response to this dilemma has been to retreat into a wildly distorted version of nature romanticism, and to absolve women of responsibility for environmental depredation by placing the blame on the shoulders of Man the Hunter. I maintain that this amounts to a strategy of intellectual dishonesty. Women at this point become identified no longer with nature *in toto*, but only with the noble and life-affirming aspects of nonhuman nature. Nature, and humanity, are split into "good" and "bad" aspects, reflecting age-old prejudices in the updated dress of popular environmentalism. Lost in this vision is any concrete sense of nature as a process of life and death in which predation plays a central role, and in which women as well as men are implicated.

ANIMAL-LOVING

Man the Hunter has conventionally depended upon the little woman to be uninterested in, even downright opposed to, his outdoor pursuits. In *The Hunt*, to cite a fairly typical example, John G. Mitchell approvingly quotes "some chauvinist" who once observed that hunting camp is "a place too good for women," even as he questions "why, if adults must be boys, they have to pretend to be hunters as well." In this widely praised critique of the culture of hunting in America, Mitchell consistently assumes that girls and women are intrinsically antihunting, and relates this directly to their love of animals and their innate opposition to aggression in any form.[2]

But what does it mean to love animals these days? We live in an age when public perceptions of nature and wildlife are arguably shaped more by Disney and by nature programs on public television, than by direct contact with the natural environment. This has been true especially for women, and raises questions about how one learns to love something one has had relatively little direct contact with. Toward resolving some of these questions, Yale University researchers Stephen Kellert and Joyce Berry during the 1970s and 1980s conducted an important study comparing women's and men's attitudes and behaviors toward wildlife. They found that women's primary relationships with animals were individualistic, in the form of emotional attachments to pets, and that women were more likely than men to express anthropomorphic feelings toward animals. Regarding wild animals, women were drawn to "large and esthetically attractive species." Not surprisingly, given the predominantly female constituency of the animal-rights movement, women also expressed "greater concern for a variety of animal cruelty issues and less support for the exploitation of and dominance over animals." Men, by the same token, were more comfortable with a "dominionistic" attitude toward animals, displaying "a greater tendency . . . to derive personal satisfactions from the mastery and control of animals."

Interestingly enough, however, the study also found that men were not only "more inclined to express a desire for direct contact with wildlife in the context of exposure to nature and the out-of-doors," they also had "a greater concern for maintaining viable relationships between wildlife and natural habitats and for ecosystem balance and functioning." Women, meanwhile, "despite strong emotional attachments to pets . . . expressed substantially more fear and indifference toward all animals, particularly in relation to wildlife." Where they did attribute value to wild animals, it was "as objects of affection." Asked to rate animals on a seven-point like-dislike scale, women expressed significantly higher preference for domestic pets (dogs and cats) and "attractive creatures" (swans, ladybugs, and robins, for example), while men gave higher ratings to predators (wolves, snakes) and game animals (moose, trout). Importantly, women also scored significantly lower than men on a test of basic knowledge about animals.[3]

A rather strange picture thus emerges, in light of Kellert and Berry's findings. Man, supposedly the alienated outsider, the enemy of nonhuman nature, appears to possess a surer knowledge of wild animals and their habitat than does nature-identified, animal-loving woman.[4] Yet she voices less sympathy for the domination of nonhuman nature, and more concern for animal protection. Where does this concern come from, one might well wonder, if not from knowledge or lived experience? Perhaps it, too, like the myths of Man the Hunter and Woman the Gatherer, is rooted in a contemporary dream of the past.

ANOTHER PARADISE LOST

"Women today," radical ecofeminist Elizabeth Dodson Gray has remarked, "are discovering the power of our own symbolic imagination to create the world afresh in imaginings of our own." What form might this recreation take? According to Gray, we are poised on the brink of a new, postpatriarchal Eden characterized by "a new vision, a vision of justice among groups, races, sexes, species . . . a vision of harmony, of wholeness." It is up to women to bring this new Eden into being, she claims, because "Women especially are being able to unfetter their deep emotional affinity with nature."[5]

We have already seen, in connection with the hunting hypothesis, that the image of Paradise Lost exerts a powerful pull on the twentieth-century imagination. This is especially true in America, where from the beginnings of European expansion the myth of a New Eden was a motive force in the shaping of a national consciousness.[6] Gray's vision of harmony and wholeness recalls the eighteenth-century ideal of a "peaceable kingdom," and like that ideal is rooted in the North American tradition of nature-based spirituality that American religious historian Catherine Albanese has described as "a kind of literalism, a fundamentalism of the earth."[7]

The notion that "paradise" consists of an absence of violence—not only human violence against animals, but animal violence against one another—is a fairly common theme in animal rights and radical ecofeminist discourse.[8] Of course, the lion and lamb never have lain down together, and never will, except in apocalyptic vision (as on Hallmark Christmas cards) or cartoon fantasy (as in any of a number of Disney films). No matter; it is nonetheless an ideal, the prospect of a "return" to which seems irresistible not only to radical feminists, but far more broadly within our culture.[9] Indeed, the paradisiacal imaginings of radical feminists bring into play themes that have come to dominate contemporary popular environmentalism, and that are in turn rooted in centuries of Euro-American cultural imagination.

The literature of radical ecofeminism is replete with the language of Edenic harmony. As in Carol Adams's depiction of vegetarian egalitarianism, there is a utopian thread running through these imaginings. New York City activist Connie Salamone, for example, sees in the coalescence of animal rights, feminism, and deep ecology, a "coming to total Organism." Salamone's activism takes the form of slide presentations juxtaposing images of the abuse of women and animals with Edenic images of a world where the lion and lamb lie down together. She closes her presentations with what she describes as "a touching earth bonding healing circle."[10] Drawing her inspiration from similar sources,

especially deep ecology's idea of the "ecological self," Deena
Metzger writes of the necessity to progressively cast off first the
individual ego, then the "gender ego," so we may finally throw
away the "species ego," this last being the most difficult task
of all.[11]

It is in the face of the manifest difficulty of this task that radical
ecofeminists universally assert that their movement is at base
spiritual. After all, in "real-world" terms, the peace and harmony
they seek is possible only on the level of visionary experience. The
problem is, they often seem to forget that there are, indeed, some
real and compelling distinctions between nature and imagination.

This is nowhere better illustrated than in Sally Abbott's essay
"The Origins of God in the Blood of the Lamb." Abbott writes
about how several years ago she had a vision of herself having to
leave her leather shoes and purse at the gate in order to be admit-
ted to the Garden of Eden. As a result of this vision, she became a
vegetarian. Eight years later, on a self-imposed vision quest involving a four-day fast, she entered into a state which she describes as follows: "I had a sense of myself as a sacred person waiting to be sacrificed and, alternatively, as a tethered animal
waiting to be slaughtered, and, in fact, I could not distinguish between the two. I was terrified that I would be put to death by God
or the collective animal kingdom—and here again I could not
distinguish between God and the animal spirits—to avenge the
animals I had eaten."[12] As a result of these visions, Abbott constructed a theory of the origin of all religion and ritual in the expi-
ation of guilt brought about by killing animals and eating their
flesh. After she had developed this theory, she had one more vision: "I was lying out in the woods and heard a rustling in the
bushes. Out came a couple of mangy, moth-eaten-looking wolves,
followed by some sheep. One of the sheep bent over and kissed
me gratefully on the mouth. It was only a dream, but I am still
reeling from that kiss."[13] On the basis of her visionary experiences, Abbott asserts that "the cultural recognition of animal
rights could . . . bring about the fulfillment of a new covenant
with animals and a restoration to the paradisiacal state."

The myth of returning to a nonviolent Paradise can be sustained only through two habits of thinking, both of which really amount to strategies of intellectual dishonesty. One is a persistent, and in some ways appalling, lack of acquaintance with the way the world of nature actually works. The other is a dangerous, because it is ill-informed, faith in the possibility of human noninterference in nature. Radical feminism in this regard distills, in many ways, some of the most troublesome tendencies in what might be termed American popular environmentalism.

THE HOUSEHOLD OF NATURE

In her important book on "ecological revolutions," Carolyn Merchant is concerned with the general pattern of the transformation and objectification of land and its inhabitants wrought by agrarianism. What is striking, Merchant asserts, about the North American case—and this surely affects all of our perceptions about the relation of nature to culture—is the fact that "what took place in 2,500 years of European development through social evolution came to New England in a tenth of that time through revolution. . . . As the American frontier moved west, similar ecological revolutions followed each other in increasingly telescoped periods of time." [14]

Merchant suggests that when Europeans arrived on the shores of New England, they encountered, in native lifeways, a culture that (at least in the wisdom of hindsight) looked something like the Edenic way of life that seems so appealing to the popular imagination today: "Before colonization the northern gatherer-hunters lived within a web of human and animal movement in interlacing cyclical space-time. . . . Space was an active place—a fusion of natural characteristics with human needs. Not demarcated by the boundary between wild and civilized as it would be for Puritans, place was identical with the natural features of Indian homelands." The settlers, of course, quickly went about marking off their towns, farms, and gardens in this new Eden, with the result of drastically altering not only the physical, but also (and ultimately, more importantly) the psychological landscape. "Mapping space," Merchant astutely remarks, "distances the observer, breaking down participation through the imposition of perspective. Through the scrutiny of the surveyor, the land is seen as a bounded object. A spatial perspective leads to its management and control." The imposition of such dominion over physical space also affects attitudes toward animal species. In the case of Native American hunter-gatherers, "the circulation of the life principle would be severed by commodity exchange. The beaver [for example] would be transformed from an equal subject outsmarted by the Indian's lure to a resource object." [15]

The patriarchal mind is comfortable with wildness only when it is under conceptual control. According to the orthodox Judeo-Christian view, when God had created Man, he placed him in a garden: a cultivated space, not a wilderness. And God told Man to "be fruitful and multiply, and fill the earth and subdue it: and have dominion over the fish of the sea and over the birds of the air and over every living thing that moves upon the earth." [16] Intrinsic therefore to the European "conquest" of this New Eden was the idea that raw untamed nature, along with both its human and nonhuman inhabitants, needed to be brought under the yoke of Western civilization. The American pioneer spirit rested on the assumption that there is a fundamental, and necessary, opposition between nonhuman nature and human civilization. [17]

Yet, as we have already seen with regard to the "pastoral impulse," in its historical development the characteristic American attitude toward wildness was less negative than ambivalent. In her study of American women and nature, Vera Norwood traces the evolution of the idea of the domestication of nature. "Wilderness" could be rendered less threatening, she finds, if it could be seen as in some ways a kind of "Home." Thus domestic images were projected upon the nonhuman world in profusion, especially by early female nature writers. Susan Fenimore Cooper (eldest daughter of James), for example, "offered her audience a bountiful nature functioning as the mid-nineteenth-century home was meant to function—as a place of harmony where citizens found security, contentment, and civility." Hence she offers the following description of songbird lifeways:

Late evening hours are not the most musical moments with the birds; family cares have begun, and there was a good deal of the nursery about the grove of evergreens in the rear of the house, to-night. It was amusing to watch the parents flying home, and listen to the family talk going on; there was a vast deal of twittering and fluttering before settling down in the nest, husband and wife seemed to have various items of household information to impart to each other, and the young nestlings made themselves heard very plainly; one gathered a little scolding, too, on the part of some mother robins.[18]

Through the nineteenth century and well into the twentieth, women naturalists described the nonhuman world as an ideal-ized version of their own middle-class society, governed by essen-tially the same rigid rules of etiquette, *and* by the same gender stereotypes. A mother bird on her nest underwent "voluntary imprisonment" for the sake of her nestling brood, a "careful mother" bee would spread a bit of flower petal "on the floor like a carpet" and make a "brilliant cradle" for her baby bee, "coquett-ish" flowers might vary their dress several times in a day, and all manner of wildlife engaged in their procreative activities dis-creetly, with an inborn sense of modesty. Nature "red in tooth and claw" rarely made an appearance.[19]

This drive to tame the natural world by projecting human values upon it was not confined to women, although, since they were homebodies whose primary (and most often only) interac-tion with nature occurred through gardening, it was perhaps somewhat easier for them to gloss over its more brutal aspects. Yet male naturalists, looking at a somewhat bigger picture, simi-larly "found morals, order, and purpose in nature." In *The Ten Commandments in the Animal World*, the influential nature writer Ernest Thompson Seton argued that the proscriptions handed down on Mt. Sinai "are not arbitrary laws given to man, but are fundamental laws of all highly developed animals." Those animals whose perceived behavior suggested adherence to these God-given laws—adults practicing "monogamy," chil-dren "obeying" their parents, and so on—were somehow more deserving of survival.[20]

Such a line of reasoning led Charles G. D. Roberts, who with Seton is credited with having originated the "realistic" animal story in the late 1800s, to observe, "The animal story, as we now have it, is a potent emancipator. . . . It helps us return to nature, without requiring that we at the same time return to barbarism. It leads us back to the old kinship of earth."[21] And what we find thus imagined is a world uncannily like our own, ourselves with fur or feathers. Even predator species, who must kill for a living, could in their own limited way be models of moral rectitude: Thornton Burgess, a popular turn-of-the-century nature writer, wrote about wolves that, although they are universally feared in the creature world, they are "the best of parents, and the little wolves are trained in all that a wolf should know."[22] Much of the motive force behind this anthropomorphizing of the natural world had to do with the rise of Darwinian science. Evolutionary theory suggested far more serendipity in nature than Victorian social convention allowed; it was reassuring to perceive in the nonhuman world a recognizably humanlike sense of decorum.

This did not, however, mean that nature was in any meaningful way equivalent to human culture. If, by the end of the nineteenth century, nonhuman nature on the North American continent had seemingly been as efficiently colonized and converted to Euro-American ways as had what remained of its original human inhabitants, it was in order to facilitate exploitation. By the time Frederick Jackson Turner marked the closing of the frontier in 1893, the plains bison had nearly been eradicated by market hunters, and the southwestern tall grass prairie all but obliterated by indiscriminate grazing. In practical terms, there was no true wilderness left.

Indeed, the ideological boundary between human culture and nature, like that between the garden and the vegetal world beyond, had become increasingly ephemeral. Wildlife biologist and outdoorswoman Anne LaBastille has sensibly remarked that, "besides being an ecological entity, wilderness is essentially a state of mind, a concept whose meaning has evolved and changed along with the changing relationship of men and women to the natural world."[23] Small wonder, then, that the desire to tame the wild frontier evoked idealized images of domestic order and tranquillity.

But predation, both by humans and wild animals, upsets the paradisiacal picture of nature's harmonious balance. Lions do not lie down with lambs in the wild, except when they are feeding off their carcasses. Market hunters and sod-busters could rationalize that they were simply enacting God's mandate to have dominion over the creatures of the earth. But to them this was obviously, and solely, a human prerogative. Nonhuman predators such as wolves, cougars, coyotes, and raptors were a nuisance to market hunters and farmers, and—with the dawning of environmental awareness—something of an embarrassment to animal-loving naturalists. Predators became, as Dunlap puts it, "a distasteful necessity at best. They might be needed to eliminate the suffering or unfit, but otherwise they had no place." In moralistic terms, they could therefore be judged to be "cruel" murderers of the more "innocent" wildlife. This provided sanction for the eradication not only of individual predators, but in some instances of entire predator populations, on much the same grounds one could argue for the death penalty. It is instructive to note that by the early twentieth century, the argument for aggressive predator control was as liable to be mounted by animal protectionists and by conservationists, as by hunters or farmers.[24]

For example, it was judged necessary (from a conservationist point of view) to extirpate the wolf from Yellowstone Park, even as farmers and ranchers were eliminating the species (for economic reasons) throughout the American West. The wolf represented, as it were, that wildness which could not be brought under the domestic yoke. The animal simply, we might even say naturally, defied such conceptualization—significantly, not because it failed the test of domesticity (we have already seen the lupine family group could be extolled), but because of the singular, and sinister, fact of its predation.

The wolf is a born killer. In popular parlance, scavenger species like hyenas, dingos, vultures, and magpies tend to be regarded as "lowlife" animal types, the implication being that they are lazy, unintelligent opportunists. Predators like wolves, by contrast, tend to be viewed as crafty and intelligent, if instinctually driven—a notion that carries over to descriptions of "predatory" human criminals, who "behave like animals." (And who may yet be devoted parents with a strong sense of family: think of any of the *Godfather* films.) This tendency to describe humans in animal terms is the obverse of the urge to anthropomorphize nonhuman nature.

The wolf thus could represent the "bad" side of wilderness, the darkly threatening aspect of nature. Via projection, wolves could simultaneously represent those ominously troubling aspects of human aggression that lurk about the edges of consciousness, much as *canis lupus* was believed to skulk in the shadows outside the boundaries of human settlement. At the same time, one of the wolf's primary "innocent victims," the deer, came to symbolize everything "good" about wild nature: grace, beauty, serenity (recalling Washburn and Lancaster's phrasing), "the peace of the herbivorous world." As sociologist Jan Dizard remarks, this tendency to define animals as either "bad" or "good"—with the concomitant drive to eliminate the bad in order to protect the good—has the effect of enormously "simplifying" the ecosystem.[25]

It also had the effect, down through the middle of the twentieth century, of giving natural history an anthropomorphic plot, complete with heroes and villains. Human intervention in nature—that is, human participation in this drama—could be seen in one of two ways. Sometimes it was benign, a heroic effort to rescue hapless victims from predacious felons. However, far more frequently, indeed characteristically, it was malicious. It was after all humanity that, from time immemorial, had upset the balance of nature. Humans had more in common with wolves than they liked to think; at base, both of them were out to get Bambi.[26]

Thus, there evolved in much popular nature writing an antipathy toward Man the Hunter. Ernest Thompson Seton wrote in 1901, "There was once a wretch who, despairing of other claims to notice, thought to achieve a name by destroying the most beautiful building on earth. This is the mind of the head-hunting sportsman. The nobler the thing that he destroys, the greater the deed, the greater his pleasure, and the greater he considers his claim to fame."[27] Fifty-five years later, philosopher Joseph Wood Krutch would write, along similar lines: "Most wicked deeds are done because the killer proposes some good to himself . . . [but] the killer for sport has no such comprehensive motive. He prefers death to life, darkness to light. He gets nothing except the satisfaction of saying, 'Something which wanted to live is dead. There is that much less vitality, consciousness, and, perhaps, joy in the universe. I am the Spirit that Denies.'"[28] While the sentiments expressed in both statements are strikingly similar, it is significant that Seton (himself a hunter and wolf-trapper) was writing against the backdrop of the environmental depredation caused by nineteenth-century market hunting, and was explicitly criticizing trophy hunting, whereas Krutch—forshadowing the contemporary animal rights movement—condemned hunting in any form, for any reason. This may in part be accounted for by the fact that in the years separating the two quotations, America was rapidly making the transition from being a largely rural to a predominantly urban society. Hunting was becoming less widely accepted, because less familiar, as a culturally rooted activity.[29]

However, it had even more to do with changing ideas about wildness in the years following the two world wars. Wilderness was becoming an issue in the popular consciousness in a decidedly new way. The closing of the frontier was history now, the lower forty-eight states efficiently marked off and settled. Yet the pioneering spirit that sets culture over against nature, using the one to define the other, was intrinsic to the American worldview. Wilderness, once feared, became highly prized. We needed our purple mountains' majesty as much as, maybe even more than, our amber waves of grain. Americans were just beginning to acknowledge the damage—some of it irreversible—that had been done to the environment in the name of subjugating nature. The modern environmental movement was born during the cold-war years, when humanity's capacity for destructiveness had become appallingly clear. In a world of heroes and villains, we had emerged as "the most dangerous animal in the world."[30]

The wolf, meanwhile, underwent a rehabilitation in popular

imagining. As wilderness came to be valued as positive, indeed necessary, in itself, the wolf—by this time threatened or exterminated throughout most of the lower forty-eight states—became a symbol of ecological health and vitality. As Dunlap puts it, "When the wilderness had been feared, the wolf had been fearsome. As the wilderness became wonderful, so did the wolf."[31]

The key idea here is that "wilderness" had come to be equated with nature "undisturbed," that is, maintaining its own harmonious balance without human incursion. The wolf became a romantic hero in several popular fictions about this "balance of nature." In his biography of the livestock-killing "Custer Wolf," Roger Caras described the world of the wolf as a place in which death was "the predator's gift to the land. Nature was in harmony, even with its thousand thousand deaths, and there was nothing savage, harmful, or tragic in all this." Everything changed, however, when humans came upon the scene: "[E]ternally guilty of crimes beyond counting—man the killer, the slayer, the luster-for-blood—has sought to expurgate himself of his sin and guilt by condemning predatory animals." Caras leaves no doubt as to who is the villain of his story: the human animal, who alone stands outside the natural world, and whose prime manner of interacting with it is destructive.

Farley Mowat carried this theme even farther in his hugely popular *Never Cry Wolf*. Purporting to give a naturalistic account of the time he spent on the tundra observing wolves for the Canadian Wildlife Service, Mowat recounted how his attitudes about wolves were transformed by firsthand experience. They were not, in fact, bloodthirsty killers at all: "George," "Angeline," "Uncle Albert," and the others he observed were playful and fun-loving, peacefully coexisting with the local caribou, except when instinctually driven to mercifully cull a sick or elderly animal. A wolf howling in the distance was for Mowat an echo from Eden, "a voice which spoke of a lost world which once was ours before we chose the alien role; a world which I had glimpsed and almost entered. . . . only to be excluded, at the end, by my own self."

Works like Caras's and Mowat's, both significantly (if questionably) based upon "real life" histories, carried forward the older tradition of domesticating the natural world, but with an important difference. The aim of these stories was to show not simply that the animals are like us, but that they are better than we are. In such fictions, as in more recent works by Barry Lopez and R. D. Lawrence, "the wolf, once pariah, has become paragon."[32] And the gap between the worlds of the human and nonhuman, which it had once seemed possible to bridge via analogies to home, hearth and higher law, has become a yawning chasm. The opposition of human culture to nonhuman nature is stronger than ever, though now the nonhuman animals occupy the moral high ground.

Against this background, ecofeminism's opposition of nature-identified Woman the Gatherer/Healer to rapacious Man the Hunter/Destroyer becomes intelligible as an attempt to exempt women from their share of responsibility for environmental devastation.[33] It also helps to account for why, as Vera Norwood points out, "in much ecofeminist literature, nature often seems to serve more as an oppositional category than as a physical space filled with plants and animals."[34] Yet the more one actually pays heed to the workings of the natural world, the less possible it is to maintain the fiction of the human (or the man) outside of nature.

In the latter half of the twentieth century, increasingly sophisticated wild-animal research has demonstrated time and again that facile projections of human law and psychology upon nonhuman animals simply do not work. Simultaneously, the environmental movement has helped us appreciate the complexity of ecosystems, and the delicate relationships and elaborate transactions that occur within them. Any attempt to remove the human animal from the natural equation is a willful distortion of the facts, and ultimately it does neither us nor the other animals much good. This is especially true, when it comes to the classification of "good" versus "bad" animals that lingers in popular imagination, with the important difference that today, only one animal—*Homo sapiens*—tends to be placed in the latter category. The negative effects of this popular bias, both on the natural environment and on human self-understanding, become clear in light of a brief consideration of the peculiar positioning of Native Americans in the contemporary debate over the use and abuse of wilderness.

A NEW, IMPROVED
PRIMORDIAL WILDERNESS

The ecosystems approach to American environmental policy that emerged in the 1960s and 1970s reflected a growing sense of uneasiness about human intervention in the natural world. In 1971 Barry Commoner stated the case on behalf of the environment bluntly: "Any major man-made change in a natural system is likely to be detrimental to that system."[35] Humans were, by definition, other-than-nature (bad). The way to safeguard (good) wild nature, therefore, was to keep hands off. In his later indictment of the mismanagement of the Yellowstone ecosystem, Alston Chase characterized the prevailing attitude of the time:

> As man was the source of all evil, expelling him became the way to restore and preserve wilderness. The Wilderness Act of 1964, which saved millions of acres of federal lands from further development, defines wilderness as "an area where the earth and its community of life are untrammeled by man." In this way the task of protecting nature was made to seem simple. By keeping man out of the woods, we would not only be protecting those woods, but also restoring them to their original condition. . . . Just so, wilderness was defined into existence.[36]

In the face of all the damage already caused by development, the idea of preserving nature through abstracting humanity was seductive. It had a comforting, Edenic ring to it. But this wilderness, "untrammeled by man," was purely an invention of the twentieth-century imagination.[37]

The idea is misguided, on two historical counts. In the first place, given the industry and ambition of the white settlers of this continent, virtually no area of North America is without their imprint: "All western lands, in particular, had been trod by the early white man. Fur trappers and gold prospectors stepped on nearly every square foot of the West at one time or another. Early settlers plowed and planted in the most surprising places. They introduced viruses, microbes, plants, and animals that centuries ago spread like wildfire to every nook and cranny of the continent."[38] Even more remarkable, however, was the erasure of the land's previous human inhabitants from the picture. In the new, improved primordial wilderness, there was no room for hunter-gatherers like the Lakota or Cheyenne, or hunter-horticuralists like the Abenaki. Having had their lands taken from them literally in the last two centuries, Native Americans by the late twentieth century were to be banished metaphorically as well.

United States Park Service publications began to refer to Indians as early "visitors" to Yellowstone Park, which was "virtually uninhabited" at its founding in 1872. Regarding the role of "primitive man" in the Yellowstone ecosystem, one biologist wrote in 1975 that "as a predator . . . that role must of necessity have been minor," despite ample archaeological evidence of *centuries* of human hunting in the area. Park publications also reinforced the idea of an ecosystem "untrammeled by man" with the oft-repeated—and racially insulting—notion that the superstitious Indians were scared off by the "evil spirits" that lived in Yellowstone's geysers (notwithstanding documentary accounts of the Nez Perce using the hot springs to cook their food!)[39]

Somewhat paradoxically, at the same time its original human inhabitants were removed from the picture of primitive wilderness, knowledge about and enthusiasm for Native American lifeways had grown exponentially in American popular culture. The American Indian Movement had considerably raised public consciousness about the history of white genocide and the plight of modern Indians, as had books that expressed the Native American point of view, like Dee Brown's *Bury My Heart at Wounded Knee* and Vine Deloria's *Custer Died For Your Sins*. But the public understanding of things Native American was arguably shaped as much, if not more, by products of Euro-American imagination: books like *Black Elk Speaks*, in which poet John Neihardt told the story of a Lakota visionary; films like *Little Big*

Man in which (as in the later *Dances With Wolves*) a white man
assimilates into native culture; and television spots like the commercial in which a buckskin-clad maiden promoted "Mazola corn
goodness" ("You call it corn, we call it maize"), or the public service announcement in which Indian actor Iron Eyes Cody shed a
poignant tear over the white man's penchant for littering.

Howard Harrod, a scholar of Plains Indian religion and culture, has referred to such popularized representations as "Eco-
Indians."[40] The problem with such idealized representations of
Indians as ecological gurus, of course, is that they in no way realis-
tically portray original Native American life. The Eco-Indian has
become a vehicle for that ambivalence toward wilderness which
is as old as the Euro-American cultural imagination.

American environmentalism grew out of a twofold interest.
On one hand, wild areas needed protection from human-caused
abuse. On the other, these lands needed to be available for
aesthetic appreciation and recreational use. Both interests, it
became distressingly clear, tended to put the environmental
movement at odds with Native American claims. Traditional
economies depend upon exploiting natural resources in a variety
of ways: netting salmon, harpooning whales, clubbing seals, or
various forms of hunting and trapping. It began to become evident that, as Chase phrases it, "Hunter-gatherers . . . were attractive to white people only so long as they were no longer hunting
or gathering."[41] The only good Indian, in short, was an invisible
one. The implications of this line of thinking have not been lost
on Native Americans.

In the late 1980s ecofeminist Judith Plant conducted an illuminating interview with Gitksan-Wet'suwet'en Tribal Council
member Marie Wilson. In the course of their conversation, Wilson rebuffed Plant's call for "a regeneration of culture . . . that
connects us to the land." That was, Wilson said, something "non-
Indians are looking for." She then went on to remark:

> I have had the awful feeling that when we are finished dealing
> with the courts and our land claims, we will then have to battle the
> environmentalists and they will not understand why. I feel quite

sick at this prospect because the environmentalists want these beautiful places kept in a state of perfection: to not touch it, rather to keep it pure. So that we can leave our jobs and for two weeks we can venture into the wilderness and enjoy this ship in a bottle.[42]

Regarding the relationship of humans to nonhuman nature, Native American novelist N. Scott Momaday has described the Indian attitude toward the physical world as "a matter of reciprocal appropriation: appropriations in which man invests himself in the landscape, and at the same time incorporates the landscape into his own most fundamental experience."[43] Such a sense of reciprocity, and mutual responsibility, arises in the Native American view from a sense of kinship with nonhuman nature (both animal and vegetal), a deep sense of the interconnectedness of things in the material world.[44]

These ideas have gained broad currency in American popular environmentalism, but only superficially. It is easy, and attractive, enough to romanticize about the Eco-Indian (a latter-day incarnation of the Noble Savage) who calls the four-leggeds and the winged-ones "sister" and "brother" and walks softly on the earth. It is rather more difficult to accommodate the notion that this understanding of kinship with nature arises from the context of killing in order to live —from, as Gary Snyder has phrased it, "an unflinching awareness of the painful side of wild nature; seeing how everything is being eaten alive."[45]

Native American attitudes toward life in nature—arising as they do from millennia of hunter-gatherer and hunter-horticulturalist experience—preclude the ready opposition of humans to nonhuman nature that so dominates the Western worldview. The kinship between humans and other beings exists in a cycle of life and death and life; the connections that relate us all one to another are, as outdoor writer Ted Kerasote phrases it, "bloodties."[46]

The conceptual banishment of the Native American from "wilderness" is the logical outcome of centuries of progressive alienation of humans from nature, in Western imagination. This alienation is reflected in attitudes, ranging from ignorance through ambivalence to hostility, toward hunting and other traditional ways of "using" life. It is symptomatic of a culture seriously at odds with itself and its world.

What have we done to our world, and to ourselves, in the process of taming the wilderness? If we can answer this question, perhaps we can learn to tell, and to live, new stories about our relation to wild nature.

4

Elk Hunting at Kill Woman Creek

The envelope looked unremarkable enough. It bore no glitzy gold seals, no currency-green lettering proclaiming "You, *MARY STANGE*, Are A Winner!!!"—just a State of Montana Department of Fish, Wildlife and Parks return address, with its familiar grizzly bear logo, and some dot-matrix print peeking through the glassine window. I shoved it into my backpack with the rest of a week's worth of mail, ran a couple of errands in town, gassed up the pickup, and drove the twenty-five miles back home. Only later, sorting through the mail, did I discover that the envelope contained treasure, in the form of an either-sex elk permit for Montana's hunting district 622. Annually, sixteen hundred hunters applied for these nontransferable permits, of which a mere thirty were issued via lottery. I had hit the jackpot.

District 622 occupies a hefty chunk of the northern shore (and several miles inland from there) of Fort Peck Lake. The lake—actually a dammed-up segment of the Missouri River—suggests, when seen from thirty thousand feet up, a blue dragon slithering its way across the northeastern part of the state. The vista at groundlevel is one of sharply undulating inlets and deep cuts, a canyon which appears abruptly in the redundant vastness of the high plains, as if the earth for some reason just dropped away there. The reason, of course, is the river. It is a stark visual lesson in the principle of erosion at work, earth and rock succumbing to the dictates of water. Given another million years or so, this might be another Grand Canyon. For now, it is the

103

heart of Missouri Breaks country, and home of the Charles M. Russell National Wildlife Refuge, or "CMR" for short.

Nothing on the million-plus acre refuge is small-scale. Creeks that feed the lake have over time cut gorges and chasms with deep, near-vertical embankments. Coulees—conventionally, creek-beds that remain dry much of the year—are so monstrously outsized as to argue that nothing could ever be a mere trickle in these parts. The vegetation tends toward the spiky and resilient: wind-gnarled ponderosa pines, yucca and prickly pear, buffalo grass and wild rye. It is an ecosystem showing scant patience for the fragile or faint-hearted, as the names of the river's tributaries reflect: Hell Creek, Devils Creek, Kill Woman Creek. The Missouri River Breaks are, as Lewis and Clark recorded when they first charted the area in 1804, stunningly beautiful. But it is beauty built on the harshness of survival; it has an edge to it.

The lake was not there, of course, when Sacajawea guided those first white explorers along this stretch of river. It is a product of the Great Depression, authorized by Franklin Roosevelt and accomplished by the Army Corps of Engineers, which still oversees the Fort Peck Dam and its hydroelectric power plant. The Corps takes pride in this project of theirs. The construction of this largest embankment dam in the United States (and second-largest in the world) was one of the most ingenious engineering feats of its time; it created thousands of jobs, and eighteen entire new towns, during the height of those economically desperate years, all in addition to taming the mighty Missouri. The legacies of that booming time (which, according to the Corps' tourist brochure, marked a rebirth of the "wild west") include the lake ("134 miles long at normal operating level," with over fifteen hundred miles of shoreline), the dam itself (which releases 6.5 billion gallons of water per day), and the Fort Peck power plant (which translates all that water into "2.8 million kilowatt hours of pollution-free energy each day, on average").

But perhaps the true marvel of the Fort Peck project is that the more some things have changed, the more others have pretty much stayed the same as they were when the only white settlement in the area was the original Fort Peck trading post. The lake may be manufactured, but the riverine wildness of its shores feels like the real thing. Today, as for untold centuries, the area is congenial to wildlife: mule deer, bighorn sheep, antelope, several species of upland birds, and—most notably—the only indigenous population of Rocky Mountain elk for hundreds of miles in any direction.

Those accustomed to thinking of elk as high mountain dwellers—as indeed they mostly are now—might think the animals out of context in the middle of thousands of square miles of shortgrass prairie. But *Cervus canadensis*, the elk or wapiti, was originally a denizen of the grasslands, with a range extending from New Jersey to California. The Plains Indians hunted them, and wapiti were said to have been their most important resource after the buffalo. But the pressure of farm and ranch settlement drove these big grazers permanently into the deep woods and mountains that had hitherto been their retreats only during mid-summer heat. By the close of the nineteenth century, elk had disappeared from the high plains in every place but one: the Missouri River Breaks—hence the specialness of an elk hunt on the CMR. Some other permits to hunt high-mountain bull elk may be as rare, and as sought after, in numerical terms. But only on the CMR are there true prairie elk. These wapiti are the ancients of days.

In recent times, the CMR itself has been the subject of vigorous debate between environmentalists and beef producers. The former have argued that it is at odds with the spirit and intent of a "wildlife refuge" to allow cattlemen to continue to lease large swaths of refuge land for seasonal grazing. The latter have argued that ranchers are the "true conservationists," and that if their livestock didn't get the grass, range fires eventually would anyway. Driving the secondary roads in this part of the country, it's not uncommon to see hand-hewn billboards enjoining travelers to "EAT MORE

BEEF!" and battered ranch trucks with bumper stickers proclaiming "Choose Lamb: A Hundred Thousand Coyotes Can't Be Wrong!" When, in the late 1980s, the dispute over cattle leases on the CMR began heating up, and theFish and Wildlife Service was in the seemingly endless throes of revising its Environmental Impact Statement on the matter, the antigrazing faction printed up their own bumper stickers: "Cattle-Free by '93!" The cattlemen's association countered with "Cows Galore in '94!" That's the way public debate proceeds in this part of the world. There isn't a whole lot of subtlety to it.

There were, however, in the summer preceding my once-in-a-lifetime elk hunt, a whole lot of cows on the CMR. It was an unusually dry season, so no one particularly missed the lightning that might otherwise have accomplished the bovine task of range management. Grassfires may be "Nature's way of doing things," but in a semi-drought year they are terrifying nonetheless. The cattle were efficient enough at chewing their way into autumn. By October there wouldn't be much vegetation left.

Toward planning my hunt, early in September I called the wildlife biologist who covered District 622 for Montana Fish and Wildlife. He was encouraging: "Oh, there's *lots* of elk in there, some really big bulls, too." I told him I intended to take advantage of the generally milder weather of the first week of deer/elk season, and asked where I might best concentrate my energy. Assuming the weather held, he advised, they'd still be in the thicker cover of the drainages they frequent during summer, venturing out into meadows to graze at darkfall. "I'd check out Iron Stake Ridge and the Timber Creek area, if I were you. Oh, and Kill Woman Creek. There've been a lot of elk around Kill Woman. 'Course, if we get some winter, they'll head off the refuge for private land. Your better bet, in that case, is to contact a rancher; several fellas around here are only too happy to give you permission, since the elk are hard on their winter hay supply."

Now, blasting a bull elk in the virtual shooting gallery of some rancher's hay yard is not my idea of hunting. Besides, if the weather took that much of a turn, we wouldn't be able to leave our own place unattended long enough for an elk hunt. No: It had to be an early season hunt, and the weather had to hold. Kill Woman Creek, I thought, had a rather intriguing ring to it.

Six weeks later, pickup laden with camping and hunting gear and a week's worth of provisions, we traced the two-lane state highway northward to ward the CMR, several hours' drive from our home. It was a bracing October day, clear-aired and cool, with crinoline clouds tumbling across the sky. There was a chance of rain or wet snow in the long-range forecast, but the next few days promised to be fine. I was fairly buzzing with anticipation; it had been a number of years since I'd even seen any elk, and that had been on a spring bear-hunting trip in western Montana. Those, of course, had been high-country elk, calf-heavy cows meandering along old logging roads, and antlerless bulls browsing the parks created by years of selective clear-cutting in the lodgepole forest. I wondered how elk would appear in the radically different, if for them more "native," habitat we were headed for now.

We took turns driving. During Doug's shift, I pored over the two maps I already knew more or less by heart, one a Bureau of Land Management (BLM) map of the Missouri Breaks region, the other a Fish and Wildlife Service map of the CMR, the boundaries of District 622 highlighted on each. Traveling from the south, we had to decide the best route around the lake, toward our destination on its northern shore. Two routes presented themselves: one entirely on gravel and unimproved roads across the northern edge of the refuge from its eastern boundary, the other a western approach mostly on paved highway, but considerably longer than the first. The sun was bright in the midafternoon sky, and since we had often taken the latter road en route to a favorite deer hunting spot, we opted for the shorter "scenic route."

By dusk, and several wrong turns and backtracks later, we were of divided opinion as to where exactly we were, except that we agreed that we were in somebody's back yard. A middle-aged rancher, and a young woman who may have been either his wife or his daughter, approached our truck, smiling affably. "Can you tell us how to get to the Sun Prairie School?" Doug asked him. He looked puzzled. "What you want to get *there* for?"

We explained that if we could get there (it being on the longer, more familiar route we had earlier eschewed), we would know where we were and could find our intended campsite. There were, predictably, two ways from here to there, one involving retracing about twenty miles, the other a "shortcut" across his cow pasture—one of those "it's hard to describe, but you'll know when you're there" routes. Since we were fast losing our light, we said we'd try the shortcut. As Doug turned the ignition, the rancher noticed our springer spaniel curled on the front seat between us. "You folks bird-hunting?" he asked, a distinct hint of concern in his voice. We explained she was just along for the ride. "I'm sorta glad to hear that," he smiled. "Sharptail numbers are way down around here this year, what with the dry summer. The birds can't take any more pressure." We nodded agreement, thanked him again for his help.

By the time we had teased our way through several cattle grates and a creek crossing or two, thence to the main road and to the abandoned rural school house where we stopped to cook up some stew on the camp stove, the stars were shimmering in the night sky, and the air had turned icy. Another hour, and we achieved our campsite on the CMR. It was a public campground on the lake shore—good enough for our first night, after which we planned to camp in the back country. Several people were gathered around a couple of campfires, listening to the World Series on somebody's boombox. The muffled buzz of the radio, the beery conversation, and sporadic cheers were not exactly what I had imagined for this first night. But no matter, I told myself as I drifted to sleep, the CMR is a huge place, and tomorrow I'll be hunting elk.

Off-road driving is strictly prohibited on the CMR. Authorized access routes are numbered. Some (though not all) of these numbered routes appear on refuge maps, but at that point ends any meaningful correlation between the CMR's unimproved tiretracks and trails more recognizably road like. We had slept in, until seven or so, in order to see the lay of the land by daylight. Now, driving Road 423 as it snaked its way up to Iron Stake Ridge, we remarked that it wouldn't take much moisture to make it virtually impossible to get around here, this being prime "gumbo" country. I'm uncertain of the derivation of that term, but whether it refers to the slimy consistency of overcooked okra or the emotional state to which a driver whose vehicle is mired in it rapidly descends, the term aptly captures the peculiar texture— a sort of slippery gumminess—of the mud hereabouts. It's often observed that the only reliable way to get out of gumbo is not to get stuck in it in the first place. Luckily for us, the sun was shining and the sky cloudless.

One of the highest points on the CMR, Iron Stake Ridge (so named, we discovered, because of the presence there of a Depression-era geological survey marker) offers a commanding view of Fort Peck Lake. We planned to spend the day scouting the area and probably camp there for the next few nights. Following the biologist's earlier advice, we reasoned it would be ideal elk habitat, and so it appeared: sheltered meadows nestled among a succession of rocky, pine-studded crests, which scaled off vertiginously toward deep, densely wooded creeks and coulees. Elk would come up to the meadows to feed at night, moving down to thick cover for the daylight hours. A predawn stand in a well-chosen spot along the ridge should therefore yield good results, the only hazard being that an animal that retreated, or tumbled, downward would be a monstrous task to bring back out. I had heard someone joke that if you shoot a bull elk in one of these coulees, you'd best bring a knife and fork down there with you. All of a sudden that didn't seem so amusing. The only "horse" we had with us was a wheeled variation on the travois, essentially useless in country this precipitous. Even bonafide equines would find this terrain tough, and frequently dangerous, going.

Equally discouraging was the relative paucity of vegetation. Cows had summered here, that much was clear. Still, in a day's worth of hiking, we saw some elk sign (though it wasn't especially recent), and at one point came within a hundred or so yards of a group of big-horned rams, who seemed fairly unruffled by our company. Game animals seem to intuit when a hunter is not in possession of a tag with their name on it.

Toward late afternoon Doug and I sat perched atop a promontory overlooking the lake, discussing strategy. We were both somewhat disappointed at the lack of wildlife, or even fresh spoor, we'd seen so far; but those rams had cheered us, and it seemed reasonable that if sheep were in their customary haunts, elk would be, too. Doug reminded me that any discouragement on my part was obviously premature.

"OK," he said, hopping to his feet, "let's circle back to the truck and set up camp!"

"Right," I replied, unfolding myself as I picked up my rifle. Something felt odd about it as I slung the strap over my shoulder. Curious, I stopped after a couple of paces to examine my gun. It took me a moment to realize there was a hole on the underside where a screw should be, securing the trigger guard. Doug, by now puzzled as to why I was standing there staring at my rifle, returned. After a less than satisfactory discussion of what had happened ("How could you lose the screw from your gun's floorplate?" "I never heard of anyone losing a screw from their gun! I didn't know that was called the floorplate . . ." "They really ought to be checked every so often, you know." "Oh really, well when was the last time you checked yours?" "Uh, never mind that. Where do you think you lost it?"), we set about combing the area where we had been sitting. We were looking for a two-inch bit of matte black hardware in the late-afternoon shadows amidst rocky scree, grass stubble, and cactus on a steep decline, where each step precipitated a minor rockslide. We didn't find it.

Cracks began to develop around the edges of my by now guardedly optimistic mood. The extent to which my Sako was effectively disabled was up to a gunsmith to determine, but I was not going to gamble on testing it. Doug offered me his Steyr; it had a bolt-action like my own, I had shot it before. It was the best of possible alternatives, indeed in the present situation the only alternative, I knew. But one's customary hunting rifle is a companion in its own right; I felt like I had lost a friend.

The cracks in my mood became ever-so-slightly wider as I noticed that what had begun an hour or two earlier as a ribbon of grayish wisps on the southeastern horizon was becoming a more pronounced cloud bank. Fortunately, I had a distinct mental image of the long-range forecast on the Weather Channel: The next big system would be coming in from the west. It was silly to get spooky over a few stray clouds. After nightfall I noted, with happy reassurance, the stars were right where they were supposed to be.

The rain set in sometime after midnight. At first, an intermittent drizzle, it evolved in collusion with the unsettled dreams of oft-interrupted sleep, into a "weather-event" of disturbingly full-blown proportions: gusting winds, sheets of enormous drops and semi-frozen slush balls. It was coming down hard when the alarm went off at 4:45. "We may be here for a while," Doug murmured, and rolled over.

By the time the day dawned a sodden gray, the rain had ceased. I threw my down vest over the long underwear I'd slept in, and ventured outside to get some tea and cereal together. "Here comes a hunter," Doug said. I didn't look up; in ten years' backcountry hunting and camping trips, Doug always said this when I was padding about outdoors in my underwear. This time, he happened to be telling the truth. In one fluid motion, I was back under the sleeping bag.

Dave was the only other hunter in this area; we'd seen his camp the day before, a couple of miles from ours, near the point where the road dead-ended. He had slogged out to glass the ridge we had spent the previous day exploring. "Saw five cow-elk headed down into the coulee a while ago," he said, "but a guy'd have to be crazy to shoot one down in there." We talked about the weather. He'd been operating on the same report we had; nasty weather wasn't supposed to hit for days yet. "Looks like the sky just might clear," he hazarded, gesturing toward a filament of blue on the eastern horizon. "I'll probably stick it out up here today, anyway." Doug and I enchanged nods. "Yeah, we probably will too."

But by midmorning, after slicking along several muddy game trails, our boots laden with gumbo, and seeing nothing, we decided to pack up and get off the ridge while this was still remotely possible. It was a white-knuckle drive, but we were relatively confident we'd make it, since Dave's still-fresh tire tracks preceded us the whole way back down.

I wanted now to head for Kill Woman Creek, in part because of the biologist's advice, but frankly more because I am drawn to places with names like that. Maps of the American West are strewn with hints of women's lives thwarted in the frontier expansion. Montana's Crazy Mountains, for example, were once called the Crazy Woman Mountains. I have heard the re-naming was in response to feminist objections, but I'm skeptical about such historical sleight of hand. The story goes that the crazy woman in question had fled a wagon train. Driven to dementia by privation and prairie vastness, she wandered off into the mountains, and to certain death.

Interstate 90 crosses a Crazy Woman Creek in northeastern Wyoming. A different woman, no doubt. It leads one to wonder how many there were, how many lost women whose stories would be remembered, if at all, with mysterious place-names. Like the Indians and the prairie elk, they too were casualties of the pioneer spirit. I try, when I can, to pay them homage, and to listen for their spirits.

I noticed now that on the BLM map Kill Woman was called *Killed Woman*. Whatever its derivation, the name seemed ominously appropriate. Unlike the other heavily wooded drainages in the area, this creekbed is a broad, deep gash of dead black earth, a jagged wound that cuts between forested slopes, eventually emptying into the lake, as if it is here that the life drains out of the landscape. I suppressed a shiver upon first seeing it.

Yet there was fresher elk-sign along the lakeshore here and in the woods overlooking Kill Woman. The sky had more or less cleared as a stiff wind came up, but as that wind might signal the advent of another storm, it seemed prudent to remain within striking distance of the gravel road about two miles from the mouth of the creek. We found a place to set up camp.

As not infrequently happens on the high plains, rather than being a harbinger of a new weather front the wind itself was the main weather event. For the next few days an unremitting gale flushed the Fort Peck canyon. It was difficult to stand still in it without wobbling, to walk without being shunted off-course. It was impossible to accurately aim a rifle, let alone to expect a bullet to fly true, even "correcting" for the gust. This was at most a hypothetical problem, however, since there was nothing to take aim at. The only large game we saw were an occasional scrawny mule deer doe, or a little spike buck, hunkered down on the leeward side of a hill.

And so it went. Kill Woman Creek got the better of me. In the course of this entire elk-hunt of a lifetime, I did not lay eyes on a single elk. What I did see was a landscape nearly bereft of viable wildlife habitat. There were surely wapiti thereabouts: I saw their droppings, although I saw much more cow manure; I saw their tracks, although these were greatly outnumbered by now-aging cowprints. Wild animals and cattle may have peacefully coexisted on the refuge throughout summer, but by October it was clear that cattle are more of a threat to the prairie wapiti than this hunter was ever likely to be. With practically no forage left, the elk had withdrawn to their deepest cover, to bide their time until the snow would come, when they would filter up onto the flats, where they could freeload off cattlemen's hay. By week's end, "once-in-a-lifetime hunt" had taken on an entirely new connotation: I did not want to ever repeat this experience.

We could not hunt the CMR indefinitely. The weather was deteriorating. And we were expecting houseguests, friends from California who were coming out for deer-hunting. I was secretly grateful for the excuse to call it quits. On our way home, I noted with more than a little irony that when I finally saw a bull elk—a nice six-pointer—it was a mount on the wall of the gunsmith's where I took my rifle for repair.

I later heard that not many elk were taken during the early season on the CMR, and most that were came from the eastern end of the lake, a different hunting district. By Thanksgiving week, the last week of deer-elk hunting, the refuge was snowbound. A neighbor of ours who is also a hunter asked if I was planning to give District 622 another try. I told him my feelings about lying in wait by a pile of hay to shoot a bull elk.

"That's not hunting," I said.

"It'd depend on the bull!" he laughed.

Because this friend runs cattle himself, I didn't tell him that I simply could not collude with the cattlemen in that way. I didn't tell him that a few weeks earlier on the CMR I had fantasized an open season on cattle just to even up the odds.

Had it been the country that had gotten the better of me? Or was it what the country had become as the result of human manipulation? Was there, at this point, any difference? Those other women—the crazy ones, the kill women/killed women, whose follies and tragedies are encoded in this harsh landscape—what portents would they have read in a prize hunt that had felt like all bad luck?

Better to have stayed at home, they might have said. Better to have owned your limitations and let the wild things be. But then again, they might have reflected, nothing ventured, nothing gained. You never know what's around the next bend in the trail or what change in the weather tomorrow will bring. That's what keeps a body going—that yearning anticipation; that belief in luck, or providence, or one's own misguided wits

They might have said all that, and more. And it might all have been the truth.

Wilderness, Alienation, and Belonging:

Learning to Live without Excuses

The sense of human alienation from nature, so prevalent in contemporary American culture, is in some ways the shadow-side of the Edenic wilderness myth. In light of the obvious damage we have done to the nonhuman environment, it is tempting to adopt a hands-off attitude and entertain the fantasy of nature's returning to a pristine state. The idea of "letting nature be nature" arises, however, from secondhand knowledge and nature-romanticism; it does not work in practice. Ultimately we are all implicated, for better and for worse, in the fate of the natural world of which humanity is, in fact, very much a part. As native and traditional cultures help to show, hunter-awareness provides a crucial way of coming to terms with the extent to which each individual life is founded upon the deaths of vibrantly alive others.

WILDERNESS AND ALIENATION

Consider the following excerpt from an obituary of a suicide, published not long ago in a radical environmental journal: "Tony was a passionate man who felt the earth's distress acutely. In a letter he left to some of his friends he explained his reason for departing. He stated his life had never been better personally. He didn't want people to be sad for him. He checked out as a response to the overwhelming toll we humans are extracting from the planet. His strategy was to lighten the load.[1]

In similar spirit, in her poem "Sanctus," Mary de La Valette, founder of the Gaia Institute and self-styled "Earthpoet of the Neopagan Age," invokes the creatures of earth, sea, and sky: cougar, whale, red-tailed hawk, tree, river, and mountain. We humans, she says, will return the Earth to these, its own. We will give it back, because, she concludes, "We do not belong here."[2]

It is hard to imagine more graphic, in some ways chilling, depictions of the alienation of humans from the rest of nature, than her poem or the obituary. In some ways their sentiments represent the shadow side of the desire for a return to paradise. The intimation that "we do not belong here" has led some radical ecologists to venture the suggestion that "the *complete* disappearance of the human race would not be a moral catastrophe at all but rather something that the rest of the 'community of life,' were it articulate, would applaud with 'a hearty "Good Riddance!"'" Viewing humankind as a "cancer" on the face of the earth, some revolutionary activists see the eradication of humanity from the "earth-organism" as the only cure to the global environmental crisis. Others, drawing inspiration from Edward Abbey's oft-quoted sentiment that he would rather kill a man than a snake, posit an "ecocentric" perspective that gives more ethical weight to the interests of soil bacteria and ocean plankton than to those of human beings.[3] Taking this line of thinking to its extreme, some have argued against humanitarian aid for victims of hunger, or research into a cure for AIDS, reasoning that outbreaks of starvation in Africa and the worldwide AIDS epidemic may be nature's way of reducing human overpopulation. Indeed, the pages of animal rights and radical environmentalist publications exude a profound sense of embarrassment over their authors' very existence.

Fantasies of self-extinction, on the collective or individual level, would seem at first blush to be an odd way for professed advocates for animals and the land to respond to the world about them. Such fantasies, however, may be seen as reasonably arising from a sense of the enormity of the offenses committed by humans against an idealized nonhuman nature. Drawing upon psychoanalytic theory, Paul Shepard's analysis of the problem leads him to ask:

Can we experience both the denial of the nature of the outer
world and an exaggerated sense of responsibility for it? The connection is a weak identity structure that cannot cope with one's
own malevolence and a poor differentiation between inner and
outer in which one projects feelings of helplessness onto the outer
world. The first results in the illusion of the peaceable kingdom,
denying the reality of predation (or self aggression), the second in
a sense of guilt for all the "badness" in the world.[4]

In the face of environmental depredation, the idea of human
nonintervention, of "letting nature be nature," is therefore seductive. It is also resolutely unrealistic.

The popular fiction is of a "balance of nature" in which the nonhuman world, left to its own wisdom and devices, reverts to equilibrium and harmony. It is a fiction that more than once has mas-
queraded as science in the shaping of wildlife management
policy, and is at back of most of the numerous disputes currently
raging over issues relating to the conservation and use of natural
resources.[5]

In a probing sociological study, Jan Dizard recounts the testing
of this fiction in the controversy that arose during the 1980s over
the Quabbin Reserve in Massachusetts—a large island of "accidental wilderness" in the midst of dense human development.[6]
At issue was severe deer overpopulation, which had resulted in a
threat not only to the indigenous flora, and to the deer themselves, but to the metropolitan Boston water supply as well. Dizard captures the excruciating complexity of the debate that
arose when a closely regulated hunting season was determined to
be the best way to preserve the Quabbin. Among the numerous
conflicting interests and viewpoints the debate engaged, two essential perspectives emerged. These two fundamentally opposed
approaches were grounded in antithetical perspectives on how
nature works, and were epitomized in the views, on one hand, of
hunters, who argued for the necessity of human involvement in
the natural world, and on the other of animal rights activists, who
argued for standing aside and letting nature take its own course.
Dizard outlines the debate:

The critics typically portrayed nature as tending toward balance: if we could just keep our hands off, equilibrium would be the outcome. . . . The proponents of the hunt, by contrast, rejected such notions of balance and equilibrium. They were much more likely to characterize nature as chaotic, given to long oscillating cycles within which disturbance and disruption are commonplace. Moreover, they resisted the temptation to see humans as foreign elements in an otherwise harmonious scheme of things. Humans, from this perspective, are just one among many of the sources of disturbance and disruption. Our effects on the environment are no less than those of the deer. The difference is that we can become conscious of the effects we are having whereas the deer cannot.[7]

As the Quabbin controversy showed, it all boils down to the task of acknowledging human responsibility for the toll our existence takes on the world about us. After millions of years of human evolution, and thousands of development, it is simply too late to entertain the question whether or not we "belong here." We *are* here. And while it is tempting to infer that we can cure the considerable damage we have done to the environment by simply walking away from it, the unfortunate fact is that there is no place for us to go.

Nor can we deny the impact our living exerts on the world of nature. As Ted Kerasote writes: "The elk in the forest, the tuna at sea, the myriad of small creatures lost as the combines turn the fields, even the Douglas fir hidden in the walls of our homes—every day we foreclose one life over another, a never ending triage, a constant choice of who will suffer so that we may live, bending a blue note into the neatness of morality. It is this tender pain between species that is the plasma bearing us all along."[8] Discomfiting as it may be to contemplate, we—as individuals and as a species—live because others die. This is a lesson that close, honest observation of nature teaches readily enough. At some point, one looks out the window. It does not matter whether it is the window of a New York City high-rise or a North Dakota prairie farmhouse. If one really looks carefully, one sees the world is not a kind and gentle place. Mothers devour their young, males bully, to the point of killing, anything that gets in their way. A few moments' candid contemplation tell you that—especially as an American, accustomed to consuming more than your fair share of the earth's resources—you are up to your elbows in blood. The question is whether you own responsibility for that fact or not.

There are no easy moral choices, in this regard—only easy evasions. One may argue the immorality of hunting wild animals, for example, on the grounds that domestic animals are raised especially for the purpose of human consumption. Yet the factory farm, feedlot, and slaughterhouse are scenes of untold animal suffering, in comparison to which the death effected by a skilled hunter is arguably infinitely more humane. One may argue for a vegetarian diet and abhor all meat-eating on the grounds of cruelty. But in a single sunny afternoon, a farmer plowing a field wreaks more carnage, in the form of outright killing and the destruction of nests and mating areas, not to mention the impacts of pesticides and herbicides on wildlife, than the average hunter does in a lifetime.

It would be nice not to have to reckon with such troubling realities, and the moral choices they entail. In painful point of fact, to the extent that one equates cruelty with killing, there is no such thing as a "cruelty-free" lifestyle. To the individual calf, deer, or cottontail, it can hardly matter much whether the immediate cause of its death is a wolf's fangs, or a bullet, or a chisel plow. The end effect is the same. And we are all implicated in each death.

Yet if we humans cannot ultimately evade the natural fact of the ways we wound the world by virtue of our mere existence, we can nevertheless be conscious about our death-dealing in ways that can significantly diminish the nonhuman suffering we cause.[9] The way to this consciousness is through breaking down the artificial boundary between human and nonhuman nature, through recovering a sense of ourselves as beings in and of this world, not alien sojourners. This is not a lesson to be learned in the abstract. As Kerasote phrases it, "In the end . . . you have to *listen*, and if you can't *listen* to the quiet sadness of this world, a lifetime of roaming the outdoors, or thinking in libraries, is not going to tell you that the country is you and you are it, and when you cause it to suffer needlessly then you have broken a cord of sympathy, which is a much more demanding tie to nature than any system of ethics."[10] Too often we have attempted to "listen" to the environment around us by projecting human laws and characteristics upon it. Yet there are, there must be, other ways of hearing. Writing as a hunter, Kerasote remarks that he is most keenly aware of his tie to the natural world when hunting elk, "walking in this forest, with the wind in my face, and pine in my nostrils, and snow under my boots." He is not talking about so-called hunting with a camera here, or about "ship-in-a-bottle" environmentalism; he is talking about the forest his very life depends upon. This is not to say that only a person who actually hunts for food can listen in this way; but it is to suggest that this mode of hearing arises from—and is in some ways primordially linked to—hunter-consciousness.

The traditional Native American view of the interconnectedness of things is instructive here, if understood aright—that is, without the romanticized trappings of the Eco-Indian. In one way or another, for the various North American hunter-gatherer and hunter-horticulturalist tribes, nature was traditionally seen as (to use environmental philosopher J. Baird Callicott's term) "enspirited." The various entities that make up the material world "possessed a consciousness, reason, and volition no less intense and complete than a human being's. The Earth itself, the sky, the winds, rocks, streams, trees, insects, birds, and all other animals therefore had personalities and were thus as fully persons as other human beings."[11] Callicott is careful to point out that, although Native Americans traditionally possessed an intimate knowledge of their environment and engaged in various practices that Westerners would label "conservation" or "wildlife management," the typical Native representation of nature was "more animistic and symbolic than mechanical and functional. The 'rules' governing hunting and fishing seem more cast in the direction of achieving the correct etiquette toward game species than *consciously* achieving maximum sustained yield of protein 'resources.'"[12] He goes on to point out, however, that such "behavioral restraints" did nonetheless have the incidental effect of limiting environmental exploitation.

Similarly, Howard Harrod observes that when Native Americans took part in rituals for calling the game or planting the earth, they were not seeing these activities in the context of economic or ecological theories. They were part of "the way their world was defined," in terms of a potent religious symbolism that linked human beings in interdependent relationships with transcendent, powerful nonhuman beings, in the cyclical renewal of life. "The idea of not taking too much—waste, overkill, bad gardening techniques—was not related to what we would understand as conservation, though these activities did issue in such consequences."[13]

The notion that a religious or ritual attitude can have practical outcomes (for good *or* ill) surely requires little elaboration. However, aside from such instances as the custom of saying a blessing before meals, or the traditional Roman Catholic proscription of meat on Fridays, or the dietary laws of diaspora Judaism, Westerners have tended not to see food as in any meaningful sense a religious "issue." Coupled with the nature/culture dichotomy, this has perhaps furthered the alienation of humans from the natural world.[14]

While it is not possible—outside of popular *Dances With Wolves* romanticism—for a contemporary Westerner to appropriate "the Native American worldview," it is nonetheless possible to learn some constructive lessons from what Indians have had to say about kinship with the rest of nature, and to use those insights to modify our by now tragically disfigured images of our human stake in nature. Harrod suggests the benefit to be derived:

> A recovery of the religious sensibility that we are deeply connected to living animals, both domesticated and wild, might lead to revisions of our moral responses. Animals are food for many of us, as they were for our Native American predecessors. But they are not, for many of us, apprehended as vibrantly alive, as *others* with depths and mystery of being. Likewise, a recovery of such

sensibilities concerning plants would lend significant dimensions of meaning to a domain of our experience that is governed now by the concept of nutrition.[15]

With such recognition of interconnectedness, comes a kindred sense of reciprocity, of "mutual obligation"[16] grounded in a sense of affection and respect. This is blood-knowledge. It is indeed ancient, and it comes from hunting.

BLOOD-KNOWLEDGE

Terry Tempest Williams recounts the Navajo story of the Deer-hunting Way, in which the Deer Gods instruct the first hunter in the knowledge necessary to kill them. It is such a story, she says, that gives the people "a balanced structure to live in." Four deer—a mature buck, a large doe, a young buck, and a little female fawn—appear in turn, each with a lesson for the hunter who awaits them in ambush. They tell the hunter how to kill and eat deer, how to speak respectfully of them, and how to properly dispose of the remains the hunter cannot use, and how to hunt only what one needs. Making it clear that the hunter's success depends upon their "approval," they also foretell the dire consequences that will befall hunters who do not approach their task in the right spirit, with an attitude of respect. Williams sums up the sense of the story as follows:

> Through the Deerhunting Way one can see many connections, many circles. It becomes a model for ecological thought expressed through mythological language. The cyclic nature of the four deers' advice to the hunter is, in fact, good ecological sense. Out of the earth spring forth plants on which the animals feed. The animal, in time, surrenders its life so that another may live, and as its body parts are returned to earth, new life will emerge and be strengthened once again. Do not be greedy. Do not be wasteful. Remember gratitude and humility for all forms of life. Because they are here, we are here. They are the posterity of the Earth.[17]

Few Americans today would dispute that ours is a greedy, wasteful culture. Those who object to hunting often see it as symptomatic of a kind of reckless cupidity. They argue that while it may once have been necessary to hunt in order to live, it certainly no longer is. This argument is misguided, however, to the extent that it assumes that hunting serves a primarily practical function. As we saw earlier, even in traditional hunter-gatherer cultures the nutrition hunting provides is far outweighed by its symbolic import. Hunting, as Williams' story amply illustrates, encapsulates a worldview that locates humans in the natural scheme of things in ways markedly different from agriculture or industry. It affords a mode of conscious participation in natural life that is unavailable elsewhere, and that—though hunting implements have changed over time—remains rooted in a primal awareness. Kerasote expresses it this way:

> I look at the rifle in my hands—walnut stock, blue-black barrel, telescopic sight. Its ancestry is more closely connected to the industrial world than to any spear a hunter-gatherer carried across this country. Yet what it does in my hands—kill wild animals for food—is connected to our ancient relationship with the earth. . . . The elk who live in these forests, the blueberries who grow in its understory, the streamside lettuce I put in my salads can't be grown by anyone. True, blueberries are cultivated, and elk are ranched in many places, but they aren't the same blueberries and elk as these wild ones, though they may bear the same genetic makeup. Wild elk, along with all the other creatures and plants of nature, are what the earth still provides from her initial grace. They can't be planted or harvested or ranched; they can only be received. Whether the means of receiving them is a spear, a gun, or one's plucking fingers matters less than the state of mind moving hands to action.[18]

It is that matter of the hunting "state of mind" that lies at the heart of this book. A common theme in Western hunting literature, as in the myths and ritual practices surrounding hunting in traditional cultures, is the fundamental identity between hunter and hunted. This is a theme to which we shall return at some length below, but bears mentioning now, because it has everything to do with the "state of mind moving hands to action" in hunting. Margaret Atwood captures a sense of its poignancy in her poem about "Brian the Still-Hunter," which reads in part:

> He said to me:
> I kill because I have to.
>
> but every time I aim, I feel
> my skin grow fur
> my head heavy with antlers
> and during the stretched instant
> the bullet glides on its thread of speed
> my soul runs innocent as hooves.[19]

The central paradox of hunting is the painful paradox of life itself: Some of us live because others die. One might, in some senses, characterize the bulk of recorded history as a catalogue of attempts to evade, or at least to camouflage, that awful truth about ourselves. A key strategem in the process has been the establishment of dualities (human/animal, warm-blooded/cold-blooded, animal/plant) that facilitate the construction of hierarchies of consumption. But those categories collapse the moment a hitherto consumer becomes the consumed. The deer's blood is as red, and as warm, as the hunter's own; her eyes, so lately luminous, as brown. Those who receive their food second- and third-hand can, if they choose, look away from this fact. A hunter cannot.

A common criticism of hunting (and, as in Carol Adams' vegetarian feminism, of meat-eating in general) is that the hunter objectifies the prey, enforcing the split between human and nonhuman nature. According to this logic, one can only kill and eat something one perceives as an inferior "other," an entity worthy of use rather than of love or mutual regard.[20] Yet from all we know about hunter-gatherer worldviews, precisely the opposite is the

case for peoples who rely upon hunting for a significant portion
(literal or symbolic) of their sustenance. For them, the animals
they hunt and the predator species that are hunters like themselves, are kindred souls, powerful and intelligent.[21] All animals,
nonhuman and human, participate together in a web of pulsating
life: birthing and nurturing, pursuing and fleeing, capturing and
dying.

By contrast, as we have seen, the conventional view of nature
that has developed in American civilization and, arguably, has
reached its quintessential expression in such movements as animal liberation and radical ecofeminism, insists upon two assumptions: that humans are not really part of nature, and that our primary way of involving ourselves with the natural world is to
destroy it. Yet perhaps the most destructive thing we have actually done is to idealize the natural world by projecting human
laws and characteristics upon it, and expecting animals to behave accordingly.

The same may be remarked of attitudes of the dominant culture toward such groups as Native Americans. It is clearly easier
for Euro-Americans to romanticize Indians[22] then to confront
the real cultural differences that have made their "assimilation"
into Western culture inadvisable, and ultimately impossible.
Ironically, this romanticizing (the Eco-Indian and all that goes
with it) is frequently done under the guise of a "progressive" point
of view. For example, at the end of her astute and influential essay
"The Power and the Promise of Ecological Feminism," philosopher Karen Warren in 1990 cited a Lakota hunting story to illustrate her thesis relating to a sense of reciprocity with nonhuman
nature. Subsequently, ecofeminist writer Greta Gaard castigated
Warren for both theoretical inconsistency and cultural imperial-
ism, claiming in the first place that her reference to the "slaugh-
ter" of an animal was itself counter to the logic of nondominance
Warren espouses, and in the second that in any event "in the
United States there can be little justification for killing or eating
animals outside the context of traditional Native American culture."[23] It is unclear to what extent, if any, Gaard believes "tradi-

tional Native American culture" exists in America today, and so in the name of sensitivity to "cultural difference" she not only denies validity to any attempt, however provisional, to entertain the Native American point of view, she also implies that Indian spirituality is fundamentally irrelevant outside Native American circles. Just as it is tempting to let nature be nature when nonhuman predation rears its toothy head, it is apparently convenient to let Indians be Indians when they behave in ways that challenge the Eco-Indian stereotype.

It is of course true that, as thealogian Carol Christ points out, "We can't just take off what we want from Native American culture and assimilate it, which is a typical imperialist posture of Americans." However, in a penetrating discussion of the question of appropriating aspects of premodern cultures, political theorist Kathy Ferguson remarks:

> Feminism needs the resources to distinguish "temporary tourism" from respectful engagement. Premodern ways, especially those that maintain a tenuous existence in the face of continued assaults, do not belong to moderns, feminist or not. But perhaps residents of modernity can learn from the histories or the descendants of premodern cultures how to curb modern society's tendencies toward expropriation and let other ways survive.[24]

It bears noting, in this regard, that contemporary Native Americans "reside" to a greater or lesser extent in modernity, too.[25] In a very real sense, it is not the business of the dominant culture to "let other ways survive;" we are all in this together, and we should be able to learn from one another. The boundaries of human culture, and consciousness, are not so readily demarcated in fact, as they appear in any "I/Other" (Anglo/Indian, human/nonhuman, male/female) scheme. This has led some environmental philosophers to argue for a model of human culture as a "mosaic of ever-changing and yet recoverable parts that can be reintegrated into the present." Such a model would make it possible to recognize affinities with the palaeolithic past, and with modern hunter-gatherer societies as well, in order to "fashion an old-new way of being."[26]

In any encounter with the "other," of course, a little knowledge can be a very dangerous thing. This is perhaps especially true, in light of the way knowledge comes packaged in our media-obsessed age. In an ever more urban-centered society, most people learn what they know about nature secondhand, from books, television, and films, supplemented at best by an occasional hike on a clearly blazed trail or a stay in a well-groomed campground with all the amenities.[27] Accustomed to being outsiders, and with the excuse of limited leisure time, most Americans are most comfortable visiting nature vicariously, usually via the screen or the printed page, in order to commune with it in discreetly measured doses, and on their preferred terms. In its own fashion, this is another way of taming and domesticating nature. And as Gary Snyder has recently written, it yields a newly distorted perspective on wildness:

> You can go about learning the names of things and doing inventories of trees, bushes, and flowers. But nature often just flits by and is not easily seen in a hard, clear light. Our actual experience of many birds and wildlife is chancy and quick. Wildlife is known as a call, a cough in the dark, a shadow in the shrubs. You can watch a cougar on a wildlife video for hours, but the real cougar shows herself only once or twice in a lifetime. One must be tuned to hints and nuances.[28]

We earlier had occasion to remark that, whatever else it may be, wilderness is a state of mind, expressing a sensed relationship between the human and nonhuman realms. For ecofeminism, as we have seen, nature too often functions more as an "oppositonal category" than as an enspirited space filled with living, breathing beings. For all its proponents' talk of identifying with an idealized nature, their identification is necessarily selective, evading the more distressing aspects of the nonhuman world. Theirs is a view devoid of a sense for hint and nuance. Willfully stumbling into that pitfall Naomi Wolf has criticized as "the old trap that women have to be better in order to be equal," they fail to see

"what should be our baseline feminist goal: laying claim to our
humanity, all of it, not just the scenic parts."[29]

Radical feminism has justly celebrated women's blood-
knowledge when it comes to such matters as menstruation and
childbirth.[30] Yet if ecofeminism is to avoid being reduced to stereotypes about "woman and nature," and the ready opposition of
biophilic Woman the Gatherer to rapacious Man the Hunter, it is
time to talk about different ways of women's blood-knowing, ways
not so specifically tied to gender or to traditional gender roles. It
is time to talk about looking at our human animal-nature un-
flinchingly, and surviving what we see, about it and about ourselves. The poet Carol Frost captures a sense of this vision in her
hunting poem, "Red Deer":

> I stand in violence, in death,
> and I am happy—with the chill of fear.
> The light withdraws; chills me; alters
> nothing. At the root of humanness
> a cup of blood
> nature spills. And this is part
> of everything I see or make or am.

The speaker here might be female or male; the voice can only be
a hunter's. The poet goes on to describe strategies for concealing,
from others if not from herself, the blood on her hands and now
her conscience. She decides against concealment:

> But this once
> let me tell the truth
> that can't be told
> outright. I had no pity.
> The deer's last breath
> crawled out like a clear beautiful ray
> of sun on stones. I kissed
> its head. I couldn't help myself.[31]

That is Woman the Hunter speaking. Her message resonates with
the Native American sensibilities discussed above, and with what
we can glean of hunter-gatherer worldviews. But we need not
look "outside" Western culture to find her. Indeed, in the figure
of the goddess Artemis, she stands at the dawn of Western civilization.

   It is time, then, to talk about Woman the Hunter. It is time to
talk about Artemis.

5

Diana's Portion

"We live our lives," the poet Rilke wrote, "forever taking leave." Lifting off from Billings into the eastward dusk one Sunday evening many Octobers ago, I recalled that elegiac reflection on the evanescence of things. I was tired; it had been a full weekend. The 727 climbed to cruising altitude above scarlet-tinged clouds, leaving the earth and daylight in its wake.

Driven by necessity to teach in the Midwest, although my heart was in Montana, I had arranged my schedule to allow a limited—and thereby more precious—amount of quality hunting time in a few weekend excursions. My carefully laid plan had been foiled at the outset when a nasty bout of bronchitis forced me to sit out the opening (and undoubtedly the best) weekend of antelope season, and to pass up pheasants, as well. So it was especially exhilarating to make this trip late in October, to rendezvous in Billings with Doug, who was also at that time living the life of a hunter-commuter. Having driven to Billings earlier in the day, he met my Friday evening flight. We ate, caught a few hours' sleep, and drove through the wee hours of Saturday to arrive in southeastern Montana well before dawn.

We would be hunting the kind of terrain I like to think of as "another-hill" country. Broad, rolling expanses of sage and grass, punctuated occasionally by deep shelter-rich cuts and jagged rock outcroppings, rise and subside in ever steeper hills, giant ripples in the prairie's surface. It is here the Great Plains begin to anticipate the mountains farther west, and it is a landscape of surprises, far more variegated than it might first appear. In this

131

topography of buttes and draws, boulder-riddled hillsides opening onto vastnesses that need to be seen to be believed, only one thing seems certain, and that is that each time one crests one of the mammoth hillsides that dominate the scene, wondering what is on the other side, the answer is always the same: another hill.

It is about the best pronghorn country there is.

There had been an early snow that year, more than a dusting, leaving patches of white on the north-facing sides of rocks and hills, and in the shade of denser growths of sage and buckbrush. This leant an extra bit of challenge to the task of sighting antelope, and coupled with the fact that pronghorns get warier as the season goes on, made for a full day of hiking and tracking. But the radiant sunshine and comfortably brisk air made it relatively easy to cover a lot of ground.

Several times, glassing the area, one or the other of us saw a herd of a dozen or so antelope, and by late afternoon we agreed that we had been chasing this same herd all day, always a half-mile or so away from them. They had the skittishness that comes with having been shot at.

Eventually, shadows grew long, the temperature dropped, and the sun poised to dip below the horizon. We decided we had best call it a day and find a place to camp. We got back to our truck, and had set off down the gravel county road, when suddenly that herd of pronghorns materialized off to our left, a mere two hundred yards or so from the road. They were grazing peacefully, but would be up and running if we stopped right there, so we continued on, parked, and circled back on foot. The approach was easy— across some sage flats, then up and over a slight hill. Doug, ever the gentleman on these occasions, suggested I take the first shot. I singled out the only buck—a nice one—and fired. We had just enough light to field-dress him and get back to the pickup before dark.

That night I slept well, knowing there was still all Sunday morning to hunt. My return flight would depart late in the day, so we wouldn't need to set out for Billings until around noon.

Sunday emerged from predawn frost crisp and mostly sunny. Doug still had his antelope tag to fill. I had my deer A-tag, but since it was still early in Montana's deer season, I intended to be very choosy when it came to taking a shot. (Deer hunting was already penciled in on my calendar for later in November.)

Saturday's antelope herd had vanished, and our first two hours of walking and glassing turned up nothing for Doug. Around nine o'clock, we took a break for tea and a snack, perched on a sunny slope, where we could see across a broad field toward another hill. Directly across from us, nestled in a brushy draw, a big mule deer buck appeared, at first more like a mirage. He had not come, he was simply there, apparition-like, standing and looking straight in our direction, yet evidently unaware of us. We noticed him at about the same instant, trained our binoculars on him, and agreed that this was a buck worth going for.

"What do you think, Mare? He's a real beauty," Doug (somewhat choosier that I) ventured.

"I don't know, it's still early in deer season," I hedged.

"But he's a *nice* one, and you never know, you might not get another chance like this." I knew this was true. After all, I could have a bronchial relapse. There could be an unforeseen airline strike. The educational economy could collapse, wiping out my travel funds. Then again, I simply might not see another buck as fine for the rest of the season. It could happen; it happens often enough.

The buck stood rock-still, within good shooting range two hundred yards away. Deciding this apparition had been conjured up for me, I eased down the slope, assumed a prone position for a solid shot, and put the crosshairs of my scope on the buck's chest. I squeezed off a shot and the buck went down like a marionette whose strings had been cut.

"Nice shot," Doug cheered as he strode up beside me. Even as he was speaking, as I was getting up and dusting myself off, the buck struggled to his feet. Unbelievably—for I was sure he was mortally wounded—he was up and loped over the hill. We raced after him. I scrambled over the hill and saw the deer sitting in a deep ravine below me. I shot again, and his head went down. Slowly, I picked my way across the thickly wooded crevice, and decided I should approach the buck more carefully from behind, in case—though I much doubted it—he still needed to be finished off. As I moved toward him his head came up again, and he stood up once more. I froze, fired a shot offhand, missed this time, and the buck was out of sight around the side of the hill. I rounded the hill after him and saw, yes, another hill and beyond that one I knew there was another, beyond which lay immense stretches of snow-dotted sage and rock and sand.

For the rest of the morning and into the afternoon, we sought the buck, using every strategy we knew. Because we were certain of the general direction in which he had fled, we determined to work a broad grid pattern, tracing several pincer movements deep into the undulating countryside. Several times we spotted blood trails or tracks in the now rapidly melting snow, but the buck, wherever he was, was invisible. About three miles into the hinterland, we funneled down opposite flanks of a broad crevasse, met, and worked our way along a gentle slope that opened out onto miles of rugged flatland, thickly overgrown with sage. The high sun was now enshrouded in steely clouds, and all the snow had evaporated. The land had a barren, hollow feel to it, yesterday's lively interplay of light and shadows replaced now by a flat monochrome of grey-brown stillness.

"It's hopeless," I whispered.

Abruptly, just a few yards from us, a large mule deer buck jumped out of the sage, bounded over a fenceline, and tore with breakneck speed away from us across that sea of sagebrush, until he was a mere speck on the horizon, and then out of sight.

The landscape resumed its former inertia. Was that the deer we had been pursuing? It seemed incredible, yet one had to entertain the possibility. Maybe the buck was invincible, a spirit of supernatural strength. Or what we witnessed could have been one final, dying burst of vigor: He might now lie dead somewhere out there. Very probably, although he bore an uncanny resemblance to the one we were chasing, this had been another buck entirely, startled into flight by our arrival.

This was the worst possible time to have to worry about needing to be somewhere else, and yet we were both beginning to feel the pressure inevitably induced by the timeframe of a weekend hunt. Nonrefundable tickets and Monday morning classes, on one hand, and the deeply felt yearning to search for a wounded animal on the other. Neither of us wanted to give up, but we both knew we really had no choice.

I looked at my watch; it was well past noon. "I've got to make that plane," I murmured, "and you have a long drive ahead." Doug nodded weary agreement. Then gazing into the distance, he said softly, "The Romans would have said that was Diana's portion. She claims some of the spoils of the hunt for her own." Disconsolate as I was, I knew what he meant.

We hastened back to the truck and civilization. A speedy, mostly silent drive back to Billings, too-quick good-byes, and I was soaring to thirty-five thousand feet, bound for Omaha, nursing the kind of mixed emotions I suspect only a hunter can know.

The weekend's experience had been bittersweet, in the deepest and most complex sense of that term. I had not wanted to leave that hunt as I did. And yet, I knew—with an inner, unshakable conviction—that if I had all the time in the world, I would never have tracked down that buck. In his seemingly magical appearance, Diana had offered the deer, and in his near-mystical disappearance she had reclaimed him. Recrimination was pointless now. It had not been bad shooting. It had not been bad judgment. It was not even bad luck. Tonight, the coyotes would feast. Diana provides for her own.

Artemis

She Who Slays

Flower lion, flower lion, flower lion,
  walking in the wilderness, flower lion.

Over there, I, in the center
  of the flower-covered wilderness,
    through this enchanted wilderness grove,
    thump, thump, I am walking.
Flower lion, flower lion, flower lion,
  walking in the wilderness, flower lion.[1]

DON JESUS YOILO'I,
"FEMALE MOUNTAIN LION"

Running throughout the first four chapters has been the theme of the quest after a lost Eden, the search to recover a sense of the innocence of beginnings. We will now turn to a discussion of yet another vision of the way things were in the beginning: but without the illusion that innocence is what we will find there. The focus of this chapter is Artemis, the goddess who, more than any other in the Western mythological traditions, embodies hunting and the world of wild nature. That the ancient Greeks recognized her simultaneously as the goddess of hunting and of childbirth, at once the protector and destroyer both of nonhuman nature and of women, suggests a different way into and through the question of the relation of women to nature, hunting, and aggression. So, too, does the fact that Artemis is clearly a vestige of hunter-gatherer sensibility. The implications of Artemis as a goddess of women are, however, lost on contemporary feminists to the extent that in current goddess spirituality her "bad" (i.e., destructive) aspects have been split off from her positive ("nature-

136

loving") side. Artemis herself allows no such easy evasions. An Artemesian sensibility with regard to women's and environmental
concerns thus appears to be precisely what feminism needs, as a
necessary corrective, at this point.

LADY OF THE WILD THINGS

"Hunting scares me," writes Barbara Kafka, in a short essay ironically titled "Diana, Goddess of the Hunt." Having grown up "in
the world of man the hunter, woman the hunted," Kafka, an unre-
pentant meat-eater, admits the inconsistency of her repulsion at
the very thought of hunting. "My fantasy remains firmly on the
side of Peter Rabbit even as I stew my hare and relish its rich
sauce." This, she avers, is possible because of her "mostly urban"
life, and because she does not depend totally upon her own land,
or hunting or fishing, to feed her family. Nor is she persuaded of
the romance or adventure of hunting. She can eviscerate a fish or
disjoint a bird, but she would rather let the first blood be on
other hands.

Kafka locates her culinary truce with the implications of her
place on the food chain in the myths of Man the Hunter/Woman
the Gatherer:

> I am of the gatherers in the hunter-gatherer dichotomy, sexually
> linked to the mushroom pickers, the dandelion and ramp uproot-
> ers, the brewers of simples from collected herbs, and I am the
> cook. Where I wonder did I lose my lineage from Diana. Diana was
> a young and beautiful goddess, who protected and nurtured young
> animals but who was also shown with bow and arrows and saluted
> with dead animals from the hunt. Is hers . . . the aristocratic pre-
> rogative, or was a tradition as strong as that of the warrior Amazons
> lost as women became domesticated along with the animals?

Kafka's conclusion implies that there is more at stake, existen-
tially, in this last question than the matter of how the hare gets
into the stewpot: "The person who hunts to eat is certainly more
of a piece than I who have no intention of becoming a vegetarian
but cannot kill. A woman who can hunt as well as any man has a

primitive quality I will always lack. I am no warrior and no hunter; I like my garden and my casserole; but some part of me mourns the lost Diana in my birthright."[2]

It is not surprising that Kafka appeals to the goddess the Greeks called Artemis, and the Romans, Diana. Hers is an image we all grew up with, an image that held a special attraction perhaps for those girls who saw Barbie as a less than satisfying ideal. Thus young feminist Sarah Carner can recall when, in the fourth grade, she chose to do a project on Artemis while her classmates opted for Athena or Aphrodite, somewhat more conventional role models for girls: "Artemis was the hunter. I thought that Artemis was tough, athletic *and* smart. She was active and so was I. She was a Tomboy and so was I. She seemed to have a little bit of both Athena and Aphrodite. I even remember liking her clothes. I suppose I felt a connection with her more so than any of the other Gods or Goddesses. She crossed certain gender barriers that as a fourth grader I felt very uncomfortable with."[3] Reflections like this one suggest that it may well be time for feminism to take seriously the implications of recovering that "lost Diana" who is our birthright. Artemis represents power—female power—that, from very early times, was perceived to be highly problematic. What follows are the essentials of her story, reconstructed from the classical sources.

The Greek goddess was indeed something of a divine Tomboy. The poet Callimachus tells of the time her doting father Zeus took her up onto his knee, and asked her what presents she might like. Artemis, still a tiny child, responded without hesitation that she should like, among other things, "eternal virginity; as many names as my brother Apollo; a bow and arrows like his; the office of bringing light; [and] a saffron hunting tunic . . . reaching to my knees." She also requested a corps of virgin nymphs for her companions, and "all the mountains in the world."[4] Her indulgent father immediately granted her every wish. Artemis thanked him, hopped off his lap, and headed for the hills.

This sentimental little tale, coming late in the development of Greek mythology (Callimachus lived in the third century

B.C.E.), relates many important facets of the popular image of
the Goddess of the Hunt. Artemis is first and foremost a virgin
(*parthenos*). That is to say she, like the other virgin goddesses
Athena and Hestia, is "one-in-herself," not the consort or property of any man (or god). Indeed, according to the *Homeric
Hymn to Aphrodite*, "in all the universe" these three *Parthenoi*
alone can resist the magical powers of the goddess of erotic pas-
sion: persuasion, alluring charm, and the bonds of love. Interpreters have taken such resolute virginity to symbolize the rejection of socially constructed norms of conventional femininity.[5]

Artemis indeed goes by many names, relating to her different
associations in myth and ritual. The Fairest (*Kalliste*),[6] she is the
luminous Maiden of the Silver Bow (or the Crescent Moon).[7] As
a moon goddess, she is simultaneously "the goddess that roves by
night," and a "light-bearer," who guides travelers toward their
destinations (hence she is a guardian of highways, crossroads and
harbors). Like the moon, she is at once "enticing, romantic, and
remote."[8]

A mother goddess in her prehistoric lineage (and thus related
to the Ephesian goddess bearing the same name),[9] Artemis is, in
some special senses, a women's goddess. She is connected to
women's blood mysteries: menstruation, conception, parturition,
and menopause. "She of the Child-Bed," Artemis the divine midwife departs her mountain home for human environs only at
those times when women are in need of her, "helper in pains
whom no pain touches."[10] Those women who survive childbirth
know her as Nurse of Youth, the protector of newborn infants.[11]
Yet childbirth in Artemis's realm "is painful and difficult and always accompanied by the threat of death."[12] Those who do not
survive it are blessed with swift demise by one of her golden
arrows. "Zeus made her as a lion among women," Homer sang,
"and let her kill them whenever she chose."[13]

Artemis is, above all, the Goddess of the Outdoor World
(*Agrotera*), that is, the world beyond the city. She is the Lady of
the Wild Things, or Mistress of the Animals (*Potnia Theron*).[14]
This is, as Christine Downing remarks, "a title that encompasses
much more than is acknowledged in the post-Homeric image of

her as the shaft-showering huntress . . . she is not only the hunter but protector of all that is wild and vulnerable." Yet hunter she inevitably is. Indeed, it is in the tension between nurturing and killing, the "mystic, primitive identity of hunter and hunted," that the goddess's identity is rooted.[15] "She of the Red Deer" is thus also "She Who Strikes or Hits the Red Deer."[16] "In the bright and flowery fields she joins in the round-dance with her maidens," and so is celebrated in the joyousness of unfettered movement. Yet this same Artemis is also "She of the Nets," she who traps and captures.[17]

Reflecting upon the myth and ritual connected with Artemis, Downing suggests what the connection between the Lady of the Wild Things and She of the Child-Bed may have meant to the Greeks:

> She is a lady of the wild things, including the instinctual wildness within herself. She teaches her worshipers to know their body, their feeling, their desire as their own. The mysteries dedicated to Artemis were specifically focused on celebrating the sacred significance of those aspects of female experience connected to the particularities of female physiology: the onset of menstruation, the loss of virginity, the discovery of one's own sexual passion, the potential for loss of the claim to one's body as one's own inherent in marriage, the bodily changes associated with conception, childbirth, nursing, menopause, and, ultimately, with death.[18]

This last, Downing remarks elsewhere, "may not seem to us a peculiarly female mystery, yet to the Greeks it was self-evident that, though Apollo's arrows bring death to males, it is Artemis who brings about the death of women."[19] Thus, in a double sense, the Huntress is "She Who Slays."

The mythology of Artemis is replete with the far-darting goddess's hunting exploits. She killed enough she-goats on Mount Cynthus for her brother Apollo to build an altar, on the shores of the sacred lake on Delos, out of their horns: his first architectural project (the divine twins were four years old at the time).[20] She herself trained the hunter Scamandrius "to bring down every kind of wild beast bred in the mountain forests."[21] She and her nymphs roamed the long ridges of Taygetus, "rejoicing in boars and swift stags."[22] When the hero Heracles was transformed into a god, becoming the porter of heaven, he eagerly awaited Artemis's return each night to the gates of Olympus, her chariot laden with the spoils of the day's hunt: sometimes goats or hares, on better days boars or bulls, or lions, or wolves. Heracles would dress out the carcasses, and feast on the meat.[23]

The virgin Huntress's death-dealing extended beyond the animal world, sometimes indeed to those she loved. She killed her hunting companion Orion, according to some accounts by accident owing to Apollo's trickery, to others because Orion made sexual advances toward her, or toward her nymphs the Pleiades.[24] His image, and theirs, were set in the stars.[25] Likewise, when she discovered that her nymph Callisto had succumbed to Zeus's seduction, Artemis transformed her into a she-bear; she would have been felled by a hunter's arrow had she not been transformed into the constellation Ursa Major.[26]

Artemis drove the hunter Broteus mad, because he refused to honor her, and she transformed Meleager's evil sisters into guinea-hens because of their complicity in that heroic hunter's murder.[27] Among her most celebrated victims was Actaeon. Out hunting one day with his hounds, he chanced upon Artemis and her nymphs bathing in a mountain spring. When Artemis caught sight of him, she retaliated for this violation of her sacred privacy by transforming him into a stag. His dogs dragged him down and tore him to pieces.[28]

In myth and cult, Artemis demanded blood-sacrifice, generally of maidens. In the most notorious instance, before the Greeks could set sail for Troy, Agamemnon had to offer up to her his daughter Iphigenia. Subsequent myth, however, claimed that at the last moment Artemis had snatched the girl up into a cloud and substituted a hind for her on the altar. This story may reflect ritual practices at sites such as Sparta and Athens, in which "maiden-sacrifices" to Artemis Agrotera were enacted, using such animal surrogates as colts and goats.[29] Also, one of her temples near Athens was a repository in which were deposited the corpses of capital criminals and the implements suicides had used to bring about their deaths. In Rhodes, at the festival of Cronia, a condemned criminal was sacrificed before her statue.[30]

The devotion of hunters to the goddess is illustrated by the historian Xenophon. Exiled from Athens to Sparta for his role in the Persian Wars, he established on his estate a hunting ground sacred to Artemis, where he built a temple resembling (in smaller scale) the temple to Artemis at Ephesus. There he held an annual festival to the hunting goddess:

> All citizens and neighbors, both men and women, took part in the festival. The goddess provided barley, wheat bread, wine, dried fruits, and a portion of the sacrifices from the holy pasture, and from the hunted animals too. For a hunt was held at the festival by Xenophon's sons and those of the other citizens, and any of the grown men who wished to also took part. They took game, some from the holy ground itself and some from Pholoe, boars and roe deer and fallow deer.[31]

Partly on the basis of evidence like this story, it has been inferred by some that Artemis's identity as Huntress was primarily a men's concern.[32] This, however, belies her equally powerful reality for women, rooted in archaic rites of blood-sacrifice and in the everyday realities of biological blood-knowledge. It is tempting to evade the truths embedded in myth and ritual: that not only does life feed upon life, but also that the woman who is virgin, one-in-herself, can demand sacrifice, and can be lethal to man and animal alike. Yet as Downing declares, "So long as I deny that she is, indeed, 'She Who Slays,' I am . . . evading Artemis."[33]

The drive to evade this truth is itself ancient. It is reflected in Callimachus's charming (and somewhat taming) image of tomboy Artemis, daddy's little girl and Heracles's Olympian pal. So, too, in the ancient stories of the Amazons, who by classical times had been safely relegated to the mists of prehistory. As historian Abby Wettan Kleinbaum observes, "Much of what the Greeks found so frightening in the idea of Amazons was their manlessness: Amazons were supposed to be creators and perpetuators of female community, which except for reproduction, was entirely separate from the world of men."[34]

Artemis was the Amazons' divine patron, leading some to see in this association a link between hunting and warfare.[35] Yet the Greeks do not appear to have drawn this connection. As Downing remarks, Artemis was "clearly out of her element" in the Trojan War. Indeed, the one time she tried to involve herself, Hera violently rebuffed her, telling her in effect to go back to chasing deer about her sacred hills and leave warring to gods who knew what they were doing.[36]

Artemis's connection, then, is to the violence—the life/death/life process—of the wild world. Indeed, she "is herself the wilderness, the wild and untamed, and not simply its mistress."[37] The wild animals especially associated with her—deer, hare, wolf, lion, boar, bear, and quail—as hunters know, are creatures of "hint and nuance," the nature that "often just flits by and is not easily seen in a hard, clear light."[38] The nature that, as Heraclitus remarked, likes to hide.

Arcadia, Artemis's favorite haunt, was for the Greeks not a "pastoral realm," but "a wild and dangerous, rude and barbarous land . . . where things are as they are in themselves, not as shaped and manipulated by humankind."[39] Yet, unlike the primordial earth goddess Gaia, Artemis is "wilderness within the human world":[40] *Agrotera*, the world *outside* human civilization. Matt Cartmill suggests that hunting has thus to do with the "boundary where the human domain confronts the wild." Perhaps, he infers, "one of the reasons why the hunt plays a large role in Greek mythology—and in later Western thought about human origins—is that it takes place on that boundary, and thus marks the edge of the human world."[41] The hunter is thus, as Artemis was, a "liminal and ambiguous figure."[42]

Intrinsic to the idea of boundaries is their permeability; in effect, they exist to be crossed over. Dawn and dusk, the boundary-times between night and day, are the best times for hunting. The best places are those edges where one kind of habitat gives way to another (forest to meadow, for example, or along a lakeshore or riverbank). Hunting the edges, one perceives that in its workings, the world is far more complex and subtle than the intellect's too-ready distinctions seek to make it: wild/tame, animal/human, nature/culture, female/male. It is therefore not surprising that the Mistress of the Beasts is a goddess of sacrifice and transformation, death and renewal, of boundary situations. As remote as the moon or the mountain-top, as intimate as a first cry or last breath, she commands recognition that in our beginnings are our ends.

ACTING THE SHE-BEAR, HUNTING THE BOAR

At Brauron Athenian girls called *arktoi* (bears) celebrated their coming-of-age by "acting the she-bear" for Artemis. At Cyrene new brides and women about to deliver were required to go to the sanctuary of Artemis Kourotrophos and there offer sacrifice to the goddess. The sacrificial emoluments—hide, head, and legs— went to the priestess of Artemis who was called by the title *Arkos* or bear.[43]

Little is known for certain about the festival of Artemis at Brauron. From fragmentary written records, and from the scenes painted on shards of ritual vessels, a scenario can be pieced together: About a hundred girls, all "select virgins," and none older than ten, participated in what was surely an initiation rite. The scenes portray the girls engaged in what appear to be athletic contests, under the direction of adults, some of whom are wearing animal masks suggesting bears. Other animals sacred to Artemis (deer, dogs) are pictured with the girls, and in one scene a she-bear occupies center stage.[44] Written sources attest that the girls were "acting the she-bear," which earlier scholarship took to mean they were dressed in bearskins.[45] Scholars have more recently agreed that their dress was symbolic: the saffron tunic of Artemis, with whom the bear was closely identified.

Why bears? Some interpreters have glimpsed the remnant of a hunting ritual here. Walter Burkert, for example, notes that "the maiden as a vicarious victim for the animal to be killed—presented in mythology as the bride of the bear or buffalo—is a very widespread motif in hunting cultures."[46] Yet in ancient Greek imagination, the bear was not only an object of the chase; she was also a symbol of procreation and motherhood. Thus in the she-bear are united the two key concerns of the Lady of the Wild Things: hunting and childbearing, the ending of some lives and the beginning of others. Classicist Paula Perlman explains:

> Both the bear and Artemis are at one and the same time savage and nurturing, and just as the bear licks her cubs into shape so Artemis, savage goddess of the wilderness, (tenderly) presides over the development of the young *arktoi* as they accomplish the transition from *parthenos* [virgin] to *gyne* [woman]. . . . To act the she-bear, then, was to propitiate both Artemis, mistress of wild animals, and Artemis the virgin goddess. It was incumbent upon the maidens to mollify the goddess, for their future as mothers depended upon the protection of Artemis Kourotrophos, patron goddess of childbirth.[47]

The festival obviously served the civic purpose of socializing "the transition from prepubescent girl to nubile woman," preparing the girls for their adult roles: civilizing wild things, in short.[48] But what additional message might this initiation have held for the "little bears" themselves, who danced before the goddess's altar?

Surely, they would have been familiar with the stories about Artemis. And they very likely would have drawn parallels between themselves, dressed in her saffron hunting tunic, and her nymphs and hunting companions.[49] One story, in particular, would have come to mind, given the context of the ritual: Arcadian Atalanta, the virgin huntress who shunned the settled life of marriage and motherhood.

Atalanta's father Iasus had exposed his infant daughter on a mountainside when she disappointed him by not being a boy. She was suckled by a bear, sent to her by Artemis, and in due time was found and raised by a clan of hunters, among whom she became proficient with arms and renowned for her fleet-footedness. Soul sister of the hunting goddess, she grew to womanhood, swearing never to marry.

Meanwhile, Meleager was growing up in Calydon, son of King Oeneus (though some said his father was the war-god Ares). Meleager's mother Althaea had worked some magic when he was a baby, to ensure his immortality so long as a certain brand from the hearth remained extinguished. Young Meleager was renowned as the best javelin-thrower in Greece, and he had a chance to demonstrate his skills when his father Oeneus committed the stupid indiscretion of forgetting to include Artemis among the Olympian gods to whom he made annual sacrifice. In retaliation, she sent a huge boar to kill all the king's cattle and farmhands and destroy his crops. And so Oeneus decided to stage the biggest hunt that Greece had ever seen, to capture and kill the Calydonian boar.

Atalanta was among those who came from far and wide to participate, spurring dissension among the manly hunters who refused to hunt in the company of a woman. Meleager, who was already married, had nonetheless fallen in love with Atalanta, and threatened to cancel the hunt altogether unless she were allowed to join in. Thus the hunt began in strife and discord.

The first blood shed was human, more or less. Two Centaurs determined to rape Atalanta, who had taken a stand isolated from the other hunters. Her arrows dispatched each in turn, and she decided to hunt thereafter at Meleager's side.

When the massive boar was finally flushed, it foiled the efforts of several of the mighty hunters: Two were killed and one hamstrung, Nestor was driven up a tree, Jason's javelin, along with several others', missed their mark. When Telamon tripped over a tree-root and Peleus stooped to help him up, the boar turned and charged them. Atalanta let fly an arrow, piercing the boar's neck. Ancaeus, sneering "That's no way to hunt!", swung his battle-axe at the angry boar, succeeding only in disemboweling himself as the boar raced by. Eventually, after further mayhem, Meleager flung his javelin, hitting the boar in the side. He raced forward and plunged his spear into the boar's heart.

Meleager immediately skinned the boar, and gave the hide and tusks to Atalanta, to acknowledge her having drawn first blood. The assembled hunters were outraged that a woman should receive such an honor. Two of them went so far as to claim that Iphicles, not Atalanta, had drawn first blood. In a lover's rage, Meleager killed them both. There followed a tale of internecine strife, in which Meleager, cursed by his own mother for killing kin, was eventually killed himself when Althaea threw the magic firebrand into the fire. She and his wife hanged themselves, and Artemis turned his surviving sisters into guinea fowl.

Returning home, meanwhile, to Arcadia, Atalanta discovered that her father Iasus—delighted with rumors of her exploits—had forgiven her, at last, for being female. But he insisted she choose a husband. Atalanta—whom the Delphic oracle had warned against marrying, for in marriage she would lose herself—said she would only marry a man who could outrun her. And she reserved the right to kill any suitor who failed the test, as several princes did, to their misfortune.

Finally, Atalanta's Arcadian cousin Melanion decided to give it a try. But first, he invoked Aphrodite (Artemis's Olympian opposite number) for assistance. She gave him three golden apples from the Garden of the Hesperides. During his race with Atalanta, Melanion cast the beautiful apples, one by one, in her path. She could not resist the temptation to pick each one up in turn. These brief pauses, compounded with the weight of the apples, slowed her down sufficiently for her suitor to win the race, and her as his wife. Thus Aphrodite took revenge for Atalanta's obstinate refusal to marry.

There is clearly an object lesson for girls in the story of the Hesperidian apples. Divine Artemis might be able to resist the wiles of Aphrodite, but no mere mortal, no matter how resolute ("Atalanta" means "Unswaying"[50]), can long evade her powers. The myth thus served the interests of a society based upon patriarchal marriage, in much the same way as did the festival at Brauron, at the end of which the girls presumably shed their robes to symbolize "the abandonment of the 'bear life' in order to enter a new stage of life, the phase of puberty, to be followed by marriage." The ceremonies, as one classics scholar suggests, could be seen as "a way of exorcising the 'she-bear' (a symbol of the savagery of childhood) in every little girl."[51]

Perhaps. But perhaps the festival of acting the she-bear, like the heroic story of bear-suckled Atalanta's participation in the Calydonian boar hunt, held another meaning, as well. Classicist Lilian Portefaix sees in the myths relating to Atalanta

> the antagonism between different stages of culture: on one side a hunting-culture, represented by females, and on the other agri-culture and town-culture represented by males. Artemis was insulted that Oeneus had forgotten his earlier means of subsistence, and she sent the boar in order to force him and the heroes to leave civilization and return for a while to the hunting stage of culture to destroy the beast. Atalanta took part in the hunt, as a fellow-sportswoman in the same conditions as the males, but they did not acknowledge her as their equal.[52]

In the sequel to the boar hunt, Atalanta the hunter is literally overtaken by the fruits of agriculture. The Hesperidian apples come from a garden, not wild nature; and they are made of gold, "a material related to a more advanced stage of culture than hunting." Eve, it seems, was not the only woman in Western mythologies to be undone by an apple:

> Agriculture defeated the hunting virgin and she had to change her life of freedom in unspoiled nature for a domestic life in dependence on a husband.
>
> Artemis, on the other hand, was not defeated by agriculture. She remained a hunting-goddess, but she did not forget Atalanta and her sisters in their new existence.... In the cult of the hunting-goddess, women returned to an earlier stage of culture, which may explain why the amazons, so nearly related to Artemis, became a frequent motif in Greek art.[53]

Portefaix discerns in the cult of Artemis (as also in the nature-cult of the "women's god" Dionysus) a yearning for a lost paradise, women's desire to leave behind their "isolated lives in their homes and exchange their tasks of weaving and spinning for group-hunting."[54] In myth and cult are reflected the fact that the agricultural triumph of human culture over nature had also been, as we saw in chapter 1, in many ways the triumph of men over women.

The historical development of sex-role specialization accounts
for what Portefaix acknowledges as "a crucial problem: why is it
that from a female point of view a hunting-culture and not agriculture is looked upon as the lost paradise?" Artemis represents
an earlier stage in culture, when labor was divided more evenly,
when women joined men in hunting. But she is much more than
that: In her dual aspect, as taker and protector of wild and human
life, she recalls a "demand for ecological balance" that would
have been familiar in hunting culture, but that had been lost sight
of in an urban culture, "evolved to such a degree that its dependence on nature has practically disappeared."[55]

What distinguishes Artemis Agrotera from the primordial
earth goddess Gaia on the one hand, and the agricultural grain-
mother Demeter on the other, is that she is, as Martin Nilsson put
it, "the Life of Nature in the measure in which it intervenes in human life and forms a necessary and obvious basis for it."[56] As the
goddess of the ecosystem, for whom "each creature—each plant,
each wood, each river—is . . . a Thou, not an it,"[57] she forces the
recognition that we can too-readily forget our roots in the "outdoor" world. Like Oeneus, we do this only at our peril.

Meanwhile, Artemis also whispers to her little she-bears that
they, too, are wild nature. The eternally youthful Huntress might
stand for the crossing of gender-boundaries that a male-
dominated culture would like to keep as clearly demarcated as its
towns and farm fields. The unleashing of female energy impacts
the patriarchal imagination like a boar tearing through fences
and trampling crops. Indeed, the history of Western patriarchy
might be said to be the history of attempts to kill or bridle that energy, or to trick it into submission.

At the close of *The Creation of Feminist Consciousness* historian Gerda Lerner declares, "the millennia of women's prehistory are at an end." What she is getting at is the fact that, although male control of social and cultural institutions is still the
norm, advances in the education and social empowerment of
women have, at long last, made it possible to imagine shattering
the patriarchal hegemony of males over females. "We stand,"
Lerner suggests, "at the beginning of a new epoch in the history

of humankind's thought, as we recognize that sex is irrelevant to thought, that gender is a social construct and the woman, like man, makes and defines history."[58] If Lerner is right, and I believe she is, then it is clearly time for women to reclaim the "lost Diana" that is their birthright. The question today is where to seek her.

Contemporary goddess spirituality is a logical place to start. Unfortunately, however, the feminist spirituality movement has fallen prey to many of the same delusions, about women, nature, and female power, that characterize radical feminism and ecofeminist theory.

THE REBIRTH OF THE GODDESS?

"The reemergence of the Goddess is a grassroots movement."[59] So Elinor Gadon writes in the introduction of her *The Once and Future Goddess*, a study of the relationship between symbolism and spirituality in the work of contemporary feminist artists, and goddess images stretching back to the Old Stone Age. Gadon shares with a number of other commentators—among them Riane Eisler, Merlin Stone, Gloria Feman Orenstein, Buffie Johnson, Monica Sjoo and Barbara Mor, Starhawk, and foundational theorist Marija Gimbutas[60]—the intimation that patriarchy's time is up. Monotheism's center no longer holds, and we are today experiencing a rebirth of the primordial wisdom of the archaic Goddess, who teaches us to live in harmony with the earth and all her creatures, to heal the breach between human and nonhuman nature forged by patriarchy so effectively, and with such dire social and environmental consequences. Proponents of this view see evidence of the rebirth of the goddess not merely in the emergence and apparently growing popularity of goddess spirituality and feminist witchcraft, but also in such various social and cultural phenomena as the peace and environmental movements, second-wave feminism, ecofeminism, New Age religion, various twelve-step recovery programs, the current popular fascination with all things Native American, and the "Gaia hypothesis" of Lynn Margolis and James Lovelock.[61]

Critics contend that latter-day devotees of the Goddess have rejected historical realities in favor of a retreat into myth and metaphor.[62] For their part, scholars of goddess spirituality counter that their point of view is actually more deeply rooted in history than the conventional wisdom of patriarchal scholarship, tinged as that inevitably is by a male-dominant imagination. As Gloria Orenstein states the case: "To call the Goddess an archetype is to relegate some 30,000 years of human history to the level of the unconscious and to negate the actual historical reality of centuries of human life. Therefore, the Goddess is anything *but* ahistorical! The history of the Goddess actually exceeds that of Father God by millennia."[63] Orenstein's remark reflects the growing consensus among scholars—and it is not confined to writings about the Goddess—that it is simply no longer acceptable to trace the dawn of human civilization to the apparent invention of writing and the contemporaneous rise of patriarchal societies roughly five thousand years ago in Egypt and the Near East. Relying largely on James Mellaart's excavation at Çatal Huyuk in Turkish Anatolia, and on Marija Gimbutas's extensive work on artifacts from the Neolithic cultures of "Old Europe," proponents of the new scholarship on the Goddess push the earliest vestiges of complex civilized life back by at least four millennia, to the eighth millennium B.C.E. They take their inspiration from the revolution in archaeological thinking about human prehistory; and so, inevitably, Man the Hunter and Woman the Gatherer lurk about the edges of their theory of beginnings: "The old view was that the earliest human kinship (and later economic) relations developed from men hunting and killing. The new view is that the foundations for social organization came from mothers and children sharing. The old view was of prehistory as the story of 'man the hunter-warrior.' The new view is of both women and men using our unique human faculties to support and enhance life."[64]

This approach, which Kathy Ferguson usefully designates "cosmic feminism," is underwritten by the assumptions of radical ecofeminism. In the cultures of the Bronze Age—most significantly Çatal Huyuk and Minoan Crete—cosmic feminism discerns an agrarian social world that was "woman-centered, peaceful and egalitarian," and in which worship of the great mother goddess reflected a reverence for women's life-giving powers.[65] According to Riane Eisler, whose *The Chalice and the Blade* is perhaps the fullest exposition of cosmic feminism, the neolithic cultures were "*not* warlike. They were *not* societies where women were subordinate to men. And they did not see our Earth as an object for exploitation and domination." Thus, they provide excellent models for what we need today, "an ecological consciousness: the awareness that the Earth must be treated with reverence and respect."[66]

Cosmic feminism's portrayal of the "lost world" of the neolithic is infused with nostalgia for paradise. "In fact," Eisler writes, "we all know of this earlier time from no less a source than the best known story of Western civilization: the story of the Garden of Eden. This biblical story explicitly tells us there was an earlier time when woman and man (Adam and Eve) lived in harmony with one another and with nature. The garden is probably a symbolic reference to the Neolithic period, since the invention of agriculture made possible the first gardens on Earth."[67] *The Language of the Goddess,* Marija Gimbutas's study of Neolithic artifacts, tells, its publisher proclaims, "a dramatic story of paradise lost and now rediscovered."[68]

What was life like in that lost paradise? Cynthia Eller sums up the "content of feminist spirituality's myth of matriarchy" as follows:

> There was no war, people lived in harmony with nature, women and men lived in harmony with one another, children were loved and nurtured, there was food and shelter for all, and everyone was playful, spontaneous, creative, and sexually free under the loving gaze of the goddess. People were in touch with their bodies and the seasons, there were no rich or poor, [and] homosexuality (particularly lesbianism) was as valid or more so than heterosexuality.[69]

This Edenic equilibrium, or so scholars of goddess spirituality believe, was disrupted by patriarchal invaders (Gimbutas named these Indo-Europeans the "Kurgans") who beginning around the fifth millennium B.C.E. "swarmed down on [old Europe] from the Asiatic and European northeast." The Kurgan invaders were supposedly aided and abetted by Hebrew "warrior-priests" who worshipped "a fierce and angry god of war and mountains." The Kurgans and the Hebrews had in common "a dominator model of social organization," characterized by "male dominance" and "male violence."[70] They destroyed the "gylanic"[71] social fabric of the women-centered early neolithic cultures, and replaced the life-affirming great Mother Goddess with death-obsessed God the Father.

There are a number of problems with this story, beginning with the fact that there is no historical evidence to support it. For its proponents this presents no great difficulty. They argue, in general, that while gynocentric prehistoric cultures cannot be proved to have existed, they cannot be disproved, either: "If ancient matriarchies are not a certainty, at least they are a possibility, and this is enough to go on."[72] Numerous studies have shown that the worship of powerful goddesses neither arises from nor guarantees the egalitarian status, let alone the high esteem, of human women. One might look, for example, at the disparity between goddess-veneration and the suppression of women in ancient Greece or in modern India. Proponents of goddess spirituality, however, have nothing to say about this rather embarrassing state of affairs.

Ironically, as seems to happen whenever Woman the Gatherer rears her lovely head, cosmic feminism manages to reinforce precisely those gender stereotypes of femininity it claims to be rejecting in the name of the Goddess. A good example is the treatment of the numerous so-called Venus figurines recovered from sites dating to as early as thirty thousand years ago, the interpretation of which formed the foundation of the late Marija Gimbutas's theory. Gimbutas traced the Great Earth Mother's roots back through the Upper Paleolithic period, seeing her image in every such figurine.[73] Her reasoning, in effect, was that anatomy was destiny. At the first awakening of human awareness, when the mechanics of reproduction were not understood, women's ability to give birth must have inspired awe and fear in men: hence not only the Goddess' supreme power, but also the multiplicity of her images throughout Old Europe. The uniformity of the figures, with exaggerated breasts and hips and swollen bellies, pointed to their function as images of a goddess associated with fertility. Women and the Goddess were both defined strictly in terms of biological determinism.

In point of fact, however, as archaeologist Sarah Nelson points out, such an interpretation of the figurines (along with the assumptions about women that give rise to it) is based largely in "a folklore of the anthropology profession." Not only is there great diversity in design among the figurines, which represent a "3,000 mile and perhaps 10,000 year spread," we have no certain evidence of the circumstances or purposes of their manufacture. Who made them? Did they reflect male or female conceptions about women? Were they in fact fertility fetishes (by far the most conventional interpretation), or key elements of a goddess-centered religion (Gimbutas's view)? Were they playthings, portraits, or even "Pleistocene pinup or centerfold girls"?[74] Or none, or all, of the above? It is difficult, perhaps ultimately impossible, to know.

The notion of a continent-wide cult of a great goddess plainly rests upon an exaggeration of the material evidence. While the archaeological record is clear that one or more fertility goddesses were venerated in Anatolia several thousand years after the figurines were produced, there is nothing to suggest that all the figurines need be interpreted in the light of these goddesses, or in the same way. A universal religion based upon a single deity would, in fact, have been highly improbable in Paleolithic Europe, owing not only to limited contact among widely dispersed human settlements, but more especially to the fact that such a religion would be foreign to modern hunter-gatherer societies.[75]

Regarding Gimbutas' theories about the "peaceful . . . art-loving peoples" of Old Europe, it amounts, to borrow archaeologist Ruth Tringham's phrasing, to a "remedial feminist study which has put women into the pot and stirred vigorously."[76] Indeed, while Gimbutas and cosmic feminism put a positive spin on the idea, the impulse to imagine a female-dominant prehistory is as old as patriarchy itself. It was reflected in the ancient Greek relegation of the Amazons, and such other female powers as the Furies, to misty prehistory. More recently, the idea of ancient matriarchies captured the masculine imagination in the form of theories of archaic "mother-rule" spawned, after Goethe and Nietzsche, by thinkers like J. J. Bachofen, Robert Briffault, Erich Neumann, and Robert Graves.[77] Greek historian Stella Georgoudi has remarked that these more recent mythologizers of prehistoric matriarchy were up to about the same thing as their ancient Greek forebears:

> Some Greek myths placed this fearsome female element at the beginning of time and endowed it with venerable primordial power. To relegate women's power to the remote past, to assign it a place in "prehistory," to associate it with barbarian, "gynecocratic" regimes characterized by the absence of law and morality—to do these things was no doubt to write women out of the picture, to exclude them from Greek history, indeed from all history. Bachofen and his followers clearly saw this legendary "reality." Their error was to take the Greeks at their word, to mistake myth for history. In so doing, they unwittingly created a myth of their own, itself a worthy object of study: the myth of matriarchy.[78]

Abby Wettan Kleinbaum mounts a similar argument about how, for the past three millennia, "generation after generation of men in the West, champions all, have enlisted in the war against the Amazons."[79]

If the patriarchal effort to disempower women by writing them out of history reflects ambivalence about and hostility toward female power, the cosmic feminist effort to write women back in seems to issue from a complacency about power in the hands of women that could only be sustained through resorting to such stereotypes as the biophilic female and the rapacious male. Both views are grounded, as we have seen, in a close identification of women with nature, and both depend upon nature/culture dualism. In the patriarchal view, culture exists to tame nature (and woman). By contrast, theologian Kathleen Sands aptly describes what happens in the cosmic feminist reinvention of the nature/culture story:

> The world of patriarchy is seen as unrelievedly evil, and alienated, male-defined rationalities are denied moral authority over women, the earth, or other endangered goods. Instead, the grounds of moral authority are defined as "nature" and "women," which function as *immanent* ideals, immediately available in women's essential, creative, and mystical experiences. . . . The language of evil . . . becomes a kind of border guard aimed outward against patriarchy and cordoning off a sacred sphere where women's mystical and aesthetic powers can be fostered.[80]

We have already seen the inherent limits of this essentialist idealization of women and nature in ecofeminist discourse. Fantasies of ancient matriarchy and patriarchal invasion rest upon an assumption that it is the male role in nature and in culture to wound the female; "femaleness" becomes equated with the inability to inflict harm. "This demonization of males, of heterosexuality, and heterosexism ," as Christine Downing remarks, "represents an enormous effort to deny the shadow side of our own lives."[81]

Patriarchy has traditionally dealt with the "shadow side" of life by splitting reality into conflicting polarities: male and female, culture and nature, mind and body, and (with regard to the Goddess of prehistory as a projection of human psychological experience) the Great and Terrible Mother. Cosmic feminism, just as dualistic in its approach, seeks to "heal" all divisions by attributing evil to the "male" (or "male-identified") side of each equation, and good to the "female" or "natural" side. As Sands point out, this makes the question of "negativity"—violence—in nature highly problematic: "If 'nature' is used as a code for the good or acceptable negativity, that is only because everything that is adjudged bad or unacceptable has already been definitionally excluded. . . . The same applies to *women*, which if used as a code for the human good will exclude all the human proclivities of which it disapproves, even if they happen to be found in females."[82] This effort at exclusion and denial is especially evident in the popular image of the Goddess. And it is perhaps nowhere clearer than in latter-day depictions of the Lady of the Beasts.

"BACK-TO-NATURE ARTEMIS"

In her *Lost Goddesses of Early Greece*, ecofeminist Charlene Spretnak tells about the virgin goddess of the wild world. Her rendering of the "lost" story is worth quoting at some length:

> When the moon appeared as a slender crescent, delicate and fine but firm in the promise of growth, Artemis roamed the untouched forests of Arcadia. The Goddess lived with Her nymphs amid the thick, wild growth where animals joined freely in Her games and dances. She loved new life. Whether at play or at rest, Artemis was ever alert for the rising moans of a mother giving birth. The wind brought to Her long, low sighs and staccato songs of pain expelled. If the mother was an animal, lying alone in a hidden cave or a sheltered pile of leaves, Artemis rushed deftly through the woods to her side. She brought leaves of Her wild artemisia for the animal to eat and spoke softly in the mother's own sounds. The goddess gently stroked the bulging womb until the wet, squirming bodies emerged. She fondled each one and placed them under Her protection: *Within these forests no harm will touch the children of Artemis.*

There follows a description of Artemis similarly assisting a human mother. "Then Artemis would smile at the new One and whisper to the mother: *You may both enter My forests without fear and join Me on any night lit by the waxing moon.*" Spretnak goes on to recount in elaborate detail how during each moon cycle, women joined Artemis and her nymphs and the animals in "Her sacred grove," to dance around the "moon tree," from which the goddess "brought forth new life."

> Sparks of energy flew from their fingertips, lacing the air with traces of clear blue light. They joined hands, joined arms, merged

bodies into a circle of unbroken current that carried them effort-
lessly. Artemis appeared large before them standing straight
against the tree, Her spine its trunk, Her arms its boughs. Her
body pulsed with life, its rhythms echoed by the silvered tree, the
animals at Her feet, the dancers, the grass, the plants, the grove.
Every particle of the forest quivered with Her energy. Artemis the
nurturer, protector, Goddess of the swelling moon. Artemis![83]

At this point in the story, Artemis disappears into her tree, the ec-
static dancers fall exhausted, and another moon goddess, Selene,
takes over the action, driving her chariot (the full moon) across
the night sky.

Spretnak's fairy tale is charming, and incorporates several important aspects of the virgin goddess: her identification with wild
nature (animal and vegetal) and the moon, her role as midwife
and protector of young life, her connection with the dance. Conspicuously absent, however, is any reference to her hunting—or,
indeed, to any of her death-dealing. Gone are her silver bow, her
golden arrows, her demand for sacrifice.[84] The Mistress of the
Beasts—in whose presence, according to a Homeric hymn, "The
crests of tall mountains/tremble, and the thick-shaded forest re-
sounds/dreadfully with the cries of beasts, while the earth/and
the fishy deep shudder"[85]—is transformed, in Spretnak's rendering, into something like the Fairy Godmother in Disney's *Cin-
derella*. Filtering her tale of the "lost goddess" through the cosmic feminist myth of ancient matriarchy, Spretnak in fact loses
much of the goddess. This is Artemis's customary fate, in the popular literature about goddess spirituality and ecofeminism.

The Greeks knew the moon as a triple goddess: Artemis (the
crescent moon), Selene (the full moon), and Hecate (the dark of
the moon). Of these three Selene was a goddess of light, Hecate
(the prototype of witches) of darkness. Both were relatively minor goddesses, subordinated in myth and ritual to Artemis, who
was one of the twelve Olympians, and who as we have seen carries
light and dark together. The crescent moon not only waxes, it also
wanes. Death feeds on life as the darkness gobbles up the light.

Popular feminist spirituality has appropriated Hecate as the patron of witches, and generally invokes her when discussing death and transformation in the natural world. This has the effect of making Hecate (the "Crone") into the "dark side" of Artemis (the "Maiden").[86] To her alone is attributed the "acceptable negativity" of the wild world, where all death and suffering are "natural."[87] Meanwhile, Artemis—when she is mentioned at all—is celebrated for her "in-her-selfness" and her nurturing, biophilic qualities.[88]

Given the extent to which she is female-identified—her association with virgin nymphs and manless Amazons—Artemis actually appears surprisingly rarely in feminist literature. This seems odd for the goddess Jungian analyst Jean Shinoda Bolen calls the "archetype of the women's movement," and the "personification of an independent feminine spirit."[89] Yet Bolen's depiction of "Back-to-Nature Artemis" may help to explain why:

> In her affinity for the wilderness and undomesticated nature, Artemis is the archetype responsible for the at-oneness with themselves and with nature felt by some women when they backpack into forested mountains, fall asleep under the moon and stars, walk on a deserted beach, or gaze across the desert and feel themselves in spiritual communion with nature.[90]

It is noteworthy that she invokes examples of "non-consumptive" experiences of ship-in-a-bottle nature here. When Bolen glancingly mentions Artemis's hunting, it seems roughly equivalent to a hearty mountain hike, and curiously, no animals are reported dead. Hunting is at best, in her analysis, a metaphor for being "goal-focused."

Bolen is careful to specify that while Artemesian consciousness may incidentally arise from "back-to-nature" experiences, the wilderness adventure is fundamentally a journey inward, to "the wilderness within us all. This may be the deepest value of such an experience, the recognition of our kinship with the natural world."[91] This is surely true, and important. However, what we encounter on the inward wilderness journey is obviously shaped by our ideas about the human experience of and relationship to nonhuman nature: ideas which, as we have seen, arise far too frequently from a confusion of alienation, romanticism, death denial, and sheer ignorance.

This point seems to be largely lost on cosmic feminists. Ecofeminist Gloria Orenstein writes:

> In contemporary societies we take the journey into our psyches and into our dream worlds rather than to the mountains and sacred sites in nature in order to gain the knowledge of the shaman who dissolves the boundaries between the worlds, the knowledge that tells us we are both "tamed" and also part of the nagual, the other world. . . . Yet, this inward journey . . . actually subjectivizes and dehistoricizes what, for primal peoples, was a literal objective and historical pilgrimage to an actual sacred site.[92]

Orenstein rightly recognizes that it is crucial to "re-exteriorize" the wilderness journey, a quest that has become increasingly problematic for Westerners. For her, the way to do this is through the arts. Yet, as her own *Reflowering of the Goddess* and other similar works help to show, art can so easily become evasion.

For example, Orenstein quotes at length "matristic writer" Diana di Prima's poem-cycle *Loba,* in which the "metaphor of the Hunt . . . pleads for a return to our human-animal nature." Confronting the Wolf Goddess,[93] the poet "learns that she is *not the Hunter* at all, but rather *the Protectress.* Her ferocious animal nature is now seen to be a means to her survival, an element integrally related to her nurturing qualities." In the wolf, she sees a "kind watchdog I could/leave the children with." This amounts, Orenstein says, to a matter of feminist "reversal . . . a feminist matristic revisioning of the Dark as the Light, which has been repressed and reversed."[94]

As we saw with regard to nature writing in Chapter 3, such "revisioning" has been all too tempting when the wolf enters the natural scene. And this domestication of wolfishness amounts to a reversal, indeed, when it is masquerading as a reconnecting with "instinctual nature." A similar dynamic is at work in Clarissa Pinkola Estes's *Women Who Run With the Wolves.* Estes writes passionately, and sometimes poetically, about recovering the "Wild Woman Archetype," about recognizing that "no matter where we are, the shadow that trots behind us is definitely four-footed." But that shadow's killings all amount to mere metaphor, occasions for self-transformation and transcendence—not too different, in the final analysis, from the older masculine impulse to conquer the Amazon. Estes's wolves, though they may "howl often," have neither fangs nor claws.[95] Viewed in this light, wolf is no longer wolf, and Artemis is no longer Artemis.

One Jungian analyst, Ginette Paris, presents a different angle of vision on the implications of this goddess. She comments, in her extended meditation on the Wolfish One:

> Artemis has nothing in common with bucolic sentiment and kindly nature. . . . The Goddess who slays the beasts, whose patron she is, has a liking for bloody holocausts. It is not only animal sacrifice that is attributed to Artemis. In the most distant times of Greek religious history, she was associated with the practice of human sacrifice. . . . For those who imagine an ancient and pre-patriarchal matriarchy that was as cozy as the home of grandma, it is shocking to have to recognize the dark and cruel side of Artemis.[96]

A key point here is that she "slays the beasts, whose patron she is." Artemis's "cruelty" may inhere precisely in the fact that in this life there are some realities—death paramount among them—which cannot be reversed. One of the lessons the natural world teaches is that there are limits to metaphor.

We had closed the first chapter with the questions: What if it all had happened differently? What if women had continued to hunt? What if nonhuman animals continued to be viewed as intelligent equals, even superiors, of human beings? What if the world of nature were not experienced as opposite to, or other than, human culture?

Disabused of attitudes grounded in fantasies about nature and dreams of the past, these questions are after all worth asking. Gary Snyder comments: "There is no 'original condition' which once altered will never be redeemed. Original nature can be understood in terms of the myth of the 'pool of Artemis'—the pool hidden in the forest that Artemis, Goddess of wild things,

visits to renew her virginity. The wild has, nay *is*, a kind of hip, re-
newable virginity." [97]

The Lady of the Beasts may indeed bring us back into ourselves, but only if we allow her to be herself: She Who Slays, as
well as She Who Calms. And certainly not some benevolent Artemis of Assisi. How well we can claim to know nature anymore is a
complex question. Clearly the effort involves looking out, at the
nonhuman world and our relation to it, as well as looking within.
Artemis knows the way, but the only way she will take us there is
as a hunter.

6

Forest Reflexes

The moon, just past full, hangs in an ice-blue early morning sky. It is the third day of a forest hunt for whitetail, something to which I'm fairly unaccustomed, being by experience and by inclination a hunter of wide-open Western spaces. Mostly, I've hunted mule deer and antelope, and the whitetail deer (all does) I have shot have been at reasonably long range. I have, I suppose, a prairie hunter's prejudice against sitting still for too long: The mystique of scents, lures, and rattling-in largely escapes me. When I do take a stand, I prefer one with a long, broad view.

Nonetheless, I have been enjoying still-hunting amid brushy Ponderosa pines and cottonwood-cluttered ravines. A mid-November snowstorm has impeded access and kept most hunters home. My partner and I have these woods virtually to ourselves. The snow is fluffy and the wind cooperative, and the rut is in full swing. I am carrying two Montana deer tags: an either-species buck tag, and a B-tag for antlerless whitetail. Our first morning out, as the snow was just starting to fall, we surprised a formidable buck, bedded down with a doe. He was up and gone in a heartbeat, and has been a phantom in the back of my mind ever since. Now, we glimpse a solitary whitetail doe a hundred or so yards off in the trees. She senses our presence and bounds toward denser cover. My companion, who grew up deerhunting the woods and field-edges of Wisconsin, remarks, "The thing about a forest stalk is, once you've seen deer, they're *really* there. Up until you see them, they're ghosts."

We only hunt the dawn and morning hours. In the last three days, we have seen several whitetails, mostly does and fawns. None of the bucks we've jumped have measured up to that phantom-buck in my mind, but my failure to take any shots at them owes, in all honesty, as much to awkwardness as to choosiness on my part. I've got to develop better forest reflexes.

We've been following game trails through knee-deep snow for two hours now, and aside from a few wary does and the departing flag of a buck whose morning courting we interrupted, have seen nothing. Birds compare notes high in the trees, and the sun begins its ascent in a clear sky. Looking up at the moon, I think, "Artemis is on the animals' side today." Instantly I make a mental correction: Artemis, of course, does not take sides.

I find that my mind, like my body, meanders differently in the forest than in open country. Glassing across broad valleys and working the edges of rocky ridges can prompt expansive thoughts, ideas large and light enough to inhabit the landscape. Or that same terrain can engender a congenial emptiness of mind, as if its agenda has been cleared of all but the essentials: the earth, the sky, myself, the deer. The openness, thinking through me.

It's otherwise, here in the forest. Everywhere except overhead, the sky hides behind the trees. I strain to discern deer closer in: a tail here, an antler there, hiding behind the same trees. My thoughts grow smaller but more distinct, my mind searching its own thickets for connections: there's a metaphor around every fallen pine, in every snapping twig. Details matter. Details, and hints of possibility.

Working downhill, I tread the dormant undergrowth and deadfall carefully, feeling them through the snow. The air is still and impossibly clear. We come upon a rub and a fresh-looking scrape not too far from where we originally jumped that big buck, suggesting he may still be somewhere nearby. Threading along well-traveled deer-runs, I cradle my .270 in readiness for a sudden surprise calling for a quick shot. But I'm skeptical, both about my chances and my reflexes. I've read too many hunting stories about monster bucks abruptly crashing through the brush and into the crosshairs to believe those things will actually happen. The whitetail I'm hunting is too smart to be a cliché, and I'm not a fancy enough shot to be one.

That big buck, the reality and nearness of which I am certain, will remain a ghost for the rest of the morning. I know that, and so, I imagine, does he.

These woods occupy a broad bowl-shaped divide, funneling steeply down from open flats. We are working our way along the hillside, well below the rim. Concentrating so hard on training my attention upwards, where a late-lingering deer might be coming down off the top, I am suddenly startled to spy a deer straight ahead. A hundred yards, no less than that, away — a *big* deer (as big, it appears to me, as a cow), but clearly a whitetail. I can see all of it, except its head.

I creep closer, the snow muffling my steps. I wait, my rifle steadied on a tree limb, the crosshairs behind the deer's shoulder. I wait some more. This is the best shot I've had in three days; I know it won't happen again, and the opportunity won't last forever. After what seems an interminable time, but is probably more like three minutes, the deer raises her head. A doe. A *big* doe. Does she have company? I wait some more, and I begin to get a cramp in my back from the rather awkward position I've been hunched in. She is still unaware of me, so I slowly lower my rifle and arch my back. This action spooks another deer, one I cannot even see; he (I am convinced it's *him*) is in too-thick cover. The doe wheels around and follows him. I manage to glimpse their tails, zigzagging down through a cottonwood swale. Thinking I was right about the kinds of things that only happen in other people's hunting stories, I rejoin my partner, who had been lingering several yards behind me.

We pace a few steps, and almost immediately notice that we are being watched. A little whitetail doe is poised at the edge of the woods, perhaps seventy yards above us. She seems oddly unruffled by our presence; one would expect her to flee, especially as convection currents are wafting our scent in her direction. She takes a cautious step, then another. "She's injured," my companion—who has a clearer view of her than I—says. "See, she's limping." This situation calls for a hunting reflex that is not so specific to the forest. I move to where I can get a clear shot, take aim, and fire.

When we make our way up to the rim, we discover the little doe's left front leg had been broken above the knee, by a bullet that cut to the bone— the result, clearly, of someone's foolish, or careless, shooting earlier in the season. Her wound is partially healed over, but the little deer would likely have been a coyote's meal before winter's end.

The next day's forest stalk is an exercise in futility. The weather had turned temperate yesterday afternoon, with bright sunshine and brisk breezes, glazing everything over. Gone are the loft and quiet of the previous days' snow. Today it sounds like we're crunching through a toppled box of Crispix. There is nothing "still" about this hunting.

We decide to try some rattling-in—to no avail. Nobody's home in the woods. After a couple of hours we concede defeat and head for more open country.

Now we are well into the final week of deer season, and although I had dedicated myself this year to the quest of the elusive whitetail, I am by no means opposed to the notion of shooting a nice mule deer buck. I do not see this as a question of "compromise," although I realize some would. I respect the animals I hunt too much to ever regard myself as settling for one because I cannot have another. I have a healthy admiration for the wily whitetail. But I have little patience with the widespread prejudice (manufactured, I suspect, by the same folks who gave us *eau de* buck-in-rut and doe-in-heat) that mule deer are, by comparison, intellectually challenged. From the vantage point of a still-hunter, mature bucks of either species are a challenge. They get to be mature *because* they are a challenge.

So I do not mind, or not too much, abandoning the quest for the phantom whitetail as we descend out of the woods into the valley below. This is more familiar country for me, rolling grassland cleft here and there by deep brushy draws and rambling creekbeds. Though the snow is crunchy, in these open spaces the sound dissipates, and I feel like I can hear myself think again. That forest was beginning to feel a bit claustrophobic. It's a pleasant change of pace to get back out into the open, where the deer don't behave like ghosts. Back to the essentials.

I am thinking this, walking fifty or so yards behind my partner, along the crest of a rise that overlooks an open pasture. It's midmorning now, so at most I expect to see mule deer fawns whose mothers are in deeper cover with their gentlemen callers, or immature bucks on the make for a stray doe. I let my mind, and attention, wander.

Suddenly, two deer leap into view at the far side of the pasture, about three hundred yards off. *"WHITETAILS!!!"* my companion explodes. I can't quite believe my eyes: a doe, with a buck—yes, my binoculars confirm, he's *that* buck—in ardent pursuit. He is not a ghost anymore. But what on earth is he doing out *here*? The terrain, and the time of day, are all wrong for a whitetail buck that's smart enough to have gotten this big, even if the rut is in progress. Either he was led astray by one dumb but beautiful doe, or this is the whitetail romance of the century and they both threw caution to the wind.

While I am expending precious seconds trying to work this out, my companion (he of the finely tuned forest reflexes, who knows opportunity when he sees it, whatever the context) has more sensibly moved a few yards into better shooting position. The deer have discovered us and are on the run. I drop to a sitting position and put my scope on the buck, but cannot steady it enough to get a confident shot off at this distance. I hear myself let out a yelp of frustration.

The whitetails reach a fenceline, the doe jumping it and heading for the trees, the buck hesitating for a mere instant. My partner fires, and the buck goes down.

He is a real beauty: a broad, heavy 5×5 with long, elegant tines. His body is as big as a mule deer. I would love to have shot him myself, but cannot begrudge my partner's success, or his superior marksmanship. A hunter for more than forty years, who has deferred to me on more than one occasion, he deserves this one.

This does not prevent me, of course, from wishing I had the last several minutes to live over again. It is a long drag back to the pickup.

The next morning, Thanksgiving, dawns overcast and frosty. As I step outside and pause to let my eyes become accustomed to the dark, a round break opens in the clouds, the moon precisely centered, shining through. Taking this as a good omen, I set off for a stretch of sage country where a series of knobs and rocky hills gradually rise into rugged buttes.

I do not have to go very far. By seven o'clock I have killed a good buck, a large robust mule deer in his prime. It was one of those rare "textbook" stalks where conditions are ideal and everything goes right—that is to say, a fine memory, but not the makings of much of a story.

Sitting on the hillside, next to my buck, I watch the sun clear the horizon. Turkeys are calling down in the creek, and a little forked-horn buck is trying to impress a doe on a neighboring hilltop. I am happy with the morning and with my deer. It has been a good season.

I find myself thinking about those days, this past week, in the woods. There are lessons I need to learn there, skills to develop, instincts to train to the altered rhythms of the understory. I notice that the moon has set. Next year I will start earlier in the season, and stay longer each day. I want to spend more time in that forest.

Woman the Hunter:

Learning to Live New Stories

Radical ecofeminism and popular environmentalism have sustained themselves for too long now on fictions of nature romanticism and on gender-essentialist fantasies. It is time to take an honest look at the world of nature and our human involvement in that world, including the blood that is on all our hands, in one way or another. Hunters may know how to do that better than anyone else. And women hunters are especially well poised to express the meaning of human involvement in nonhuman nature right now, in ways simultaneously quite new and very old. The changing demographics of female hunting (which have led some to suggest that women are "the future of hunting") may represent a seismic shift in popular consciousness that has implications far broader than the "hunting fraternity" has begun to comprehend.

The quest for a new cultural sensibility (Gary Snyder calls it a "culture of nature"[1]) need not end in either a rehashing of the myths of Man the Hunter and his enabler Woman the Gatherer, or in a burst of New Age spirituality infused with pseudoscience and mythohistory. Artemis may indeed be the goddess of the women's movement, but in ways not yet imagined.

"THE WOMAN WHO HUNTS"

Consider: a woman is on her way home from work, and from her after-work personal safety course. Stopping at the supermarket for some steaks to grill for dinner, she sees the latest Jean Auel novel on the paperback stand and happily tosses a copy in her cart. What appeals to her in these stories is their strong central character, Ayla, the Woman Who Hunts. Whether or not our

169

shopper identifies herself as a feminist (and many of the novels' fans do not), whether or not she consciously enjoys her vicarious participation in Ayla's death-dealing, this reader's contribution to the popularity of the Auel's novels itself may signal an advance in the evolution of female consciousness as decisive, in its own way, as the fictional Ayla's first determination to break the taboo against women's hunting, and to fashion a sling for herself.

At the end of the millennium, it seems everything in American society is more or less after-the-fact: The latter third of the twentieth century has variously been labeled post-modern, post-industrial, post-feminist, post-historical. This may help to account for the popular and scholarly fascination with the Old and New Stone Ages. It is as if to say, if we could only go far enough back in prehistory, maybe we could start over and get things right this time. Apropos of fictions such as Auel's *Clan of the Cave Bear*, and in light of such social phenomena as goddess spirituality and the scholarship ostensibly undergirding it, archaeologist Margaret Conkey has warned against the "aesthetic colonization" of Ice Age Europe.[2] Her words of caution are certainly warranted, considering the way theories about the past can be used to reinforce stereotypes grounded in the present. In this sense, the longer ago, the better. The Paleolithic period becomes an ideal screen— even better than the Neolithic—on which to project fantasies, because so little material evidence is available to challenge them. When fantasy masquerades as fact, as we have seen with regard to the myth of matriarchy, the result can only be bad history; or, as in the hunting hypothesis, questionable science.

Imagining the past can, nevertheless, make for some good fiction. And, interestingly enough, if the goddess the ancient Greeks would have recognized as She Who Slays never makes a recognizable appearance in contemporary goddess spirituality, she seems to provide a considerable amount of inspiration for authors of the Paleolithic fictions that have been so commercially successful in the last few years. While mass-market commercial fiction may seem at first blush a less likely place to seek a genuine rebirth of an Artemesian sensibility than ecofeminism or goddess spirituality, it may also be a more reliable indicator of significant trends at work in the popular imagination. What is it, exactly, that draws readers to these stories?

Most noteworthy, by far, among the fictions of the Upper Paleolithic are Jean Auel's enormously popular *Earth's Children* series.[3] Auel's first novel introduces Ayla, a Cro-Magnon girl orphaned and raised by the Neanderthal Clan of the Cave Bear. At a climactic moment in the story, the Clan has gathered to decide her fate, after she has transgressed their law by hunting. When the shaman announces that "Long ago, before we were Clan, women helped men to hunt," his remark is greeted by a collective "gasp of disbelief." The shaman counters the men's incredulity by explaining that long ago, people were guided by different spirits than the ones guiding them now. Indeed, those spirits guiding the women hunters were even more powerful and greatly to be feared than the men's totem spirits. What the Clan men now fear in the idea of women hunting, the shaman tells them, is the reassertion of that primordial power in the women who, over time, have been so successfully domesticated.

Because the shaman understands the politics of the Clan, he is quick to reassure the men that they needn't fear that any of their own women will take up weapons: The ability and desire to hunt has been successfully bred out of Clan women, but Ayla, being one of "the Others" (a Cro-Magnon) is different. Her hunting should, therefore, prove no threat to their collective manhood. After considerable debate, Ayla receives the special title, "The Woman Who Hunts." It is at once an acknowledgment of her talent with a sling and of her peculiarity as an outsider.

Auel surely intends her tale to strike an ironically familiar note. Ayla is a "new woman," a challenge to traditional conceptions about femininity. She is blonde, beautiful, upright and strong. Yet the Clan find her ugly (even grotesque) in appearance, and willfully stupid and nonconforming. Auel writes: "The whole concept of a woman hunting was so unique, so thought-provoking, that several of the men had been jarred into making the small incremental step that pushed the frontiers of their comfortable, secure, well-defined world."[4] Auel is on to something here. Her description might as easily apply to a room full of anthropologists as

to a cave full of Neanderthals. This in fact may help to account for
the immense popularity[5] of her books chronicling the adventures
of Ayla, the Woman Who Hunts. The novels are patently anti-
intellectual; Auel is writing for an audience that wants a "good
read," that is, a fast-moving plot, reasonably believable characters, and love and death in approximately equal proportions.

When *The Clan of the Cave Bear* was first published, it was
hailed as a feminist novel, and Ayla as a protofeminist, a reading
surely intended by Auel. Here is her description of the typical
Neanderthal man's reaction to this strange young girl: "Females
were supposed to be docile, subservient, unpretentious, and
humble. The domineering young man took it as a personal affront
that she didn't cower a little when she came near. It threatened
his masculinity. He watched her, trying to see what was different
about her, and was quick to cuff just to see a fleeting look of fear in
her eyes or to make her cringe."[6] For her part, like many a young
woman awakening to her own inner capabilities, Ayla experiences herself as a social outsider. Certainly much of the broad
appeal of Auel's fiction lies in the facility with which she uses
Neanderthal society to critique conventional assumptions
about women's place, and such arbitrarily defined categories as
"beauty" and "femininity."

Ayla is an explicitly evolutionary figure, whose life-journey
comprehends both human evolution (she is a transitional figure,
with cultural roots in both branches of *Homo sapiens*), and the
geographical extent of Late Paleolithic human settlements (she
begins her life in the Ukraine, venturing westward to follow
the Danube across the European continent, toward the region
around Lascaux in southern France). Auel portrays Ayla and
her mate Jondalar (another Cro-Magnon) as culture-bringers,
and they thus represent for her the emergence of recognizably
human culture. Ayla and Jondalar's Cro-Magnon culture is fairly
egalitarian, although familiar gender roles are more or less
in place: Women rear the children, men do the heavy lifting.
Significantly, though, one activity—hunting—is not gender-
determined among Ayla and Jondalar's people. Among them,
Ayla the Woman Who Hunts is recognized as an expert, but not

an oddity. She is equally valuable to the community as healer/ midwife and as hunter. In both spheres of activity, Ayla is serving "Doni," the Mother of all, and here Auel incorporates the idea of a primordial Mother Goddess based on the "Venus" figurines. Her portrayal of the relationship of "Earth's Children" to their mother reverberates with a distinctly twentieth-century ecological sensibility.

Another novelist drawn to the Upper Paleolithic is anthropologist Elizabeth Marshall Thomas, whose *Reindeer Moon* (1987) and *The Animal Wife* (1990) are set in Siberia twenty thousand years ago. Thomas—perhaps owing to her professional training—posits less egalitarianism among her people, but similar to Auel takes up the themes of hunting and invention as work for women as well as men. The Goddess (Thomas calls her "Ohun") is ever-present in human interactions with nature; indeed, she is nature in all its forms. Of key importance to Thomas are two themes: the continuity between human and nonhuman nature, and the death-dealing side of the Goddess. Like Auel, Thomas posits a Paleolithic Earth Mother among whose attributes are those a later time would recognize as attaching to Artemis: in Gimbutas's phrasing, "the Lady of free and untamed nature and the Mother, protectress of weaklings, a divinity in whom the contrasting principles of virginity and motherhood are focused into the concept of a single goddess."[7] It is she who reminds her people of the central, inescapable fact of human existence—that life feeds on life, and for some to live, others have to die.

Both Thomas and Auel give their heroines Artemesian attributes. Yanan, the heroine of *Reindeer Moon*, who narrates her story from the spirit world after having died in childbirth, takes on the forms of various Artemesian animals—wolf, lion, deer— in her after-life journey through the world of nature. Ayla's totem animal is the cave lion, and via the Clan she has a special relation to the cave bear; she travels with a wolf by her side. Like Artemis she is tall and fair, and most importantly, she combines the two crucial roles of hunter and midwife.

Both writers portray the poignancy of the hunting life. After her exile from the Clan, Ayla for example realizes that now she must hunt in order to live through winter. She kills a mare, and then—discovering it had a young foal—reflects: "I'm sorry for you, Ayla thought. I didn't want to kill your dam, she just happened to be the one who got caught. Ayla had no feelings of guilt. There were hunters, and there were the hunted, and sometimes the hunters were hunted. She could easily fall prey, in spite of her weapons and her fire."[8] The narrator of Thomas' *The Animal Wife*, an adolescent boy named Kori, similarly reflects on killing in order to live. Having speared a reindeer and wrestled it to the ground, he says:

> I freed myself and stood up. The wind had died. The day was ending, and into the depth of the quiet thicket cold air was creeping from the lake. My reindeer lay at my feet with its head on the ground, mouth open, and a pool of blood forming. I could smell it. He lived a little longer, watching me, knowing at last who was the stronger of us.
>
> Ah, well. Our eyes met, and I held his gaze until his pupils widened in an empty stare. Then I was alone, with meat.[9]

If the passage from Auel reflects something of the goddess as Protectress (Ayla adopts and raises the little filly whose mother she has killed for meat), the passage from Thomas confronts more directly the uncompromising harshness of She Who Slays. Neither writer loses focus on that hairbreadth between life and death that makes living possible at all.

Both passages are noteworthy for their matter-of-factness. Although Ayla and Kori each reflect on the meaning of their killing, neither writer attributes feelings of guilt or remorse to her character. Far from being a mark of moral failure, this absence of guilt feelings suggests a highly developed moral consciousness, in tune with the realities of the life-death-life process of the natural world. The simplistic analogy of hunting to such forms of male aggression as rape and warfare breaks down at precisely this point, where a kinship is perceived between the hunter and the hunted.

So, too, does the distinction between hunting's practical purpose (as a means of survival) and its symbolic function (as the center of a particular way of life). As Gary Snyder observes, "To acknowledge that each of us at the table will eventually be part of the meal is not just being 'realistic.' It is allowing the sacred to enter and accepting the sacramental aspect of our shaky temporal personal being."[10] The hunter serves as an agent of awareness for society at large, both by forging that most elemental conceptual connection between human and nonhuman animals, and by locating the essence of that connection in the good food that sustains life. Such awareness is only available, though, to the extent that some people are actually hunting; otherwise, it is mere nostalgia (a non-Artemesian emotion if ever there was one), an empty metaphor.

One of the earliest surviving representations of the goddess of the hunt is a rock engraving dating to the Mesolithic, from the Algerian Sahara.[11] It suggests that at the heart of hunting lies the mystery of regeneration. A hunter, armed with bow and arrow, takes aim at an ostrich. Behind him stands the goddess, her arms upraised in a gesture of blessing. A "line of force" flows from her genital area to his, and to his arms. Significantly, though the goddess is often described as "presiding over" the hunt, she is here pictured on a continuum with hunter and prey: They are equivalent participants in the cycle of life and death and renewal. Absent from the image is any suggestion of domination, conquest, or exploitation—those patriarchal dynamics against which ecofeminism justly argues. The power of hunting, as imaged here, is the generative power of life which comes through death. It is a power intimately connected to sexuality, its force a "bloodtie" uniting goddess, hunter, and hunted.

Ironically, this archaic sense of the inherent connection between death and regeneration is captured far more acutely in contemporary popular fiction, than in cosmic feminist writing about the goddess. In *Mother Earth Father Sky*, Sue Harrison tells the story of Chagak, a prehistoric Aleut girl who, like Auel's Ayla, is orphaned young and must make it on her own in the world. After her home village is destroyed by fire and all its inhabitants killed by marauders, when her sole surviving relative (a baby brother) dies, Chagak is at the point of suicidal despair. What brings her slowly back to life is hunting— something she had seen the boys and men of her village do, but until now she herself has never attempted. She takes up the bolas and spends hours each day practicing so hard she raises blisters on her hand, making her feel "as if she were again part of the things of the earth." Hunting eider ducks, Chagak kills two drakes. "They were her people's spirits, she had no doubt. She had taken two of them. Two spirits would stay with her."[12] She cooks and eats their meat and preserves their hides and feathers. Chagak begins to live again. Harrison's use here of the idea of hunting affording a way through suffering to renewed life reflects Artemesian blood-knowing about the way of the world.

Why fictions such as these, and why now? Readers of these novels may well recognize in them a refreshingly realistic perspective. Auel, Thomas and Harrison all clearly read the archaeological and mythological records differently than do cosmic feminists. For these writers, there are no easy evasions. Everything that lives will die. And out of its dying, others will live. Although it has always been so, it is easier now than ever before in history to shield ourselves from this knowledge.[13] Yet, given the state of worldwide environmental depredation, now more than ever we need to disabuse ourselves of dangerous illusions about the nature of the wild "outdoor world," and about our involvement in and impact upon it. We need to learn to tell ourselves, and to live, new stories. Some women are doing just that.

THE WOMEN WHO HUNT

In August 1990, Professor Christine Thomas of the University of Wisconsin-Stevens Point College of Natural Resources, organized a conference on the subject of "Breaking Down the Barriers to Participation of Women in Angling and Hunting." Thomas and her colleague Tammy Peterson were working from the hunch that women's nonparticipation in traditionally male-identified outdoor activities often had less to do with lack of interest than with negative peer pressure, lack of access and of encouragement. Their intimation proved correct.[14] Subsequently, in light of the vigorous interest the conference had generated among the public and the press, Thomas the following summer organized a three-day outdoor-skills training workshop especially for women. In August 1991, at Treehaven Field Station in Tomahawk, Wisc., just over a hundred women attended the first "Becoming an Outdoors-Woman" workshop. "They ranged in age from 18 to more than 65. Their annual incomes ran the gamut from college students living below the poverty level to professionals earning more than $55,000 annually. They ranged in education from high school graduates through advanced graduate degrees. They were married, single and divorced. Some had children, some didn't. They came from a variety of vocational and personal walks of life."[15] What united them was their desire to learn hunting and fishing skills in the noncompetititive, supportive atmosphere the workshop planners had promised.

To ensure such a female-friendly atmosphere, as many sessions as possible were instructed by women. The sessions were hands-on; participants learned by doing such activities as shotgunning and riflery, archery, flyfishing, canoeing, backpacking, orienteering, various hunting techniques for different species, and wilderness survival. The workshop was a resounding success, and the Becoming an Outdoors-Woman (BOW) program of women's outdoor skills training workshops was born. Since that modest start, the program has mushroomed nationwide; workshops have to date been held in forty states and three Canadian provinces,[16] and by the close of 1996, approximately twenty thousand women had participated.[17]

The exponential growth of the BOW program is perhaps the best indicator of a rising interest in hunting among American women, but far from the only one.[18] The last few years have witnessed the establishment of several regional women's hunting and fishing organizations, some with a national outreach.[19] Traditionally male-dominated prohunting organizations like the National Wildlife Federation and the National Rifle Association have marked sharp increases in their female membership.[20] Hunts designed specifically for women are becoming increasingly common, some sponsored by organizations like the Women's Shooting Sports Foundation, others by state fish and wildlife agencies. Hunting and angling clinics are increasingly being offered by merchandisers who, newly alive to the potential of this growing market, are also stocking clothing and gear designed for women. Similarly, outfitters are increasingly advertising all-women hunting opportunities, ranging from elk hunts in Colorado to safaris in South Africa.

Industry spokespeople and wildlife agency personnel have simultaneously taken to characterizing women as the "future of hunting," given the rise in female-headed single-parent households and the shift in American demographics from a rural/suburban to an urban focus. Some have seen in all this nothing more than a crass attempt by the shooting sports industry to manipulate women in order to drum up new business, in the face of slowly eroding numbers of male hunters. But the women involved do not see themselves as the unwitting dupes of unscrupulous advertisers; and as *Newsweek* pointed out in a 1995 "Lifestyle" article on the phenomenon of more women taking to the field, "none of the easy stereotypes fits these wilderness women." That article addressed not only the broad range in age, education, and background among outdoors-women, but also their complex motivations for taking up hunting.[21]

Some significant differences seem to exist between the typical female and the typical male hunter. Women as a group tend not to be as interested as men in acquiring trophies; their emphasis is consistently on having a more intimate connection with their food, on using as much as they can of the animals they kill.[22] Women, despite all the propaganda to the contrary, approach firearms use with a higher level of responsibility than males do. Firearms safety instructors commonly attest to their preference for working with female students. Women and teenage girls, they report, are typically more teachable than men or teenage boys, who tend to think that for them firearms use is supposed to "come naturally." And not only are women more open to instruction, they also appear more concerned about the ethical implications of firearms use.[23] Christine Thomas remarks that, from the beginning of the BOW program, its participants "said they wanted to know more than just how to do something. They also wanted to know why it should be done a certain way."[24]

These differences may owe, at least in part, to the fact that females typically take up hunting later in life than do males, at a time when ethical decision-making amounts more to integrating new knowledge or ideas into an already established moral perspective, than to simply learning a series of dos and don'ts. It may also owe, of course, to the fact that females are socialized differently than males, in such a way that moral decision-making happens in the context of relationship.[25] Whatever the reasons, and they are surely complex, the possibility clearly exists for those women who venture afield to create new models of hunting and outdoor ethics. Such possibility is not lost on Thomas, who with her colleagues begins each BOW workshop with three "ground rules:" that political differences be left at the door, that safety always be the primary consideration, and that ethical behavior based in reverence for the natural environment be a central concern. "Women," she tells participants, "are starting with a clean slate." The implications of all this for women hunters as cultural agents of awareness are indeed considerable. For in constructing new models of hunting and outdoor ethics, these women are also in a position to suggest new models of female power, and relationship to nature. But before getting to those implications, we must banish from view—one last time—the spectres of Man the Hunter and Woman the Gatherer.

HUNTING WITH A DIFFERENCE

The plain facts are that roughly ten percent of American hunters overall are female, that in some regions the proportion of women hunters is significantly higher (twenty percent in some of the Rocky Mountain states, for example), and that these numbers seem to be growing exponentially. The precise number of female hunters nationally is impossible to determine; the most widely quoted estimates, drawn from various governmental and industry sources, placed the figure at between 2.5 and three million as of 1995. And all observers agree that the number is growing annually.[26] Numbers like these are obviously unsettling to those adherents of the Man-the-Hunter/Woman-the-Gatherer school—macho hunters and feminists alike—who would rather see women at home tending their herb gardens.

Significantly, macho resistance to the idea of women hunters is not limited to the pages of "hook and bullet" outdoor publications. In 1994, for example, the *National Law Journal* ran a story about a group of women judges and attorneys in Houston, Tex. who had formed a hunting club (El Club Cordoniz Sin Cabeza, "The Headless Quail Club") with the following stated purposes:

> To facilitate bonding among female lawyers and jurists, to obtain fresh game for post-hunting trip celebrations, to get out into the great outdoors and find out why men have been hunting together for millenia.[27]

While some of their male colleagues were reported to be supportive of their networking strategy, far more were appalled by it. Dick DeGuerin probably spoke for the majority: "I think it's a dangerous trend. . . . If they want to network then they ought to have a quilting bee—hunting is a male avocation. I don't think the women's networking needs to be a simple emulation."[28] One male attorney remarked that the club "gives new meaning to the term 'lady-killers' "; another attributed it to "penis-envy"; yet another (invoking the Lorena Bobbitt case) quipped that maybe guns were at least preferable to knives.

All of these responses echo the too-familiar resistance outlined above (in chapter 2), to the very *concept* of women appropriating men's (literal and symbolic) tools. And in this light, it must be emphasized that the attorneys interviewed were bothered not merely by the women's hunting, but also by their professional networking: Judge Carolyn Garcia, a club member, said her male colleagues were "constantly asking, . . . 'What did you talk about on the trip? What did you do?' "[29] The leitmotif in all the men's responses is that these women have violated traditional gender boundaries; one attorney asked, "Why do they think they have to mimic the men?"[30]

Women hunters, from all class levels and walks of life, have encountered similar "glass ceilings" at traditionally all-male shooting ranges and hunting camps. They have, until quite recently, had to make do with ill-fitting clothing and other gear designed for men or boys. Yet they persist in the face of intense negative pressure. Indeed, noting the considerable obstacles facing women in the "man's world" of hunting, sociologist Robert Jackson reported that in his survey of Wisconsin women deer hunters, "Seventy percent stated they would miss hunting more than most or all other recreational activities. It should be noted," Jackson went on, "that most of them reported that their most obvious role model, their mother, didn't even have recreational interests. Their development as hunters is almost revolutionary."[31]

The notion that women breaking out of traditional gender roles merely want to "mimic the men" is, at the close of the twentieth century, frankly silly. Indeed, this criticism only makes sense if one grants the essential validity of gender-determined roles, and the best feminist analysis has gotten well beyond that. This leaves ecofeminist critics of hunting with two options. The first is to simply ignore the fact that a significant proportion of hunters are women, and persist in defining hunting as a male activity.[32] This strategy, by far the more common one in their writings, is fundamentally flawed. What, after all, are the implications of a feminist critique that intentionally brackets out the experiences of millions of women?

Dimly cognizant, perhaps, of this problem, some activists have opted to focus on phenomena like the BOW program, all-women hunts, and the increased marketing of hunting merchandise to women. These are evidence, they charge, of the shooting industry's underhanded intent to seduce women into buying hunting-related merchandise, coupled with the desire of state fish and wildlife agencies to increase license sales. In the name of feminism, these critics mount their argument that women's active participation in traditionally male outdoor activities amounts to nothing more than a huge deception. Women hunters, according to this line of reasoning, are victims of crass ("malestream") corporate and governmental interests.

The chief spokesperson for this point of view has been Heidi Prescott, national director of the Fund for Animals. In December, 1995, she sent a letter to the fish and wildlife agency directors of all fifty states, demanding they cease support of the BOW workshops. It read, in part, "The Fund for Animals requests that your agency decline to host any program designed to entice women to hunt—whether the enticement is blatant or subtle. . . . Although these programs are spin-doctored as an opportunity to 'get-acquainted-with-nature,' the obvious intention is to recruit women hunters or, at the very least, to increase women's acceptance of hunting."[33] Embedded in Prescott's widely quoted comments is the stale stereotype of the naive female "enticed" into "sin" by the nefarious male. Using a similar logic, ecofeminist Maria Comninou suggests that perhaps the fact that modern hunting involves all sorts of "paraphernalia and other products or services one can buy," means women who subscribe to the " 'shop 'til you drop' credo" might well be attracted to hunting.[34]

Criticisms based in such trivializing female stereotypes are an insult to the intelligence, and integrity, of women who hunt; so are the facts that feminist critics of hunting are otherwise virtually silent about women hunters, and that they quite obviously have not made any serious attempt to acquaint themselves with the actual views and experiences of women hunters. While hunting commentary by women is hardly abundant in the outdoor press, over the past several years there have been a number of articles and stories by women hunters, many of them specifically intended to convey either why they became hunters in the first place, or what is it like, specifically, to be a woman hunter. There is also an extensive historical literature by women who have hunted, sometimes with husbands or lovers, sometimes on their own (and sometimes after jettisoning their husbands!).[35] References both to the historical and the contemporary literature are conspicuously, and consistently, absent in ecofeminist criticism of hunters and hunting.

How might we account for this glaring omission? Feminists for Animal Rights founder Marti Kheel unwittingly implies an answer. In her essay "License to Kill: An Ecofeminist Critique of

Hunters' Discourse," Kheel develops a threefold typology of hunters: the "happy hunter," who hunts for sport; the "holist hunter," whose motivation is located in environmental ethics; and the "holy hunter," for whom hunting is a quasireligious experience.[36] Acknowledging that the divisions among the three types are not hard and fast—indeed, that there is considerable overlap among the three—Kheel writes that her major concern is with the "holy hunter." There are two reasons for this. The first, she says, is that "the spiritualization of violence engaged in by this category of hunter is particularly insidious." Indeed, it must look that way from the vantage point of cosmic feminism's emphasis on the moral purity of women, in conjunction with "good" nature. In this regard Kheel brings into play all the familiar arguments about man the rapacious dominator, over against passive, biophilic woman.

Kheel's second reason for focusing on the "holy hunter" is more interesting, however. It is, she says, because "the language and ideology that surround the 'holy hunt' bear a disturbing resemblance to that of ecofeminist thought."[37] Why, precisely, is this resemblance "disturbing?" Kheel cites the ideas of the hunter's identification with the hunted, the symbolic tension between killing and giving birth, and men's aggression against women and nature. All are, in her analysis, either/or propositions, grounded in biologically rooted gender identity. According to her logic, women give life, and men take it. Period. With recourse to object relations theory, Kheel sums up hunting as "the quest to establish masculine identity in opposition to the natural world."[38] And she concludes that we must identify the roots of our "violent culture" in "the masculinist mind," recognizing that "the perpetrators of violence throughout the world are, by and large, men, and the victims of this violence are primarily women and the natural world."[39]

It is the same old story, then, but with one intriguing variation: the matter of that "disturbing" similarity of some hunters' discourse to ecofeminism. Kheel is reading the right sources (many of them have been cited in this book); but she is reading them through essentialist lenses. She winds up employing a dualistic framework that any patriarchal theorist would be proud of. And her characterizations of hunting consistently miss the mark.

For example, she describes hunter-consciousness as "diffuse" (since "attention" implies "caring," which is an obviously female prerogative in her system). Yet in actuality a hunter with "diffuse" awareness could hardly to be successful. Regarding the identity of hunter and prey, she castigates hunters for their "abstraction." Yet there is nothing "abstract" about intentionally taking a life, let alone about the business of getting up to one's elbows in blood, field-dressing a large animal. Hunters are, as a group, necessarily more comfortable with ambiguity—and in a sense, more comfortable with being *un*comfortable—than are Kheel and her ecofeminist colleagues.

The inability to tolerate the complexity of human interactions with nonhuman nature—so characteristic not only of radical ecofeminism, but of upbeat popular environmentalism as well—is nowhere clearer than in Kheel's discussion of the symbolic relation of hunting to childbirth. She quotes Paul Shepard: "The value of the hunt is not in repeated trips but a single leap forward into the heart-structure of the world, the 'game' played to rules that reveal ourselves. What is important is to have hunted. It is like having babies; a little of it goes a long way." Kheel, inexplicably, sees in this statement an example of "the mental construct of masculinity that is fed by violence and death." [40] If giving life is inevitably something women do, and taking it what men do, it is no wonder Kheel does not talk about women who hunt. Not only is there no conceptual room for them in her theory, their very existence calls that theory radically into question.

The similarity of hunters' discourse to that of ecofeminism can be disturbing only to those who, like Kheel, insist upon women's moral purity in relation to the nonhuman world, coupled with men's tendency toward depravity. Not only is theirs a resolutely unrealistic perspective, it is also maddeningly simple-minded when it comes to the intricacies of human existence.

Those moments when we are most fully alive, and arguably most completely ourselves, are never instances of unalloyed emotional, ethical or aesthetic experience. Depth and richness do not come prepackaged, in emotions or values readily labeled, sorted out and categorized according to an approved, ideologically freighted checklist. There is an infinity of meaning in the beating of a heart, as well as in its stopping. But that meaning is something we bring to it, one beat at a time, each time: each pulse a new event, a once-in-a-lifetime encounter. To squeeze the trigger or not, to embrace that bittersweet burden of mutual mortality and make a meal of it, or to let be. These are decisions not lightly, or easily, undertaken—especially, perhaps, when the gun is in a woman's hands.

We have seen what men have to fear when destructive power is in female hands: the loss of their masculine hegemony, and of their ability to keep women in check. Given millennia of male privilege, men's uneasiness at the closing of the patriarchal frontier at least makes historical, and psychological, sense. Women's resistance to "owning" their aptitude for aggression is more problematic, however, since it amounts to a flight from self-knowledge, as well as from responsibility. Before the rise of feminist consciousness, it was of course possible for women to retreat into traditional images of passive, nonthreatening femininity, while the men about them smiled benignly and soldiered on, in the male-defined "real" world beyond the home. But for feminists, at the end of the second millennium, to adopt essentially the same posture, in the name not only of feminism but also of identification with nature, simply defies rationality.

The question at issue is not whether women are as capable of violence as are men. Obviously we are, though traditionally female aggression has taken different forms, more often psychological than physical, and far more often directed inward toward the self rather than outward toward others. In a society where women are widely viewed as incapable of healthy aggressiveness, female aggression as a result is almost invariably deemed pathological. Yet just as violence is a fact of nature, aggressive tendencies are necessary components of human personality. We could not get along without them. We would, among other things, starve to death.

Hunters know this from lived experience. And that is why

hunters attest that what they do in the field, when they do it well, is not only right, but healthy, meaningful, and deeply satisfying. This is true whether the hunters are men or women. But when they are women, because of the social and psychological barriers they have to overcome, and because of their transgression of the cultural taboo against women's using men's tools of power, they are up to something else as well. Whether they are self-conscious about it or not, whether they call themselves feminists or not, they are rewriting history.

THE END OF WOMEN'S PREHISTORY

After recounting the Navaho story of the Deerhunting Way,[41] Terry Tempest Williams tells about how she was sixteen years old before her father invited her to go deerhunting along with him and her brothers. After days of stalking the ridges of Colorado's Dolores Triangle and evenings under the stars listening to hunting stories by the campfire, Williams realized how much she had missed: "My brothers had been nurtured on such tales, and for the first time I saw the context they had been told in. My education was limited because I had missed years, layers of stories." Williams had, in essence, missed the lived dimension of the Deerhunting Way; as she states it, poetically:

> *Walk lightly, walk slowly,*
> *look straight ahead*
> *with the corners of your eyes open.*
> *Stay alert, be swift.*
> *Hunt wisely*
> *in the manner of the deer.*[42]

Such lessons cannot be learned in the abstract: context, as she suggests, is everything. Yet surprisingly, in the right context—that is, in the forest one's living depends upon—one may well discover these skills are not "learned" at all. In a sense, they come with acting naturally.

A few years ago, a writer for *Petersen's Hunting* magazine recounted a conversation he had had with a friend, a professional hunting guide in South Africa. His friend had remarked an interesting fact of his experience: that, when stalking an animal, people visibly changed, their pace becoming more stealthy and deliberate, their breathing and facial expressions altered. Asked if this was apparent only in seasoned hunters, "he replied that it was a constant in all his hunters, beginners and old pros alike. He added that it was interesting that women and children who had never hunted before had all the instinctive movements that many people think they learn only through years of experience."[43]

Context is everything, then, but so is intention. It is not simply the fact of being in nature that excites the body's instinctive response, it is the natural action of stalking. The training that makes it work more efficiently, and the stories that give that action meaning, come later. In one sense, women have, over the past several thousand years, indeed missed experiencing layers of stories. Yet in another and more primary sense, the encounter with oneself in nature, is as new, and as pregnant with possible meanings, as it ever was. Every hunt is a first time.

And every hunter brings a world of human meaning to bear upon her participation in the cycle of life and death. As was remarked much earlier, the hunter confronts the nonhuman world *in person*, an animal like the others, but one with a particular knack for crossing boundaries, and an obsession for making sense of things. She returns with blood under her fingernails, and with meat—which, later on, lusciously sauced and served with wine and the story of the hunt, is indeed the best of foods.

It all comes down to accepting responsibility for the totality of one's existence: not, as Naomi Wolf has remarked, just the "scenic parts." Feminists have long, and legitimately, called upon men in American culture to own their full range of emotions, to develop their capacities for nurturing and tenderness, for vulnerability. Too often, however, this has been taken to mean that men have to own up to those elements of human personality that have traditionally been labeled "feminine," even as women need to express their "masculine" qualities (and, in the process, risk being charged with trying to act like men). This, as has been widely re-marked, has the unfortunate effect of perpetuating gender distinctions, under the guise of overcoming them.

It is, in addition, difficult to embrace what one perceives (in the light of culturally determined stereotypes) to be negative qualities: "feminine" weakness, "masculine" aggression. The latter is especially problematic, not only because of deeply ingrained prejudices about appropriate gender roles and behaviors, but also because, in a society as violent as our own, there are precious few positive images of human aggression to begin with, and none of female aggression.[44]

Hunting is one key instance in which, as we have seen, natural aggression can be positively valued. Women hunters are indeed "starting with a clean slate;" they are not burdened with the cultural baggage men are, all that macho-paraphernalia. In a very literal sense, they have nothing to prove, in their hunting. This is something men—hunters and nonhunters alike—can learn from Woman the Hunter: that the rites and symbols of male initiation are far from the heart of the matter.

Yet if in one sense Woman the Hunter gives the lie to conventional gender categories, in another—having to do with the heart of the matter, with blood-knowledge—she transforms them. In hunting, the dual functions of giving and taking life are fused; hence the frequent comparison of hunting to childbirth, and the complex symbols and rituals attaching to Artemis. Male hunters can, if they choose, downplay the "feminine" side of things, but in this regard women—if they are being honest with themselves, anyway—cannot. Blood is a fact of female life, a continual reminder of our rootedness in the life-death-life process. By virtue of the interplay of biological identity and socially imposed role, the manifold implications of killing in order to live are for women necessarily very close to the surface of consciousness.

The perspective such awareness affords has to date been sorely lacking in discussions of the variety of ethical and environmental issues that confront American society at the close of the twentieth century. The important idea of an "ethic of care" with regard to the nonhuman environment has recently been advanced by a

number of environmental theorists, as a way of reconceptualiz-
ing the relation of humans to the nonhuman environment. However, within feminism, as well as more broadly, the conversation
about "earthcare" has been dominated by Woman the Gatherer
and her macho mate.[45] As long as this continues to be the case, all
the old stereotypes of appropriate gender roles and behaviors are
bound to define the terms of the dicussion. Woman the Hunter
defies and recontextualizes those traditional stereotypes.

One of the strengths of ecofeminist theory, and its best potential for making a lasting contribution to the debate over environmental issues, lies in its grasp of the importance of context, both
with regard to framing philosophical positions, and charting political courses of action. We have heard enough, by now, of male
domination of women and of nature. The point, to be sure, is well
taken. The question for the future is, where do we, women and
men together, go from here—as a society, as a species, as diverse
members of variegated communities of life? The contexts for environmental thought and action are as big as the globe itself, and
as intimate as a kitchen herb garden. Whatever forms our conversations take, though, now more than ever we had better be sure
we are talking about the real world of living breathing experience, not about fantasies of a pristine nature that never existed
and never will. This real world, in all its harsh complexity and
dangerous, heart-rending beauty, is ours for the loving. So our
blood tells us, if we will listen carefully.

The paradoxes of life and death admit no ready solutions: they
should not. This is the only world we have to make meaning out
of, and it would be a shame—indeed, a tragedy—if in any context
that meaning turned out to be simple, or single. Intricate realities
demand multiple perspectives. It is time to welcome the hunter-
woman back into the community of discourse; she has been waiting, like the wolf (though perhaps not so patiently) outside its
boundaries for far too long now. She obviously deserves a place at
the table, and she comes bearing good food for thought.

Sister Predator

A young juniper is nestled here, where I am sitting on the ground by a fence corner. The tree provides camouflage for me, the fence a rest for my rifle. On the other side of the fence, a large rolling hay field; behind me, ponderosa pine woods. I am waiting, in the frosty predawn stillness, for the deer—whitetails and mule deer—to filter down off the field, where they have spent the night feeding, into the daytime shelter of the forest. They will materialize any moment now, nothing more at first than tiny shadows, barely distinguishable in the greyish frost. I know they are sniffing the air, training their ears for unfamiliar sounds, shrugging ice crystals from their thick, fragrant coats. I know this, even though they are still too far away to see clearly and will be for several minutes.

I am not the only hunter to have taken a stand here this morning. Atop a wooden power pole a few yards beyond the fence, a great horned owl scans the field below. She too is alert for the movement of tiny shadows, and is surely aware of me, though I do not imagine she cares much one way or the other about my presence. We are not intent upon the same quarry, she and I.

This start of my hunting day is the close of hers. We share the symmetry of this boundary situation, during the quarter-hour or so that it takes for the air to begin to lighten, the stars to fade. Then, soundlessly, she swoops down from her perch, traces a swift, graceful arc across my line of vision, disappears.

A pinkish glow suffuses the horizon, a ruby filament begins to burn along the buttes to the southeast. I continue my vigil. The shadows grow in size, begin to move, to breathe.

Notes

INTRODUCTION

[1] Aldo Leopold, "The Deer Swath," in *A Sand County Almanac*, 223–24. Leopold's classic collection of essays on hunting, ecology, and the "land ethic" was originally published in 1949. His remark about these habits of mind belonging to both sexes is characteristically forward-thinking. In the passage quoted, therefore, each "he" should be read as "he or she."

[2] Heidi Hall, "Never Give Up," *Turkey & Turkey Hunting* (Spring 1994), 68.

[3] Quoted in Mary Zeiss Stange, "Women in the Woods," *Sports Afield* (June 1995), 102.

[4] Susan Ewing, "To Each Her Own," *Gray's Sporting Journal* (September 1994), 25. Italics in original.

[5] Gary Snyder, "Survival and Sacrament," in *The Practice of the Wild*, 184.

[6] Paul Shepard, "A Post-Historic Primitivism," in Max Oelschlaeger, ed., *The Wilderness Condition*, 82.

[7] Snyder, "Survival and Sacrament," 179. Snyder here is invoking John Muir's remark that "Culture is an orchard apple; Nature is a crab." However, he is less convinced than Muir of the ready opposition of nature to culture. Elsewhere in the same volume, Snyder remarks that "We are always in both worlds, because they aren't really two" ("The Woman Who Married a Bear," 165).

[8] Stephen Kellert cites several sources regarding "the myth of nonconsumptive use." See *The Value of Life*, 194–95, and 245 n. 8.

[9] Margaret Atwood, *Surfacing*, 222–23. In the climax of Atwood's novel, widely regarded as a signal text of second-wave feminism, the protagonist undergoes a kind of nature-initiation, involving a regression to a prehuman animal state, through which she comes to understand that she must "give up the old belief that I am powerless and because of it nothing I can do will ever hurt anyone."

[10] Shepard, "A Theory of the Value of Hunting," *Transactions of the Twenty-Fourth North American Wildlife Conference*, Washington, DC: American Wildlife Institute, 1959, 510–11. On Leopold's idea of the "split rail value" of activities like hunting, see his essay "Wildlife in American Culture," in *A Sand County Almanac*.

Stephen Kellert, in his important sociological study of the attitudes of hunters and antihunters, "Attitudes and Characteristics of Hunters and Anti-Hunters and Related Policy Suggestions," quotes this passage as an illustration of what he terms the "naturalistic hunting attitude," which "more than any other motivational source for hunting, is compelled to confront and rationalize the death of the animal," and the "essential paradox of inflicting violence on a natural world cherished for its quiet beauty." Kellert, "Attitudes and Characteristics," 11. Kellert remarks in the same study that one of its most striking findings was the much greater naturalistic attitude of hunters compared to nonhunters. "Hunters generally revealed far more interest in the outdoors, and more affection and desire for contact with wildlife. Hunters reported significantly greater desire for exposure to wilderness areas and living in proximity to wildlife. . . . Hunters also revealed substantially less fear, indifference and disinterest in animals than nonhunters. . . . Additionally, hunters reported significantly greater affection for pets and generally more recreational involvement with animals. Thus, although hunters killed wild animals for food, recreation or other purposes, they appeared to be characterized by substantially greater affection, interest and lack of fear of animals than those who had never hunted" (6).

[11] Clarissa Pinkola Estes, *Women Who Run with the Wolves*, 461.

[12] Snyder, "The Etiquette of Freedom," 17. Italics in original.

[13] Ann S. Causey, "On the Morality of Hunting," *Environmental Ethics 11* (Winter 1989), 343. Causey writes: "Most anti-hunters, except the most extreme animal rights advocates, agree that for some traditionally subsistence-based cultures hunting is necessary for spiritual, if not physical, survival. Why should the modern sport hunter, similarly seeking spiritual enrichment, not be given the same consideration? By focusing on modern man's physical needs and ignoring his spiritual needs, we threaten to eliminate elements in our collective cultural background that should, instead, be nurtured. We have moved in most aspects of our lives so far away from our roots, placing so many middlemen between us and the land, that we have become increasingly arrogant and ignorant of our place in and dependence upon the land pyramid. We should not, by reducing their genuine sport to one more modern management or conservation tool, discourage the earnest attempts of those who try to keep this contact alive." For the idea of the "land pyramid" see Leopold's "The Land Ethic" in *A Sand County Almanac*.

[14] On the problematic idea of "sport hunting," see James A. Swan, *In Defense of Hunting* (San Francisco: HarperCollins, 1995). Swan, a psychotherapist, observes that "Like his predecessors, the modern hunter hunts for meaning, to express himself as a member of the human race" (144).

[15] I am, of course, echoing Henry David Thoreau's oft-quoted declaration in *Walden* that "[I]n wildness is the preservation of the world."

[16] I am borrowing this provocative phrase from feminist historian Gerda Lerner; see chapter 5 in this book.

CHAPTER 1

[1] Frances Dahlberg, ed., *Woman the Gatherer*, 1.

[2] Desmond Morris, *The Naked Ape*, 53.

[3] See Robert Ardrey, *The Hunting Hypothesis: A Personal Conclusion Concerning the Evolutionary Nature of Man*, 65–67.

[4] Julian H. Seward. The single most important source of information on the hunting hypothesis is *Man the Hunter*, eds. Richard B. Lee and Irven DeVore. See especially the essays by Lee and DeVore, James Woodburn, Hitoshi Watanabe, Joseph P. Birdsell, Glynn L. Isaac, Lewis R. Binford, William S. Laughlin, and Sherwood Washburn and C. S. Lancaster.

[5] Washburn and Lancaster, "The Evolution of Hunting," 296.

[6] Lee and DeVore, "Problems in the Study of Hunters and Gatherers," 7. They note in this context that "only in the arctic and subarctic areas where vegetable foods

are unavailable do we find the textbook examples of mammal hunters." See also Lee, "What Hunters Do For a Living, or, How to Make Out on Scarce Resources," 30–48.

[7] Lee and DeVore, "Problems in the Study," 7.

[8] See, for example, Julian H. Steward, "Causal Factors and Processes in the Evolution of Pre-farming Societies," in Lee and DeVore, *Man the Hunter*, 321–34.

[9] Hitoshi Watanabe, "Subsistence and Ecology of Northern Food Gatherers with Special Reference to the Ainu," in Lee and DeVore, *Man the Hunter*, 69–77.

[10] Washburn and Lancaster, "The Evolution of Hunting," 299. This passage may be the most frequently quoted excerpt from the essay, both in literature for and against the hunting hypothesis.

[11] Washburn and Lancaster, "The Evolution of Hunting," 299.

[12] William S. Laughlin, "Hunting: An Integrating Biobehavior System and Its Evolutionary Importance," in Lee and DeVore, *Man the Hunter*, 305–7. In Laughlin's analysis, the hunting "behavior pattern" has five sequential components: 1) programming the child, 2) scanning or collecting information, 3) stalking and pursuit of game, 4) immobilization of game, including the killing or capture of game, and 5) retrieval of the game.

[13] Watanabe, "Subsistence and Ecology," 74. (Watanabe's assumption that women in hunter-gatherer cultures never hunt "individualistically" has been proved wrong by subsequent field research.) Laughlin similarly recognized females' restricted capacity for tool development and use. The bolas, he observed, being "simple enough for women and children to manipulate," helped to account for some of their contributions to ancient and modern hunting economies—presumably their occasional taking of small game. "Hunting: An Integrating Biobehavior System," 314.

[14] Laughlin, "Hunting: An Integrating Biobehavior System," 318. Laughlin goes on to muse, regarding one of the australopithecine lines that preceded the emergence of *Homo sapiens*, "If *A. robustus* was a vegetarian, it is difficult to imagine what he was doing with tools. On the other hand, tools become useful to a bipedal hunter because they do facilitate killing and the reduction of the dead animal for food and fabricational purposes" (319).

[15] Watanabe, "Subsistence and Ecology," 77.

[16] Watanabe, "Subsistence and Ecology," 73. Joining women in their sedentary life were the other "less able-bodied," that is, children and old people.

[17] Laughlin, "Hunting: An Integrating Biobehavior System," 319.

[18] Margaret Ehrenberg, *Women in Prehistory*, 41.

[19] Lee and DeVore, "Problems in the Study," 7.

[20] Laughlin, "Hunting: An Integrating Biobehavior System," 311. The verb tense in his observation is noteworthy in itself!

[21] George P. Murdock, in *Social Structure*; quoted by Patty Jo Watson and Mary C. Kennedy in "The Development of Horticulture in the Eastern Woodlands of North America: Woman's Role," in Joan M. Gero and Margaret W. Conkey, eds., *Engendering Archaeology: Women and Prehistory*, 256.

[22] To put water-fetching further in perspective, it is illuminating to note that among the Hadza people of Tanzania, "three or four miles [are considered] the maximum

distance over which water can reasonably be carried and camps are normally sited within a mile of a water source." See James Woodburn, "An Introduction to Hadza Ecology," in Lee and DeVore, *Man the Hunter*, 50.

23 Watson and Kennedy, "The Development of Horticulture," 268–69.

24 The debate between "gender essentialism" and "the social construction of gender" is at the heart of contemporary feminist theory. As we shall be seeing throughout this inquiry, the distinction between "nature" (or biodeterminism) and "nurture" (or environmentalism) is more elusive than it might at first appear.

25 This has led anthropologist Cheryl Claasen to argue that "until we inspect the division of labor more carefully, we have written into prehistory a time management crisis for women, and an inventory of activities tacitly assumed to have been 'women's work' produces superwomen, carefree children, and sportsmen." Claasen, "Gender, Shellfishing, and the Shell Mound Archaic," in Gero and Conkey, eds., *Engendering Archaeology*, 286.

26 Sarah Blaffer Hrdy, *The Woman That Never Evolved*, 5. One possible explanation, of course, is that for many of the anthropologists involved, intelligence was not a conspicuous component of female biopsychology.

27 See especially Dahlberg's anthology, *Woman the Gatherer*. See also Sally Slocum, "Woman the Gatherer: Male Bias in Anthropology," in *Towards an Anthropology of Women*, ed. Rayna R. Reiter; Nancy Tanner and Adrienne Zihlman, "Women in Evolution. Part I: Innovation and Selection in Human Origins," *Signs: Journal of Women in Culture and Society* 1:3 (1976), 585–608; and Adrienne Zihlman, "Women in Evolution. Part II: Subsistence and Social Organization among Early Hominids," *Signs* 4:1 (1978), 4–20.

28 The most noteworthy case is the Agta of the Philippines; see Agnes Estioko-Griffin and P. Bion Griffin, "Woman the Hunter: The Agta," in Dahlberg, *Woman the Gatherer*, 121–51. Other frequently cited cultures in which women regularly join in the hunt include the Mbuti pygmies of Africa and the Tiwi aborigines in Australia.

29 Ehrenberg, *Women in Prehistory*, 43.

30 Dahlberg, *Woman the Gatherer*, 12.

31 Hrdy, *The Woman That Never Evolved*, 6.

32 Donald Johanson and James Shreeve, *Lucy's Child: The Discovery of a Human Ancestor*, 224.

33 Michelle Z. Rosaldo, "The Use and Abuse of Anthropology: Reflections on Feminism and Cross-cultural Understanding," *Signs* 5:3 (1980), 393, 412.

34 Gerda Lerner, *The Creation of Patriarchy*, 12–13.

35 Tim Ingold, *The Appropriation of Nature: Essays on Human Ecology and Social Relations*, 79.

36 Ingold, *The Appropriation of Nature*, 80.

37 Ingold discusses the various terminological permutations operative in anthropological discourse on the subject in some detail in *The Appropriation of Nature*, 82–91. Fundamentally he argues that the terms "hunting" and "gathering" imply purposive intentionality, whereas "predation" and "foraging" (which is sometimes used as an umbrella term for "hunting and gathering") do not, or at least not necessarily. In this discussion, following his lead, I use the terms "hunting" and "gather-

ing" to refer to human purposive activities of pursuit and collection, and "hunter-gatherer" to refer to human societies that procure their food resources in these ways.

38 Ingold, *The Appropriation of Nature*, 80.

39 Ingold, *The Appropriation of Nature*, 88.

40 Ingold, *The Appropriation of Nature*, 87. By the same token, proponents of the gathering hypothesis, while they acknowledge that gathering involves collecting various animal foods, tend in general to discuss the gathering of plants over against the hunting of meat. See, for example, Ehrenberg, *Women in Prehistory*, 51.

41 Ingold, *The Appropriation of Nature*, 89.

42 See Ehrenberg, *Women in Prehistory*, 46.

43 Ehrenberg, 55. In "Genderlithics: Women's Roles in Stone Tool Production," in Gero and Conkey, *Engendering Archaeology*, 163–93, Joan M. Gero convincingly demonstrates that nothing in the archaeological record argues against women's stone-tool production: "There are no compelling biological, historical, sociological, ethnographic, ethnohistorical, or experimental reasons why women could not have made—and good reason to think they probably *did* make—all kinds of stone tools, in all kinds of lithic materials, for a variety of uses and contexts. On the other hand, direct gender attribution of individual tools remains problematic" (176).
　The question of gender-divided access to tools in general, and to weapons technology in particular, appears, however, to be more complicated in modern hunter-gatherer societies than it may have been in prehistory. In contemporary hunter-gatherer cultures, women generally work with their hands or with rudimentary tools, and are prohibited access to more complex tools, and especially to weapons, which are reserved for male use. (Recall Watanabe's comment above, that women "have no weapons of their own," and therefore are excluded from hunting.) Paola Tabet writes of these cultures: "The forms of hunting practiced by women are in fact probably closer to the schemas of archaic hunting: because of the rudimentary character of the means used, the captured animals are most often sleeping, slow, sick or small. . . . Thus the constraints linked to child care, lesser mobility, or women's physical inferiority don't seem to explain women's place in the sexual division of work. It is not hunting which is prohibited to women, it is weapons; it is access to weapons, or more precisely, to technological development, as represented by weapons of greater complexity than clubs or sticks, that is denied to them." "Hands, Tools, Weapons," *Feminist Issues* (Fall 1982), 3–62. This is a theme to which I return in chapter 2.

44 Glynn Isaac, "The Food-Sharing Behavior of Protohominids," *Scientific American* (April 1976), 90–108. See also Richard E. Leakey and Roger Lewin, *People of the Lake: Mankind and Its Beginnings*, which was heavily influenced by Isaac's thesis of human origins. In *Man the Hunter*, Lee and DeVore had anticipated Isaac in seeing food as predating women as "the original medium of exchange," with a nod to Levi-Strauss, "Problems in the Study," 12.

45 In Lee and DeVore, *Man the Hunter*, Binford had urged caution when making archaeological and ethnographic comparisons, noting that experts from the two specialties can readily draw quite different inferences from the same data. See "Methodological Considerations of the Archeological Use of Ethnographic Data," 268–73.

[46] See Lewis Binford, *Bones: Ancient Men and Modern Myths*. As for the role of hunting in human adaptation, Johanson notes that "in Binford's final analysis, the adaptation to hunting, far from forging humanity for millions of years, did not play a significant part in our evolution until a mere seventy thousand years ago, when fully modern humans began to cope with the harsh conditions of Europe by systematically hunting large game." Johanson and Shreeve, *Lucy's Child*, 240.

[47] Johanson and Shreeve, *Lucy's Child*, 242. Johanson implies that this return to "Brave *Homo*" is in some ways reminiscent of the mighty-hunter model.

[48] See Pat Shipman, "Scavenger Hunt," *Natural History* (April 1984), 20–27, and "The Ancestor That Wasn't," *The Sciences* (March-April 1985), 43–48; Henry T. Bunn and Ellen M. Kroll, "Systematic Butchery by Plio-Pleistocene Hominids at Olduvai Gorge, Tanzania," *Current Anthropology* 27 (December 1986), 431–52.

[49] Rosaldo, "The Use and Abuse of Anthropology," 392. Rosaldo used the phrase with regard to cross-cultural comparisons between "advanced" and "primitive" societies.

[50] Johanson and Shreeve, *Lucy's Child*, 252.

[51] See, for example, Ehrenberg, *Women in Prehistory*, 50.

[52] Margaret Conkey deconstructs one such depiction of early human society, an artist's reconstruction of Cro-Magnon reindeer hunters of the late Ice Age, which accompanied an article published in 1986. These hunters, who that article tellingly claimed "were really us: working out strategies for survival," look remarkably like contemporary Eskimo caribou hunters using Stone Age harpoons. This has the effect, Conkey notes, of "collapsing the distinctions between ethnographically documented hunter-gatherers and 'our' Upper Paleolithic ancestors, and presenting their lifeways as a single homogenized 'bloc'." Margaret W. Conkey, "Contexts of Action, Contexts for Power: Material Culture and Gender in the Magdalenian," in Gero and Conkey, eds., *Engendering Archaeology*, 57–92. See illustration and text, 84.

[53] Johanson and Shreeve, *Lucy's Child*, 243–44.

[54] Donna Haraway, "Modeling the Human Way of Life: Sherwood Washburn and the New Physical Anthropology, 1950–1980," in *Primate Visions: Gender, Race and Nature in the World of Modern Science*, chap. 8. In Haraway's analysis, the hunting hypothesis was politically driven, and developed in large part to support post-war Free World capitalism by positing a fundamental identity between "Early Man in Africa" and "UNESCO Man."

[55] Regarding communism, Haraway speculates that "Man the Hunter was liberal democracy's substitute for socialism's version of natural human cooperation." "Modeling the Human Way of Life," 187.

As to the Judeo-Christian bias undergirding the hunting hypothesis, Ehrenberg points out that the widespread notion of a "Mother Goddess," deduced from the so-called Venus figurines found at numerous Paleolithic sites, is supported neither by the figurines themselves, nor by the fact that in modern hunter-gatherer societies, religion typically centers on spirits and forces, rather than personified powers like gods or goddesses. *Women in Prehistory*, 73–74. (See chapter 5 in this book.)

[56] In "The Evolution of Hunting," Washburn and Lancaster acknowledge that collecting and sharing food obviously required the development of "some sort of receptacles" and this "may have been one of the most fundamental advances in hu-

man evolution." They completely erase the role women may have played in this advance, however, and in the same paragraph reiterate that it was "hunting large animals" that required the complex of behaviors (cooperation and so on) "which separate[s] man so sharply from the other primates." Lee and DeVore, 297.

57 Washburn and Lancaster introduce another important variation on the theme of tool use: Fossil evidence suggests to them that it took large-brained men to produce "beautiful, symmetrical tools"; thus hunting indirectly "created the skills that make art possible." "The Evolution of Hunting," 298.

58 Ehrenberg traces archaeology's fixation on hunting and male dominance to nineteenth-century European anthropologists, among whom male social and economic dominance were givens, and hunting an activity of the upper classes. *Women in Prehistory*, 51.

59 "And so came about this sexual segregation in the daily life; the males to their hunting range, the females and young to their homesite. (We think of it today as the office and the home.) Her collections of food were undoubtedly important in terms of vitamins, but it was low-calorie. The survival of the reproductive group depended on the return of the males with whatever bacon they had managed." Robert Ardrey, *The Hunting Hypothesis*, 91–92.

60 A highly accessible rendering of the early history of paleoanthropology detailing these various fossil discoveries is found in Donald Johanson and Maitland Edey, *Lucy: The Beginnings of Humankind*, 27–70. See also Johanson's more recent *Ancestors: In Search of Human Origins*, coauthored with Lenora Johanson and Blake Edgar.

61 Quoted in Matt Cartmill, *A View to a Death in the Morning: Hunting and Nature Through History*, 10. Dart had deduced his "ape-man's" predatory violence and cannibalism chiefly from a number of fossil skulls, some of baboons and some australopithecines, damaged in such a way as to suggest blows to the head. Some heads even appeared to have been punctured, in order to extract their contents. Subsequent research suggested far more plausibly that the damage was caused by predators. The puncture wounds in some of the skulls turned out to match precisely the gap between a leopard's lower canine teeth. As Johanson puts it, "far from being the chief consumer on the ancient South African savanna, *Australopithecus* appeared to be merely one of the consumed." See his discussion of Dart, *Lucy's Child*, 215–20.

62 Quoted in Cartmill, *A View to a Death*, 11. Dart was reasoning from the assumptions that higher apes neither eat flesh nor hunt, whereas field research has shown that in fact chimpanzees—our closest primate relatives—do both.

63 See Robert Ardrey, "The Basic Drive—for Territory," *Life*, September 1966, and "Man—The Territorial Animal," *Life*, October 1966, 50–59. Among his several books, see especially *African Genesis* and *The Hunting Hypothesis* (The latter volume is dedicated to Raymond Dart.)

64 Ardrey, *The Hunting Hypothesis*, 11. Italics in original.

65 Ardrey, *The Hunting Hypothesis*, 30. Compare this passage to Ardrey's characterization of the "syndrome of qualities" that evolved as human "courage," p. 24 above.

66 Faced with evidence of hunting behavior among chimpanzees, Ardrey somewhat grudgingly acknowledged that male chimpanzees had indeed been observed to hunt, but only "for fun," not for meat. For them, hunting was a mere "souvenir" of

the "time of our common ancestors." *The Hunting Hypothesis*, 32–33. Presumably the poor creatures had not taken hunting seriously enough when it counted, in evolutionary terms.

[67] Rene Dubos, *Man Adapting*, 28.

[68] See Washburn and Lancaster, "The Evolution of Hunting," 299. What they have in mind here is the absence in humans of biologically encoded submission gestures that other animals exhibit when attacked by dominant members of their own species. The conclusion that other carnivores do not engage in intraspecies assault/murder does not necessarily follow, however. Such behavior is widely reported, for example, among lions, as well as among some primates. It is, of course, true that humans engage in intraspecies violence on a scale apparently unequalled in the nonhuman world.

[69] Washburn and Lancaster, "The Evolution of Hunting," 299–300.

[70] See Julian Steward, "Causal Factors and Processes in the Evolution of Pre-farming Societies," *Man the Hunter*, 333–34. One way to link hunting to warfare is the notion of territoriality—a central idea in Ardrey's thinking. Steward refutes that argument in this essay, with particular reference to Ardrey's "sensational articles in *Life*," 330. As we shall see shortly, territoriality is less a feature of the hunting than of the agrarian worldview.

[71] On the social implications of representations of male aggression as normal (and the corresponding abnormalcy of aggression in females), see Anne Campbell, *Men, Women, and Aggression*.

[72] Cartmill develops the theme of the hunter's estrangement from nature at some length in *A View to a Death in the Morning*. Although he rejects the hunting hypothesis, he nevertheless adopts its language of warfare and combat to mount his antihunting argument, characterizing human hunting as "a war waged by humanity against the wilderness" (30). Like Haraway, Cartmill sees the hunting hypothesis of the fifties and sixties as politically driven. However, in his view the politics involved are reactionary, and the rejection of the man-the-hunter model in the seventies came about as a result of the fact that anthropologists "tend to be left-wing, pacifist, and feminist" (18).

[73] Washburn and Lancaster, "The Evolution of Hunting," 299.

[74] Nor is it clear from their account whether it was the Hadza hunter, Woodburn, or themselves who described his reaction to what he saw in terms of his being an "enemy" to the animals. There is every reason to suspect that this was the anthropologists' interpretation of the Hadza's excitement, which might more reasonably be assumed to have been due simply to his having "never seen such a quantity and variety of animals close at hand." He would not have, because they can only congregate in such fashion in the protected enclave of a reserve.

[75] Ingold, *The Appropriation of Nature*, 153, 155. Italics in original. Tabet further points out that in the process of gathering, women accumulate information about the presence and movement of animals that in turn contributes to the eventual success of hunting in the area. "Hands, Tools, Weapons," 11.

[76] See Ingold, *Evolution and Social Life*, 252. Italics in original.

[77] A concomitant view, espoused by adherents of the gathering hypothesis, had to do with women's relative closeness to nature, a theme to which I return in chapter 2.

78 Rosaldo notes that something the gathering hypothesis fails to take into account is the fact that "in no report are we informed of women celebrated for their gathering skill or granted special recognition because of their success as mothers." "The Use and Abuse of Anthropology," 411.

79 See, for example, Richard Lee's discussion in "What Hunters Do for a Living, or, How to Make Out on Scarce Resources," *Man the Hunter*, 30–48.

80 Susan Kent, "New Directions for Old Studies," in Susan Kent, ed., *Farmers as Hunters: The Implications of Sedentism*, 131–32.

81 Susan Kent, "Cross-Cultural Perceptions of Farmers as Hunters," in *Farmers as Hunters*, 13.

82 *Genesis* 3, grounded in a very ancient oral tradition that has many features in common with tribal mythologies, recounts the story of an obviously intelligent serpent matching wits with an equally savvy woman. It was only with the development of Christian theology, from about the second century of the common era forward, that the serpent was identified with Satan, and the woman Eve blamed for the fall of humanity into sickness, pain, and death.

83 Kent, "Cross-Cultural Perceptions," 13–15.

84 Washburn and Lancaster, "The Evolution of Hunting," 295. This period of "final adaptation" occurred between roughly thirty thousand and ten thousand years ago.

85 Shepard, *The Tender Carnivore and the Sacred Game*, 9. The description here was echoed in a 1986 "Far Side" cartoon by Gary Larson, in which three Upper Paleolithic wolves are spying on a human encampment outside a cave entrance. There, by the fire, sits another wolf, along with three skin-clad cave men. In the caption, one wolf is saying to the other two: "It's Bob, all right . . . but look at those vacuous eyes, that stupid grin on his face—he's been domesticated, I tell you."

86 Shepard, *Nature and Madness*, 35.

87 Boyce Rensberger, *The Cult of the Wild*, 17–18. On farming as a war against nature, see also Shepard's *Nature and Madness*, chap. 2, "The Domesticators."

88 The themes of the "happy hunter" and "the original affluent society" pervade discussions of prehistoric and modern hunter-gatherer cultures, lending a certain weight to Shepard's intimation that the lost paradise reflected in the *Genesis* myth of Eden was in fact a "gathering paradise" (*Nature and Madness*, 27). While it is obviously easy to romanticize the hunter-gatherer lifestyle, there is sound evidence that in fact it is less stressful than agrarianism. Too much rain, too little, or even rain at the wrong time can wipe out a year's crops, as can an insect invasion; disease, parasites, or drought can decimate a herd. The food resources available to the hunter-gatherer are, by contrast, more reliable even in lean years.

89 Ehrenberg, for example, traces the origins of warfare to the advent of large-scale herding: "For the first time people owned a resource which it was both worthwhile and fairly easy to steal." *Women in Prehistory*, 105.

90 There is, of course, a broad spectrum of power and status arrangements among these cultures. For an excellent summary of anthropological findings in this regard, see Ruth Bleier, *Science and Gender*, chap. 6, "The Subordinance of Women: A Problematic Universal," 138–61. See also Karen Sacks, *Sisters and Wives: The Past and Future of Sexual Equality*; and Peggy Reeves Sanday, *Female Power and Male Dominance*.

[91] In this connection, Elizabeth Wayland Barber has recently proposed women's discovery of spinning as the key innovation that propelled humanity forward. Regarding the impact of the multiple uses of string to catch, hold, and carry, to tie and tether, and to create more complex tools such as nets, she writes: "So powerful, in fact, is simple string in taming the world to human will and ingenuity that I suspect it to be the unseen weapon that allowed the human race to conquer the earth, that enabled us to move out into every econiche during the Upper Paleolithic. We could call it the String Revolution." *Women's Work: The First Twenty Thousand Years*, 45.

[92] Ehrenberg, *Women in Prehistory*, 119. Ehrenberg argues that these sites provide the first certain evidence that sex was "a primary factor of social differentiation."

[93] On this theme, see especially Gerda Lerner's summary discussion in *The Creation of Patriarchy*, chaps. 2–5.

[94] Ingold, *The Appropriation of Nature*, 254: "Though I cannot prove it, I would speculate that hunting societies in which the sexual division of labour contains a strong element of subordination of women to male heads of households will also entertain ideas about (masculine) spirit masters who are supposed to guard and control their (feminine) wild animal charges. . . . Combining the analogy, between human and spirit guardians as masters in their respective households, with the substitution, of animal for female wards in the human household, we obtain the parallel between spirit and human mastery—of wild and domestic animals— by virtue of which each may stand as a model for the other. Rather than the former being derived from the latter, or *vice versa*, both are derived from a common source, having their roots in the internal relations of the human family."

[95] Conkey presents a powerful argument against the "aesthetic colonization" of the hunting cultures of the Ice Age, and imagines a number of ways in which hunting parties and foraging groups, each comprised of both women and men, would have been far from edenic in *their* atmosphere. See "Contexts of Action, Contexts for Power," in Gero and Conkey, *Engendering Archaeology*, 78–86.

[96] In this regard Lerner asserts that women are just now emerging from their own "prehistory." See *The Creation of Patriarchy* and its sequel, *The Creation of Feminist Consciousness*; her remark about women's prehistory being at an end is on p. 283 of the latter volume.

CHAPTER 2

[1] Ernest Hemingway, *Green Hills of Africa*, 72–73.

[2] Annette Kolodny, *The Lay of the Land: Metaphor as Experience and History in American Life and Letters*, 8.

[3] The literature on this subject is extensive, and much of it will be cited in the notes that accompany this and the next chapter. An excellent summary statement of the woman/nature identification is to be found in Sherry Ortner's influential essay, "Is Female to Male as Nature is to Culture?" in Michelle Zimbalist Rosaldo and Louise Lamphere, eds., *Woman, Culture, and Society*, 67–87. In Ortner's view, the woman/nature vs. man/culture dichotomy results in women being considered of "a lower order of being" than men: "[W]omen are seen 'merely' as being *closer* to nature than men. That is, culture (still equated relatively unambiguously with men) recognizes that women are active participants in its special processes, but at the same time sees them as being more rooted in, or having more direct affinity

with, nature" (73). Italics in original. Ortner assumed this to be a universal phenomenon. Other researchers have pointed out that it is more accurate to say that it is a characteristic of *Western* cultures.

4 On the history of the development of this idea in the West, see especially Carolyn Merchant, *The Death of Nature: Women, Ecology and the Scientific Revolution.*

5 Kolodny, *Lay of the Land*, 9. Kolodny confines her discussion to the European conquest of North America, however the "pastoral impulse" spawned on this continent readily translates, as in the Hemingway passage cited above, to the "dark continent" of colonial Africa about which he was writing.

6 Hemingway, *Green Hills of Africa*, 64, 73.

7 Hemingway, *African Journals*, in Charles Scribner, Jr., ed., *The Enduring Hemingway*, 580.

8 The phrase in quotes is Kolodny's; see especially her discussion of John James Audubon's "The Lost One," *Lay of the Land*, 80–87.

9 Hemingway, "The Short Happy Life of Francis Macomber," in *The Enduring Hemingway*, 545–46, 567.

10 See Kenneth M. Cameron, "Rogue Male," *Sporting Classics* 12:1 (January/February 1993), 30–38.

11 *The Macomber Affair* (1947), directed by Zoltan Korda, and starring Gregory Peck as Wilson, Robert Preston as Macomber, and Joan Bennett as Mrs. Macomber. In a sense, Hollywood gave Mrs. Macomber a chance to redeem herself in *The Snows of Kilimanjaro* (1952, directed by Henry King), in which Peck plays a Hemingwayesque writer in search of his lost soul. In a plot devised from a pastiche of Hemingway narratives, Ava Gardner plays the writer's first wife who, like "Miss Mary," harbored an inborn inability to shoot straight; it is she who, having died as a nurse in the Spanish Civil War, haunts the writer's memory. His second wife, played by Susan Hayward, is a tougher character and an expert hunter; in one early scene she feigns missing a shot, just as Pauline had been prone to do. The film ends happily, in a reconciliation in which she saves her husband's life. (It is quite otherwise in the title story, in which the writer dies alone.) Hemingway reportedly referred to the film as "The Snows of Zanuck."

12 Donna Haraway, *Primate Visions: Gender, Race and Nature in the World of Modern Science*, 387 n. 32, and 209.

13 Recall Watanabe's suggestion that prehistoric women would not have hunted because they have no weapons of their own. See Paola Tabet's important article, "Hands, Tools, Weapons," *Feminist Issues* (Fall 1982), 3–62. Tabet sees in the proscription of women's use, either of weapons themselves or even of tools which might double as weapons, the foundation of women's dependence upon men and men's domination of women: "[T]he hypothesis of an *underequipment* of women and of a technological *gap* between men and women, which appears in hunting and gathering societies, has become progressively deeper with technological evolution, and still exists in industrialized societies" (8). Viewed in this light, Audre Lorde's oft-quoted statement that "The Master's house cannot be dismantled using the Master's tools" takes on an entirely different connotation.

14 See David D. Gilmore, "The Manhood Puzzle," in Caroline B. Brettell and Carolyn F. Sargent, eds., *Gender in Cross-Cultural Perspective*, 164, 170.

15 Paul Shepard, *The Tender Carnivore and the Sacred Game*, 122–23.

16 Gilmore, "The Manhood Puzzle," 170–71. See Lionel Tiger, *Men in Groups*.

17 Gilmore, "The Manhood Puzzle," 172.

18 The popularity of *Thelma and Louise* notwithstanding, the conventional view promoted by the mainstream media—and echoed in much feminist literature— is that women and firearms are inevitably a bad combination. A number of studies are typically invoked to support the argument that women should, for their own good, eschew the use of weapons of any sort, but especially guns: chief among them A. Kellermann, et al., "Gun Ownership as a Risk Factor for Homicide in the Home"; A. Kellermann and D. Reay, "Protection or Peril? An Analysis of Firearms-Related Deaths in the Home"; A. Kellermann et al., "Suicide in the Home in Relationship to Gun Ownership"; and A. Kellermann and J. Mercy, "Men, Women and Murder: Gender-specific Differences in Rates of Fatal Violence and Victimization." For critiques by medical and legal professionals of the methodological problems raised by these articles in the medical literature, see Edgar A. Suter, MD, "Guns in the Medical Literature—A Failure of Peer Review"; Miguel A. Faria, MD, "Second Opinion: Women, Guns and the Medical Literature—A Raging Debate"; and Don B. Kates, Jr., et al., "Bad Medicine: Doctors and Guns," in David Kopel, ed., *Guns: Who Should Have Them?*

The debate about women and firearms, while complex, generally centers around the issue of women's self-defense. On this subject, see especially Kates, "The Value of Civilian Handgun Possession as a Deterrent to Crime or a Defense Against Crime," and *Guns, Murders and the Constitution: A Realistic Assessment of Gun Control*; Carol Ruth Silver and Don B. Kates, Jr., "Self-Defense, Handgun Ownership, and the Independence of Women in a Violent, Sexist Society," in Kates, *Restricting Handguns: The Liberal Skeptics Speak Out*; Ann Japenga, "Would I Be Safer with a Gun?"; and Sayoko Blodgett-Ford, "Do Battered Women Have a Right to Bear Arms?" See also Mary Zeiss Stange, "Arms and the Woman: A Feminist Reappraisal," in Kopel, *Guns: Who Should Have Them?*

19 This instrumental view of aggression, and its social consequences regarding "acceptable" norms of male and female social behavior, is developed at length by Anne Campbell in *Men, Women, and Aggression*.

20 See *Newsweek* (June 24, 1991), the cover of which depicts a shirtless man in jeans and necktie, holding a baby in one hand and a bongo drum in the other, with the caption, "What Do Men Really Want? Now They Have a Movement of Their Own." The accompanying story, "Drums, Sweat and Tears" (46–53) tells of how men "fed up with leading lives of quiet desperation" feel they have been "duped by feminism into surrendering their natural birthrights of righteous anger and self-assertion."

21 Indeed, Robert Bly, the guru of the men's movement, implies in *Iron John: A Book About Men* that for modern men to engage in actual hunting would be to regress to an infantile form of acting-out behavior.

22 George Reiger, "Instinct and Reality," 12, 14. The *Newsweek* piece in question is the one cited in item 20.

23 Reiger, "Instinct and Reality," 16. In their highly influential article on "Hunting and Human Evolution," Sherwood Washburn and C. S. Lancaster related a questing urge among male hunters to the fact that "[i]nterest in a large area is human." While theoretically women might also range widely to exploit plant resources and fetch water, in practice it made more evolutionary sense for them to

settle down and let the men cover greater distances. See Lee and DeVore, *Man the Hunter*, 297. Robert Ardery had struck a kindred note when he observed that "[t]here had to be ancient winds within us, old primate curiosities, newer predator demands for exploration. These were not so much the biological consequences of cultural advance, but very old biological demands—that inhabit us still, to become a dominant quality in the life of our species. Adventure." *The Hunting Hypothesis*, 154.

24 Reiger, "Instinct and Reality," 16.

25 *Cynegetes* is the Greek word for "hunter." For a detailed description of Shepard's ideal society of the future, see *The Tender Carnivore and the Sacred Game*, 235–78.

26 Shepard, *The Tender Carnivore and the Sacred Game*, 278.

27 Shepard, *The Tender Carnivore and the Sacred Game*, 277.

28 Shepard, *The Tender Carnivore and the Sacred Game*, 120. "Frugivorous" means "fruit eating." Significantly, Shepard is writing here about the preponderance of women in primate studies. He mentions Jane Goodall and Dian Fossey, as well as "the women whose part in husband/wife teams has been significant." He goes on to remark that perhaps women's similarities to apes "evoke an empathy which gives women an insight into and an advantage in studying, even joining, ape groups."

29 *The Tender Carnivore and the Sacred Game*, 120. It must be emphasized that in many respects Shepard concurred with the emergent feminist critique of contemporary Western culture, especially with the line of thinking that would develop into ecofeminism.

30 Adrienne Rich, *Of Woman Born: Motherhood as Experience and Institution*, 19.

31 Indeed, Lerner's analysis of the development of slavery and private property in the rise of patriarchal society, in *The Creation of Patriarchy*, is quite similar to Shepard's, although she does not cite any of his works. Kolodny does, however: she relies upon his analysis of "man in the landscape" to develop her critique of the pastoral impulse in *The Lay of the Land*.

32 Kolodny, *The Lay of the Land*, 137. Her explication here is in fact quite similar to Shepard's in *Nature and Madness*. On the theme of male violence in response to the closing of the frontier, and with explicit reference to the symbolic role played by firearms as expressions of male power, see also Richard Slotkin, *Gunfighter Nation: The Myth of the Frontier in Twentieth-Century America*.

33 Susan Griffin, *Woman and Nature: The Roaring Inside Her*, 103.

34 The term *ecofeminisme* was originated by French feminist Françoise d'Eaubonne in the mid-1970s, and gained currency in America during the 1980s, owing largely to the work of activist Ynestra King, and following the publication of Carolyn Merchant's *The Death of Nature* (1980). Ecofeminism is in many ways a logical amalgamation of the women's and environmental movements of the 1970s. However, at least one commentator—Anne Cameron, author of *Daughters of Copper Woman*—has objected to the term, on the grounds that the women's movement has, from its inception, been deeply involved in environmental and ecological issues: "To separate ecology from feminism is to try to separate the heart from the head." See "First Mother and the Rainbow Children," in Judith Plant, ed., *Healing the Wounds: The Promise of Ecofeminism*, 54–66.

35 An excellent introductory discussion is to be found in Carolyn Merchant, "Eco-feminism and Feminist Theory," in Irene Diamond and Gloria Feman Orenstein, eds., *Reweaving the World: The Emergence of Ecofeminism*, 100–5. There and elsewhere in her writings Merchant develops a fourfold typology of liberal, Marxist, radical, and socialist ecofeminism. See also Vera Norwood, *Made from This Earth: American Women and Nature*, chap. 8, " 'She Unnames Them:' The Utopian Vision of Ecological Feminism," for a summary discussion of contemporary ecofeminism in its various American manifestations.

36 Along with Griffin's *Woman and Nature*, Mary Daly's *Gyn/Ecology: The Metaethics of Radical Feminism* is generally cited as a foundational text for radical ecofeminism. Other key resources include Elizabeth Dodson Gray, *Green Paradise Lost*; Andrée Collard with Joyce Contrucci, *Rape of the Wild: Man's Violence Against Animals and the Earth*; Carol Adams, *The Sexual Politics of Meat: A Feminist-Vegetarian Critical Theory*, and *Neither Man Nor Beast: Feminism and the Defense of Animals*; Greta Gaard, ed., *Ecofeminism: Women, Animals, Nature*; Carol Adams and Josephine Donovan, eds., *Animals and Women*; also see literature produced by Feminists for Animal Rights in New York, founded by Marti Kheel and Batya Bauman. See also in Plant, ed., *Healing the Wounds*, the essays by Kheel, Deena Metzger, and Joanna Macy; and in Diamond and Orenstein, *Reweaving the World*, the essays by Sally Abbot and Kheel.

37 Owing perhaps in part to the relative poverty of liberal/progressive thought in the late twentieth century, animal activism has become something of a cause celebre among left-leaning intellectuals. That radical feminists feel drawn to animal advocacy may further be symptomatic of their sense of marginalization and alienation, in an age too readily regarded by some to be "post-feminist." Whatever the reason, radical ecofeminism has gained fairly broad—if mostly uncritical—acceptance in the feminist press. Articles advancing its perspective regularly appear in *Ms.* and *On the Issues* magazines. Adams's *The Sexual Politics of Meat*, which despite its inventive theme is based on questionable evidentiary sources and is jargon-heavy and sloppily argued, was awarded the 1989 Continuum Women's Studies Award by its publisher. A number of prominent feminist theorists—among them Mary Daly, Rosemary Ruether, Judy Chicago, Gena Corea, Merlin Stone, and Robin Morgan—are listed as members of the advisory board of Feminists for Animal Rights, although none of them write for or appear to be especially active in the organization.

38 Andrée Collard with Joyce Contrucci, *Rape of the Wild*, 1. The term "biophilic," or "life-loving," derives from the work of Mary Daly, a close associate of Collard's; by contrast, in Daly's lexicon men are "necrophiliac," or death-loving.

39 Ingrid Newkirk, *Save the Animals! 101 Easy Things You Can Do*, 14.

40 Marjorie Spiegel writes in *The Dreaded Comparison*, "[A]ny oppression helps to prop up other forms of oppression. That is why it is vital to link oppressions in our minds, to look for the common, shared aspects, and fight against them as one, rather than prioritizing victims' suffering. For when we prioritize, we are in effect becoming one with the oppressor. We are deciding that one individual or group is more important than another, deciding one individual's pain less important than that of the next." Achieving such impartiality of perspective is, of course, easier in the abstract than in concrete personal or political action. Carol Adams, the leading theorist of radical ecofeminism, has acknowledged that in fact activism on behalf of animals does tend to distract women in the animal rights movement from working for women's causes. See her dialogue with Merle Hoffman, "Do Feminists Need to Liberate Animals, Too?" in *On the Issues* (Spring 1995), 21.

[41] Adams, *The Sexual Politics of Meat*, 70. In Adams's analysis, one of the key indicators of the "fusion" of the oppression of women and animals is the use of animal terms to refer to women as sex objects or in some demeaning way, e.g., chick, kitten, bunny, cow, fox, vixen, bird, and so on. She does not deal with such parallel terms, commonly used to refer to men as weasel, rat, skunk, snake, louse, leech, ass, pig, turkey, polecat, wolf, buck, stallion, stud, beefcake or egghead.

[42] Batya Bauman has, for example, argued in the *Feminists for Animal Rights (FAR) Newsletter* (Winter-Spring 1990) that feminist consciousness needs to be "stretched" to include animals, along with proclaiming that the " 'leather culture' to which some feminists and lesbians adhere, is counter to feminist ideology and principles" (7). In another issue of the *FAR Newsletter* (Fall-Winter 1991–1992), Rebecca Taksel asserts that "animal rights is not only a woman's movement, but *the* women's movement, or certainly the most interesting and vital sector of it" (5). Italics in original.

Regarding feminist vegetarianism, Bauman wrote in the tenth anniversary issue of the *FAR Newsletter* (Fall-Winter 1993), "Our vision of the future must focus on feminism and feminists of all persuasions. Ten years from now it should be unthinkable that an evolved feminist theory would exclude consideration of non-human animals. Ten years from now it should be unthinkable that scientists who call themselves feminists still experiment on animals. Ten years from now it should be unthinkable to consider it a feminist achievement for a woman to win a dogsled race. And ten years from now the feminist movement should have adopted vegetarianism as a prerequisite to its most basic precept that the personal is political" (2).

[43] Ingrid Newkirk and with C. Burnett, "Animal Rights and the Feminist Connection," *Woman of Power* 9 (Spring 1988), exploits this idea at some length. In the same article she remarks, "The time has come to reject cavewoman fashion [fur and leather] and barbarian dining habits for 'ethical chic' " (67).

In *A View to a Death in the Morning*, Cartmill, explicitly taking his inspiration from Adams and Griffin, suggests that "perhaps the real social pathology linked to hunting is not war, as the hunting hypothesis would have it, but rape" (240). In an implicitly racist analogy, he calls hunting "the rural equivalent of running through Central Park at night, raping and murdering random New Yorkers" (239).

[44] Collard and Contrucci, *Rape of the Wild*, 33–40.

[45] Collard, *Rape of the Wild*, 34. Italics in original.

[46] Collard, *Rape of the Wild*, 40. Tellingly enough, she also remarks that her "purpose is "not to understand hunters but to situate hunting in the culture that spawned it" (46). It is, therefore, perhaps not overly surprising that her descriptions of hunters and hunting ring more of sensationalism than of reasoned inquiry.

[47] Collard, *Rape of the Wild*, 15.

[48] Similarly, there is nothing in the substance of Reiger's remarks about active, exploration-oriented men and passive, home-loving women that a radical ecofeminist like Collard or Adams would find serious disagreement with.

[49] Adams, *The Sexual Politics of Meat*, 35. She is basing her discussion on anthropologist Peggy Sanday's work on pretechnological cultures, *Female Power and Male Dominance: On the Origins of Sexual Inequality*, a work deeply influenced by the gathering hypothesis. In her broad generalizations about "meat-based" and "plant-based" societies, Adams does not convey any sense of the numerous distinctions between different kinds of hunter-gatherer and hunter-horticultural so-

cieties that figure in Sanday's discussion, nor does she seem to grasp that, as we have seen, meat is symbolically important in hunter-gatherer cultures not because of the protein it provides, but because of the hunting activity that produces it.

50 Tabet, "Hands, Tools, Weapons." The quotations appear on pages 15, and 45–46 n. 14, respectively.

51 "Any act of self-actualization can be very threatening to others in her life. Vegetarianism is not a simple decision. I have had many women over the past twenty years tell me, 'I would be a vegetarian if it wasn't for my husband.' By believing they must feed their husbands meat, they perpetuate the whole sexual politics of meat that says men need meat to be strong. They also fear that men's reaction to the absence of meat is greater than their ability to actualize their desire to be vegetarians." Adams, quoted in "Do Feminists Need to Liberate Animals, Too?" 21. In this statement, characteristic of the logic of her argument, Adams manages not only to establish meat-eating males as ipso facto dominators, but also to blame women for their own oppression.

52 For framers of the hunting hypothesis, the prehistoric sexual division of labor was reflected in the twentieth-century dining room: "Thus to this day in the American family dinner the meat is placed in front of the father to be served and the vegetables in front of the mother. This is a folk memory of the days when the father collected the meat with his spear and the mother the vegetables with her digging stick." Ralph Linton, *The Tree of Culture*, 71.

53 Recall that after his remarks about women's close affinity with apes, Shepard went on to speculate that perhaps women's similarities to apes "evoke an empathy which gives women an insight into and an advantage in studying, even joining, ape groups." *The Tender Carnivore and the Sacred Game*, 120. The close affinity between female and nonhuman animal consciousness is a dominant theme in Griffin's *Woman and Nature*, and an increasingly prominent idea in Daly's writings. See especially Daly's *Outercourse: The Bedazzling Voyage*; see also her citations of "nonverbal conversations with 'dumb' animals" that influenced her theorizing, *Gyn/Ecology*, 466, n. 47.

Science historian Londa Schiebinger points out that the association of women with "lower" animal nature, and men with "higher" rational intellect is a foundation of patriarchal science, and is even reflected in the taxonomical classification of the human species: "a female characteristic (the lactating mamma) ties humans to brutes [i.e., as mammals], while a traditionally male characteristic (reason) marks our separateness [i.e., as *homo sapiens*]." *Nature's Body: Gender in the Making of Modern Science*, 55.

54 The 75 percent figure is Adams's (*FAR Newsletter*, Summer–Fall 1990); in her interview with Merle Hoffman ("Do Feminists Need to Liberate Animals, Too?" 21) she says women comprise "at least 80 percent" of the movement. *The Animals' Agenda* magazine (March 1991), relying on data from a University of Utah doctoral dissertation, places women's participation at 78.3 percent. (The same survey found the movement to be 97 percent Caucasian, urban-based, and affluent.) It is important to note, as Adams herself does, that while the grassroots constituency of the movement is predominantly female, the leadership is predominantly male. This—coupled with the absence of feminist activism, or even consciousness, on the part of many women in the movement—may well suggest that many if not most of them actually buy into masculine definitions of appropriate female concerns and behaviors.

[55] Kheel writes, "For many women, identification with animals entails not an aggressive drive but rather the desire to avoid causing them harm." She goes on to sharply criticize deep ecologists Bill Devall and George Sessions for suggesting that hunting, performed properly, is a psychologically healthy activity. See "Ecofeminism and Deep Ecology: Reflections on Identity and Difference," in Diamond and Orenstein, *Reweaving the World*, 135.

[56] Ynestra King, "Healing the Wounds: Feminism, Ecology and the Nature/Culture Dualism," in Diamond and Orenstein, *Reweaving the World*, 111.

[57] Vera Norwood, *Made from This Earth*, 282.

[58] Merchant, "Ecofeminism and Feminist Theory," 103. See also her remarks about the "inherent contradiction" within radical ecofeminism, in *The Death of Nature*, xvi.

[59] While there are precedents for this in European cultural history, I think Kolodny is accurate in calling it a uniquely American proclivity.

[60] Linda Vance, "Ecofeminism and the Politics of Reality," in Gaard, *Ecofeminism: Women, Animals, Nature*, 136.

[61] For a representative example of this line of reasoning, see Ann Jones, "Living With Guns, Playing With Fire," *Ms.* (May/June 1994), 38–43.

[62] For an especially forceful presentation of this point of view, see D. A. Clarke, "A Woman With a Sword: Some Thoughts on Women, Feminism and Violence," in Emilie Buchwald, Paula R. Fletcher, and Martha Roth, eds., *Transforming a Rape Culture*. Clarke insightfully argues that the feminist ideal of nonviolent resistance is vitiated by the fact that women in American culture are not perceived to be really capable of aggression; i.e., a nonviolent stance is meaningless if the person adopting it is believed to be incapable of violence in the first place. Clarke also suggests, with equal insight, that were more women to shoot abusive husbands and boyfriends, fewer men might become abusers. Naomi Wolf mounts a similar argument in *Fire With Fire*.

For an extended discussion of the question of women and guns, in relation to the issue of women's self-defense, see Stange, "Arms and the Woman: A Feminist Reappraisal," 15–52.

[63] This is why, for example, Reiger is at pains to assert that the only reason a woman might conceivably want to go hunting is to garner male approval or acceptance; any other motivation is obviously too threateningly unfeminine.

[64] An insight not confined to ecofeminist circles, this is also an important theme in Shepard's *Nature and Madness*.

CHAPTER 3

[1] Boyce Rensberger, *The Cult of the Wild*, 247.

[2] John G. Mitchell, *The Hunt*, 47, 67. Mitchell writes as a former hunter, who "might have been more of a hunter" had he not been distracted from the pursuit by, among other influences, "female children who would acquire their mother's loathing of guns and would stare at their father with ill-concealed contempt as he ineptly explained how he had once enjoyed walking in the woods with a rifle in the crook of his arm" (5). On women's fundamental (and apparently inborn) opposition to hunting, see also 15, 19, 80, 135.

3 Stephen R. Kellert and Joyce K. Berry, "Attitudes, Knowledge, and Behaviors Toward Wildlife as Affected by Gender," *Wildlife Society Bulletin* 15:3 (1987), 363–71. Their database came from personal interviews with over three thousand adult Americans, in the forty-eight contiguous states and Alaska, with additional interviews conducted in Alaska and the Rocky Mountain region. The interviews were conducted in 1978. "Animal-related knowledge was assessed with a true-false and multiple choice scale. . . . The knowledge scale included questions based upon personal experience, books, practical encounters with animals, and folk knowledge. Knowledge questions covered a variety of topics including 'taxonomy' (e.g., 'koala bears are not really bears'), 'biological characteristics of animals' (e.g., 'spiders have ten legs'), 'superstition' (e.g., 'when frightened, an ostrich will bury its head in the sand'), 'endangered species' (e.g., 'timber wolves, bald eagles and coyotes are all endangered species of animals'), 'domestic animals' (e.g., 'veal comes from lamb'), and 'injury to humans or their property' (e.g., 'North American tarantulas are extremely poisonous to man')" (364). Kellert and Berry note that the only category in which the difference between male and female knowledge about animals was insignificant was "domestic animals." They conclude that "gender is among the most important demographic factors in determining attitudes about animals in our society" (370).

4 To be fair, it must be pointed out that neither sex did awfully well on the "knowledge of animals" scale, the mean score for males being 55.4 (out of a possible 100), for females 51. But the areas of significant divergence between males and females are what matter here: Differences were greatest (with females consistently considerably less knowledgeable than males) with regard to knowledge about rare and endangered species, and about several "relatively prominent wildlife issues," including the leghold trap issue, the coyote-sheep controversy, and steel-versus-lead-shot for waterfowling. Kellert and Berry note that the only issue on which there was no significant difference was the killing of harp seal pups for fur. This apparently would tie into women's attitude of affection toward "esthetically attractive" animals.

5 Elizabeth Dodson Gray, "Nature as an Act of Imagination," 19. In the second citation, she is quoting her own *Green Paradise Lost*.

6 For especially effective treatments of the well-established theme of the function of the myth of the Garden of Eden in American history, both written from feminist perspectives, see Kolodny, *The Land Before Her*; and Merchant, *Earthcare: Women and the Environment*, chap. 2.

7 Catherine L. Albanese, *Nature Religion in America: From the Algonkian Indians to the New Age*, 177. Albanese treats such New Age phenomena as the self-help movement, green politics, and goddess spirituality as "decidedly new and decidedly twentieth century" instances of American nature religion. Much of her analysis clearly applies to radical ecofeminism as well, especially in its intersection with goddess spirituality, a topic I address in chapter 5.

8 See especially Griffin's *Woman and Nature*, and Daly's *Outercourse*, for radical feminist visions of the peaceable kingdom. In animal rights literature, animal violence is to be understood against the background of (and even, in some cases, directly attributed to) human hunting. Desmond Morris, for example, writes about those who have adopted wild animals such as leopards and trained them as pets: "All too often in the past the savagery of such animals has been caused by the brutal way they have been treated by humans rather than by some inherent viciousness in their characters. The 'savage beast' is largely the invention of the cow-

ardly big-game hunter." (*The Animal Contract*, 65) When Fund for Animals founder Cleveland Amory was asked, in 1992, to describe for *Sierra Magazine* what things would be like if he ruled the world, he projected a future utopia in which "animals . . . will be protected—not only from people but as much as possible from each other. Prey will be separated from predator, and there will be no overpopulation or starvation because all will be controlled by sterilization or implant." If any human shot an animal, "They themselves would be shot." ("Now, If I Ruled the World," *Sierra*, May/June 1992, 136–37.)

9 The etymology of "Paradise" is instructive in this context. The word derives from the Persian for "park" or "enclosure," and was originally used in the *Septuagint* to refer to the Garden of Eden, as "a pristine state of perfection free of suffering." See Bruce Metzger and Michael Coogan, eds., *The Oxford Companion to the Bible*, 570. However, after the more familiar definitions of "paradise" as "the Garden of Eden" and "the Mohammedan heaven or elysium," the *Oxford English Dictionary* records the use of the word to refer to "an Oriental park or pleasureground, *esp.* one enclosing wild beasts for the chase." This manifest echo of the word's original connotation lends weight to Paul Shepard's intimation that the myth of Eden reflected a yearning on the part of "disillusioned tillers" for a lost world of hunting and gathering. See Shepard, *Nature and Madness*, 26–27, 136. See also Nigel Calder, *Eden Was No Garden: An Enquiry into the Environment of Man*, whom Shepard cites in this connection. The obvious inference here is that in its original connotation, "Paradise" referred to *human* freedom from suffering.

10 This information on Salamone's work is from promotional materials provided by World Women for Animal Rights/Empowerment (616 6 Street, Brooklyn, NY 11215), in 1991. Another New York City-based ecofeminist group, Ecofeminist Visions Emerging, plays off the return-to-Eden idea in its acronym, EVE.

11 Deena Metzger, "Invoking the Grove," in Plant, *Healing the Wounds*, 122. On the "ecological self," see John Seed, et. al., *Thinking Like a Mountain: Towards a Council of All Beings*, 21–29; also Joanna Macy, "Awakening to the Ecological Self," in Plant, *Healing the Wounds*, 201–11. Like radical ecofeminists quoted already, Seed and Macy both emphasize that attainment of the "ecological self" forges an identification with nature which is itself liberating. As Seed puts it, suggesting a return to pre-lapsarian harmony: " 'I am protecting the rainforest' develops into 'I am part of the rainforest protecting myself. I am that part of the rainforest recently emerged into thinking.' What a relief then! The thousands of years of imagined separation are over and we begin to recall our true nature." (*Thinking Like a Mountain*, 36) Macy suggests the practical outcome of such self-realization: "There is the experience of being acted 'through' and sustained by something greater than oneself . . . One simply finds oneself empowered to act on behalf of other beings—or on behalf of the larger whole—and the empowerment itself seems to come 'through' that or those for whose sake one acts." ("Awakening to the Ecological Self," 210.)

12 Abbott, "The Origins of God in the Blood of the Lamb," 36.

13 Abbott, "The Origins of God in the Blood of the Lamb," 39, 40. Reality can sometimes collide with vision in instructive ways. In 1991, I read this passage in a paper I delivered at a women's research conference at the University of South Dakota. Afterward, one of the women there remarked that she had been especially struck by it. "I've raised sheep," she said, "and believe me, if one of them kissed you on the lips, you *would* be reeling from that kiss!"

[14] Merchant, *Ecological Revolutions*, 1–2.

[15] Merchant, *Ecological Revolutions*, 50–51. On mapping, and the transformation of human interaction with the landscape from "tenure" to "territory," recall Ingold's discussion of hunter-gatherer appropriation of nature, and Kent's observations about animals as intelligent subjects in hunter-gatherer cultures in chapter 1 of this book.

[16] *Genesis* 1:28. The idea of a divine mandate for human dominion over the earth is a persistent theme in American "nature religion," and seems to occur most frequently in discussions where politics, economics, and religion intersect. In the 1980s, Secretary of the Interior James Watt appealed to this idea to justify aggressive resource development on federal lands and the expansion of private concessions in national parks. More recently, the so-called wise-use movement has picked up on the idea, as (in their view) a self-evident refutation of protectionist animal-rights and nature-rights arguments. See, for example, the literature distributed by Putting People First, a wise-use advocacy group based in Helena, Mont.

[17] Religion scholar David Chidester remarks that for the "European explorers, colonists and administrators in the New World . . . there were basically three categories by which the *other* might be classified: (1) savage, (2) slave, or (3) subhuman." This gave the colonizers intellectual license, under the rubrics of "Christianization" and "civilization," to ride roughshod over the land and its prior inhabitants. See Chidester, *Patterns of Power: Religion and Politics in American Culture*, 110–38. Merchant notes, along the same lines, that an important factor in the breakdown of Abenaki subsistence was "a new symbolic system in which the transcendent God of Christianity replaced Abenaki animism." *Ecological Revolutions*, 52. On the religious roots of colonial development in agrarian hostility to the idea of wilderness, see Roderick Nash's important study, *Wilderness and the American Mind*, chap. 2.

[18] Vera Norwood, *Made from This Earth: American Women and Nature*, 33, 37. The quotation is from Susan Fenimore Cooper's *Rural Hours* (1850).

[19] American ecofeminism continues the theme of nature as "home." For a pointed criticism of the negative implications of this idea, see Janet Biehl, *Rethinking Ecofeminist Politics*, 141–50.

[20] Thomas R. Dunlap, *Saving America's Wildlife*, 24. Seton's *Ten Commandments* was published in 1925.

[21] Dunlap, *Saving America's Wildlife*, 23. Roberts and Seton were to become embroiled in what came to be called the "Nature Faker" controversy, which pitted them against naturalist John Burroughs and President Theodore Roosevelt in a series of public exchanges over what Burroughs called "real" versus "sham" natural history. At stake in this controversy was a question still very much alive in the debate between wildlife protectionists and environmentalists/conservationists: To what extent does anthropomorphism distort our perceptions of nature and non-human animals? (27–33).

[22] Dunlap, *Saving America's Wildlife*, 32. Burgess specialized in writing nature stories for children, and is thus a direct precursor of Disney.

[23] Anne LaBastille, *Women and Wilderness*, 3. See also Nash, *Wilderness and the American Mind*, on the definitional tension between wilderness as a "specific area" and as a "state of mind."

[24] Dunlap notes, for example, that in the early twentieth century the Audubon Society "cheerfully recommended" killing hawks and owls to save songbirds. The extermination and subsequent move to restore wolves in the western U.S. is a major theme in *Saving America's Wildlife*. On this subject, see also Alston Chase, *Playing God in Yellowstone: The Destruction of America's First National Park*. Another important treatment of the effect of eliminating predators from an ecosystem in order to protect other wildlife is Jan E. Dizard's *Going Wild: Hunting, Animal Rights, and the Contested Meaning of Nature*. Chase's study of Yellowstone Park, and Dizard's of the Quabbin Reserve in Massachusetts, are two powerfully presented treatments not only of the complexities of wildlife management, but also—and especially—of the ways economic and political factors intrude upon scientific judgment about what is in nature's "best interests."

[25] Though with often unforeseen consequences: The deer, that "emblem of a highly stylized popular notion of the wild," might indeed be "graceful, pacific, 'charismatic mega-herbivores'." Dizard, *Going Wild*, 85. They also turned out, however, to be the environmental "bad guys" in the story of the Quabbin Reserve, destroying the original eastern old growth forest and endangering the watershed. The problem was severe deer overpopulation, brought on by the fact that predators had been removed from the reserve, and hunting forbidden. Chase recounts a similar story of "good" elk and bison overpopulation and severe overgrazing in the Yellowstone ecosystem, thanks to the eradication of "bad" wolves and mountain lions, in *Playing God in Yellowstone*.

[26] Antipathy toward the wolf is indeed ancient: "This is the animal that has had a price on its head for at least 2,700 years—the earliest recorded bounty having been offered in ancient Greece. For at least 135 generations of man, bounty hunters have been chasing, trapping, poisoning, stoning, shooting, spearing, and clubbing wolves all over Europe, much of Asia, and for the last three centuries, North America." Rensberger, *The Cult of the Wild*, 61.

Interestingly, lycanthropy (wolf-man disease) was, like hysteria, diagnosed in antiquity; in the early twentieth century one of Sigmund Freud's landmark case studies was that of the "Wolf Man." See Roy Porter, *A Social History of Madness*. The popularity of that case among intellectuals, along with a series of "Wolf Man" horror films spanning the forties through the eighties, suggests that the possibility of ready transformation of man into wolf exerts considerable power on the popular imagination. (Note also that "wolf" is a common term for a sexually predacious man.)

[27] From Seton's *Lives of the Hunted*, quoted in Dunlap, *Saving America's Wildlife*, 25.

[28] Joseph Wood Krutch, *The Great Chain of Life*, 147–48. Regarding this passage, Cartmill notes that Krutch "identifies the hunter as a literally satanic figure, by putting into his mouth the words of Goethe's Mephistopheles: 'Ich bin der Geist, der stets verneint'" (*Faust*, 1·1338). *A View To a Death in the Morning*, 284 n.3.

[29] On the effects of increased urbanization on public perceptions and approval of hunting, see Outdoor Recreation Resources Review Commission, *Hunting in the United States: Its Present and Future Role*; A. E. Luloff and R. S. Krannich, "Demographic Correlates of Outdoor Recreation: Trends and Implications," in J. T. O'Leary et al., eds., *Proceedings: Natural Outdoor Recreation Trends Symposium III*; T. A. Heberlein, "Changing Attitudes and Funding for Wildlife: Preserving the Sport Hunter"; and D. J. Decker, J. Enck, and T. L. Brown, "The Future of Hunting—Will We Pass on the Heritage?" in *Proceedings: Second Annual Governor's Symposium on North America's Hunting Heritage*.

30 In the old Great Apes House at the Bronx Zoo, one could observe through bars one's fellow primates, each in their respective enclosures. One exhibit involved a mirror, placed behind the bars, so that when you looked in, you saw yourself. You also saw a legend reading, "You are looking at the most dangerous animal in the world. It alone of all the animals that ever lived can exterminate (and *has*) entire species of animals. Now it has achieved the power to wipe out all life on earth." This exhibit has frequently been cited in animal rights literature; see, for example, Gerald Carson, *Men, Beasts, and Gods*, 203.

31 Dunlap, *Saving America's Wildlife*, 105.

32 See Dunlap's discussion, *Saving America's Wildlife*, 106–08. Caras' *The Custer Wolf* is an "idealized life reconstruction," told from the wolf's point of view, of the life and times of an animal that for ten years preyed upon stock in Custer County, S.Dak., by the time it was trapped and killed in 1920, there was a five-thousand-dollar bounty on its head. Caras describes the Custer Wolf as a "strange, tormented animal," implying that man has made him what he is. (Compare the quotation from Morris in item 8.) Regarding *Never Cry Wolf*, wildlife biologists have vigorously debated whether Mowat's observations are more properly regarded as fiction than science. But as Dunlap observes, "the book's influence [on popular conceptions about wolves and the wild] would not be affected even if they were completely made up" (202 n. 20).

33 For a perceptive discussion, from a deep-ecological perspective, of this tendency within ecofeminism, see Warwick Fox, "The Deep Ecology-Ecofeminism Debate and Its Parallels," in George Sessions, ed., *Deep Ecology for the Twenty-First Century*, 267–89. Fox takes ecofeminism to task for focusing on male dominance of women and nature as not only the root, but at least by implication the sole cause, of environmental despoliation: "Empirically, such thinking is simplistic (and thus descriptively poor) because it fails to give due consideration to the multitude of interacting factors at work in any given situation. (While on a *practical* level it can be perfectly reasonable to devote most of one's energy to one particular cause—if only for straightforward reasons having to do with time and energy—that, of course, is no excuse for simplistic social *theorizing*)" (275). Italics in original. Janet Biehl argues, from the vantage point of social ecology, that owing to its theoretical shortsightedness in this regard, ecofeminism fails even on the pratical level of political organizing and action. *Rethinking Ecofeminist Politics*, 131–57.

34 Vera Norwood, *Made From This Earth: American Women and Nature*, 330 n.45.

35 Barry Commoner, *The Closing Circle*, 37.

36 Chase, *Playing God In Yellowstone*, 45.

37 On the ways in which people have contrived Edenic wildernesses "by keeping the animals in and the humans out" (conceptually, though not literally), see Simon Schama's superb historical study, *Landscape and Memory*. Shama begins with the assertion that "it is difficult to think of a single natural system that has not, for better or worse, been substantially modified by human culture" (7). As a case in point, quite relevant to the present discussion, he invokes the example of Yoscmitc Park: "Even the landscapes that we suppose to be the most free of our culture may turn out, on closer inspection, to be its product. . . . The brilliant meadow-floor which suggested to its first eulogists pristine Eden was in fact the result of regular fire-clearances by its Ahwahhneechee Indian occupants" (9).

[38] Chase, *Playing God in Yellowstone*, 46. Merchant makes much the same point about the European impact on the northeastern United States, with regard to not only exploration and settlement but also the introduction of diseases and non-native flora and fauna, in *Ecological Revolutions*, chaps. 2 and 3.

[39] Chase, *Playing God in Yellowstone*, 107–9. In a case of scholarship replicating popular fantasy, the noted Native American expert Ake Hultkrantz had repeated the century-old "evil spirit in the geysers" idea in a study published in 1952.

[40] See Howard Harrod, "Is There a Native American Environmental Ethic?" *The Spire 14*, 14; see also his *Renewing the World: Plains Indian Religion and Morality*.

[41] Chase, *Playing God in Yellowstone*, 111–13.

[42] J. Plant, "Wings of the Eagle: A Conversation with Marie Wilson," in Plant, *Healing the Wounds*, 216–17.

[43] N. Scott Momaday, "Native American Attitudes to the Environment," in Walter H. Capps, ed., *Seeing With a Native Eye: Essays in Native American Religion*, 80.

[44] On this idea, see Rodney Frey, *The World of the Crow Indians: As Driftwood Lodges*.

[45] Gary Snyder, "The Rediscovery of Turtle Island," in Sessions, ed., *Deep Ecology for the Twenty-First Century*, 460.

[36] Ted Kerasote, *Bloodties: Nature, Culture, and the Hunt*.

CHAPTER 4

[1] From an obituary notice of a suicide, *Earth First! The Radical Environmental Journal* (May 1, 1996), 3.

[2] Mary de La Valette, "Sanctus," reprinted in *Feminists for Animal Rights Newsletter* (Winter-Spring 1990), 12.

[3] Roderick Frazier Nash, *The Rights of Nature: A History of Environmental Ethics*, 153–59. In the first example cited, Nash is characterizing, and quoting, Paul Taylor's views on "biocentric" morality; in the second, the reference is to the British activist group called "Gaia"; the idea of an ecocentric perspective is developed by J. Baird Callicott, with heavy indebtedness to Aldo Leopold's idea of the "land ethic."

[4] Shepard, *Nature and Madness*, 170–71 n.25.

[5] On the major perspectives at work in the debate over "saving" versus "using" natural resources, and the conceptions of nature these perspectives arise from, see John Rodman, "Four Forms of Ecological Consciousness Reconsidered," and Snyder, "The Rediscovery of Turtle Island," in George Sessions, ed., *Deep Ecology for the Twenty-First Century*, 121–30 and 454–62.

[6] The Quabbin is one of the largest areas of undeveloped lands in the Northeast, though the term "undeveloped" is in this case deceptive. In fact, this part of the Swift River Valley was farmed in the nineteenth century, and housed several communities; and of course it had been home, long prior to that time, to Native American inhabitants. Owing to the growing water needs of the metropolitan Boston area by century's end, however, the valley was evacuated, the river was dammed,

and the area around the resulting reservoir was allowed to revert to wildness. Predators were eliminated, and hunting was forbidden. With the pressure of increased human development in the surrounding area, the Quabbin came to be valued not only as the watershed for the reservoir, but as a nature preserve.

[7] Dizard, *Going Wild*, 65. Those supporting the hunt turned out to be more closely in line with contemporary developments in environmental theory. On the problems with the idea of the "balance of nature," and the shift toward chaos theory, see Merchant, *Earthcare*, and Oelschlaeger, *The Idea of Wilderness*.

[8] Kerasote, *Bloodties*, 240.

[9] Dizard states the case with insight: "Those who hold that nature, left to itself, balances out deer, geese, and seals with supplies of fish, trees, water, and bacteria seem to occupy a moral high ground. But it is a high ground of their own creation, fabricated out of a particular set of beliefs about nature and its processes. Theirs is a morally simplified world, like the world of the laissez-faire economist. It is a world freed of the troubling need to take responsibility for outcomes." *Going Wild*, 166.

[10] Kerasote, *Bloodties*, 240. Italics in original.

[11] J. Baird Callicott, *In Defense of the Land Ethic: Essays in Environmental Philosophy*, 189. Several of Callicott's essays in this volume constructively develop the relationship of traditional Native American attitudes toward the environment to contemporary Western environmentalism. See especially Chap. 10, "Traditional American Indian and Western European Attitudes Toward Nature: An Overview," and Chap. 11, "American Indian Land Wisdom? Sorting Out the Issues."

[12] Callicott, *In Defense of the Land Ethic*, 193. Italics in original.

[13] Harrod, "Is There a Native American Environmental Ethic?" 16.

[14] Shortly after I had written the original draft of this paragraph, the *Journal of the American Academy of Religion* published a special issue on "Religion and Food." All of the articles dealt with Western religious perspectives and practices. Only one—"There's Nothing Like Church Food," by Jualynne E. Dodson and Cheryl Townsend Gilkes, about the role of communal eating in Black Christian churches—stressed the positive function of food in the religious context. All the others dealt, in one way or another, with dietary proscriptions and the ways in which people's relationship with food can be perceived as a problem, even as a pathology. See *JAAR* LXIII: 3 (Fall 1995).

[15] Harrod, "Is There a Native American Environmental Ethic?" 16. Italics in original.

[16] The phrase is Callicott's, *In Defense of the Land Ethic*, 189. On the perception of all nature as alive and holy, in hunter-gatherer cultures, see especially Oelschlaeger, *The Idea of Wilderness*.

[17] Terry Tempest Williams, "Deerskin," in Pam Houston, ed., *Women on Hunting*, 82–83.

[18] Kerasote, *Bloodties*, 229.

[19] Margaret Atwood, "Brian the Still-Hunter," in Pam Houston, ed., *Women on Hunting*, 82–83.

20 See, for example, Peter Singer's elaboration of this idea in *Animal Liberation*, which many regard as the book that spawned the animal rights movement in America upon its original publication in 1975; and Adams, *The Sexual Politics of Meat*. One need not be an avowed animal rights activist to espouse the view that hunting equates directly with objectification: Basing his analysis on the "Killer Ape" idea that informed some versions of the hunting hypothesis, Matt Cartmill also develops this theme at length in *A View to a Death in the Morning*.

The opposition between things that are to be "used" and those that are to be "loved," derives from ancient Greek philosophy, and was developed in its definitive theological form by St. Augustine. Underlying this distinction is the assumption that one cannot simultaneously love and use another being. The simultaneous use and love of plants and animals is thus a theme in Native American worldviews that strikes westerners as paradoxical, as indeed it is, from a Judeo-Christian point of view. As Callicott observes, such an apparent self-contradiction, while nettlesome from an orthodox Western philosophical perspective, is not an insurmountable problem from the Native American point of view.

21 It is worth pointing out, with regard to hierarchies of consumption, that the popular fantasy of humans at the "top of the food chain" is mistaken. Predators like wolves and grizzly bears, more truly omnivorous than we are, occupy that position.

22 An excellent example here is Disney's *Pocahantas*, which in 1995 accomplished for Native Americans what *The Lion King* did for wild animals a year earlier.

23 Karen Warren, "The Power and the Promise of Ecological Feminism," *Environmental Ethics* 12:125–46; Gaard, "Ecofeminism and Native American Cultures," 296–99.

24 Kathy E. Ferguson, *The Man Question: Visions of Subjectivity in Feminist Theory*, 116. Ferguson's citation to Christ is from Ellyn Ruthstrom, "Feeling the Power of Nature, an interview with Carol B. Christ," in *Woman of Power* 9 (Spring 1988), 23. Christ, a prominent spokeswoman for goddess spirituality, coined the term "thealogy" (Gr. *thea*=goddess) for her thinking, in order to distinguish it from male-defined "theology" (Gr. *theos*=god).

25 The story of Yup'ik Eskimo Charles Hunt illustrates this point. Hunt is Native liaison for the Yukon Delta National Wildlife Refuge. In the face of severe decreases in certain migratory waterfowl populations, he worked with the United States Fish and Wildlife Service and the Alaska Department of Fish and Game to negotiate some limitations on hitherto unlimited Native spring hunting of these species, and the gathering of their eggs. As a result, some Yup'ik villagers accused him of "becoming a white man," to which he responded, "Yes, I am part of the Western culture. . . . We all are." Citing new technologies and changed living circumstances, he remarked that the relationship of Yup'ik culture to the land and wildlife were in some ways forever changed. See Roger Kaye, "Saving Geese, Saving Himself," *National Wildlife* (June/July 1995), 38–42.

26 Oelschlaeger, *The Idea of Wilderness: From Prehistory to the Age of Ecology*, 7. In this important work, Oelschlaeger lays the theoretical foundation for a "new-old way of being" rooted in a radical revisioning of the relationship of human culture to nature. While his inquiry represents a significant advance beyond the hunting hypothesis, vestiges of Man the Hunter remain, as for example in his references to the "Edenlike condition of hunting and gathering" (24), and in his treatment of ecofeminism. Noting that the debate over the gendered division of labor in the

palaeolithic "lies beyond the scope of our inquiry," Oelschlaeger adds that "though some have argued that environmental crisis is rooted in male characteristics, such a theory must be seen as a useful simplification" (365 n. 73). This is too often true, as we have seen; unfortunately, Oelschlaeger's depiction of ecofeminism (see especially 309–16) is itself an oversimplification, based on the ready identification of women and nature.

[27] And unfortunately, the trend toward increasingly second-hand knowledge about and experience of the natural world appears to be accelerating. In his recent book, *The Value of Life: Biological Diversity and Human Society*, Stephen Kellert notes that teenagers especially are getting their knowledge from books and school; and while adults are more prone to rely on personal experience of the wild, "for the majority of Americans . . . the vicarious experience of animals through zoos, film, television, and other indirect means remains the predominant basis for encountering nature and living diversity" (65). Kellert has been tracking Americans' attitudes toward nature and wildlife for more than a generation.

[28] Snyder, "Cultivating Wildness," *Audubon* (May–June 1995), 71. In this connection, it is illuminating to note that the preponderating majority of animal-rights advocates are urban dwellers; the survey reported by *The Animals' Agenda* (March 1991), based upon a University of Utah doctoral dissertation, profiled the movement as 97 percent Caucasian and 73.4 percent urban residents.

[29] Wolf, *Fire With Fire*, 232.

[30] The feminist literature on the subject is quite extensive. For an evocative discussion that captures the force of the radical feminist analysis yet maintains a steady sense of the hazards of gender-essentialist claims about women's "blood mysteries," see Christine Downing, *Women's Mysteries: Toward a Poetics of Gender*, chap. 4, "Body and Soul."

[31] Carol Frost, from "Red Deer," in Houston, *Women on Hunting*, 245.

CHAPTER 5

[1] "Female Mountain Lion," by Yaqui deer singer Don Jesus Yoilo'i, in Larry Evers and Felipe S. Molina, *Yaqui Deer Songs/Maso Bwikam*, 146.

[2] Barbara Kafka, "Diana, Goddess of the Hunt," in Houston, *Women on Hunting*, 291–93.

[3] Sarah Carner, from her journal for Women's Studies 301, Feminist Theory Seminar, Skidmore College, Spring 1994. Used by permission.

[4] Callimachus, *Hymn to Artemis*, quoted in Robert Graves, *The Greek Myths*, vol. 1, 83.

[5] See Jean Pierre Vernant, *Myth and Thought among the Greeks*, 131–32; and Nicole Loraux, "What Is a Goddess?" in Pauline Schmitt Pantel, ed., *A History of Women in the West: Volume I, From Ancient Goddesses to Christian Saints*, 23–25. Loraux observes that in the Homeric Hymn, Artemis "is the most eroticized of the three."

[6] H. J. Rose, *A Handbook of Greek Mythology*, 114.

[7] Graves, *The Greek Myths*, vol. 1, 85.

[8] Walter Otto, *The Homeric Gods: The Spiritual Significance of Greek Religion*, 85.

[9] See Marija Gimbutas, *The Goddesses and Gods of Old Europe*, 195–200; and Rose, *A Handbook of Greek Mythology*, 113. Christine Downing points out that

the apparent contradiction between "mother" and "virgin" in the figure of Artemis is resolved if one realizes that for the Greeks, "virginity" related less to an intact hymen than to a woman's condition of "in-her-selfness," that is, her physical and psychological integrity. See Downing, *The Goddess: Mythological Images of the Feminine*, 175. It is important to note in this connection that the strict equation of virginity with sexual innocence (and physical "intactness") is a product of Christian theology, from roughly the second century of the common era forward; this concept would have made little sense to the Greeks. On this latter point, see John A. Phillips, *Eve: The History of an Idea*.

10 Rose, *Handbook of Greek Mythology*, 113; Otto, *The Homeric Gods*, 87.

11 Rose, *Handbook of Greek Mythology*, 113; Louise Bruit Zaidman, "Pandora's Daughters and Rituals in Grecian Cities," in Pantel, *A History of Women in the West*; 366.

12 Downing, *The Goddess*, 161.

13 Otto, *The Homeric Gods*, 87. The citation to Homer is from *Iliad* 21.483.

14 A. J. Butler relates *Potnia Theron* (*Iliad* 21.480) to Oppian's reference to Artemis as "Sovran [sic] Queen of the Chase," *Sport in Classic Times*, 21 n. 2. *Agrotera* points more directly to Artemis's association not simply with wild animals, but with the entire realm of living nature outside civilization. Zaidman stresses, along similar lines, that Artemis was a protector of plants as well as animals ("Pandora's Daughters," 366). Transposing the Greek view to modern terms, one might call Artemis the goddess of the ecosystem.

15 Downing, *The Goddess*, 164.

16 Marija Gimbutas, *The Language of the Goddess*, 113.

17 Otto, *The Homeric Gods*, 83; Graves, *The Greek Myths*, vol. 1, 301–2; Rose, *Handbook of Greek Mythology*, 117. This title derives from Artemis's close association with the nymph Britomartis (they share the title Dictynna, from *dictyon*, the sort of net used for hunting or fishing). Britomartis was thought to have invented hunting nets; she was also the keeper of Artemis's hunting hounds.

18 Downing, *Women's Mysteries*, 69.

19 Downing, *The Goddess*, 175.

20 Graves, *The Greek Myths*, vol. 1, 342.

21 A. J. Butler, *Sport in Classic Times*, 19–20.

22 J. K. Anderson, *Hunting in the Ancient World*, 10, 29.

23 Callimachus' *Hymn to Artemis*, cited in Graves, *The Greek Myths*, vol. 2, 203.

24 See, for example, Graves, *The Greek Myths*, vol. 1, 151–54.

25 Meanwhile, by some accounts, his spirit eternally roams the Asphodel Meadows, a sort of hunting paradise to which the spirits of great hunters go after death. (See Butler, *Sport in Classic Times*, 20.) The meaning of "Pleiades" is uncertain. Graves (*The Greek Myths*, vol. 1, 154) suggests "Flock of Doves" or "Sailing Ones" (which might refer to birds in flight), so that the celestial Orion who trains his bow toward the seven sisters is perpetually hunting as well.

26 Among variant renderings of the Callisto story, the bear is rescued from the arrows of Artemis herself, or from her hounds, or from the hunter Arcas, Callisto's

son by Zeus. Arcas subsequently became the ancestor of Artemis's people, the Arcadians. See Rose, *Handbook of Greek Mythology*, 118; Graves, *The Greek Myths*, vol. 1, 84, 86.

[27] Graves, *The Greek Myths*, vol. 2, 26; vol. 1, 266.

[28] This is the most popular outline of the story. In other variants, Actaeon was killed by Artemis because he boasted of being a better hunter than she, or because he sought to marry her. See Rose, *Handbook of Greek Mythology*, 185.

[29] Walter Burkert, *Homo Necans: The Anthropology of Ancient Greek Sacrificial Ritual and Myth*, 65–67. Such sacrifices frequently were preliminaries to hunting or war. Burkert plausibly suggests that in offering blood sacrifices to Agrotera, "the goddess of the outdoor world," the Greeks sought to mediate the tension between the indoor and outdoor worlds (63).

[30] Otto, *The Homeric Gods*, 86.

[31] Xenophon, *Anabasis* 5.3.7–10, quoted by Anderson, *Hunting in the Ancient World*, 31.

[32] There is some scholarly disagreement as to the role, if any, women may have played in ancient Greek hunting. Butler argues that there are indications in classical art and literature that women in the fifth century (Xenophon's period) in fact participated in the chase, and that such participation is also reflected in myths of female hunters. *Sport in Classical Times*, 22–26. Anderson, evaluating the same materials, dismisses the possibility of female hunting; for him, "hunting in archaic and classical Greece was . . . a masculine end and, in the best sense, a manly activity." *Hunting in the Ancient World*, 29–29. In any event, hunting in the classical world was the activity of aristocrats, and any female participation would have to be viewed in that light. Anderson does discern the likelihood that a few aristocratic Roman women took to the field, "but there can only have been a very few of them" (91).

[33] Downing, *The Goddess*, 164.

[34] Abby Wettan Kleinbaum, *The War Against the Amazons*, 27–28. On this same theme, see also Page duBois, *Centaurs and Amazons: Women and the Prehistory of the Great Chain of Being*, 38. My colleague Leslie Mechem has pointed out to me that the Amazons were not entirely manless: They kept male slaves.

[35] See, for example, Burkert's analysis in *Homo Necans*, which is explicitly informed by the hunting hypothesis, and makes the standard assumption that warfare arose out of hunting. However, the fact that the Greeks sacrificed to Artemis Agrotera before setting out to war arguably had more to do with her role as "goddess of the outdoor world" into which warriors ventured forth, than with any parallel between hunting and warfare.

    As to her association with the Amazons, it is readily apparent that only a virgin goddess would do for them, and of the three available, female-identified Artemis was far more appropriate than male-identified Athena, or Hestia, goddess of the hearth and of sacrificial fires.

[36] Downing, *The Goddess*, 165; *Iliad*, 21.479 f.

[37] Downing, *The Goddess*, 165. It is important to note here that for the Greeks, the gods were "powers, not persons." See Loraux, "What Is a Goddess?" 25, quoting Jean Pierre Vernant.

[38] See Snyder, quoted above, chapter 4, note 28.

[39] Downing, *The Goddess*, 166–67. Anderson points out that by the late Bronze Age most of the Greek plains had been turned over to cultivation or pasture. Thus the only really wild country left was in the rugged mountainous regions, where hunters pursued game on foot, as did Artemis and her nymphs. *Hunting in the Ancient World*, 10. "Orion" means "Dweller on the Mountain" (Graves, *The Greek Myths*, vol. 2, 403).

[40] Downing, *The Goddess*, 165.

[41] Matt Cartmill, *A View to a Death in the Morning: Hunting and Nature through History*, 36. In Cartmill's view, this interpretation hinges on the "mirror-image" opposition of Artemis to Dionysus, her "restraint" over against his "excess." This seems to me a misreading of the myths (there is nothing "restrained" about Artemis), though his intimation about the "boundary" situation is sound (and indeed is confirmed from classical sources by Vernant). For an alternative reading of the relation of Artemis to the boundary between nature and culture—one that captures the necessary interrelationship between the death-dealing and life-affirming sides of the goddess—see Hans Peter Duerr, *Dreamtime: Concerning the Boundary between Wilderness and Civilization*.

[42] Cartmill, *A View to a Death in the Morning*, 31. Cartmill extrapolates that the hunter, who "swears no perpetual allegiance to either side" of the nature/culture split, is really at war against nature, or against the animal side of his own personality. In a similar vein, Burkert sees in the hunt human intraspecific aggression turned outwards; this is how he accounts for the attribution of "quasi-human" characteristics to the hunter's quarry (*Homo Necans*, 20). Both of these readings are grounded on the oppositional logic of male-defined experience, and depend upon the concept of the natural world's fundamental "otherness" than the human realm. I aim to suggest that an interpretation grounded in female-identified experience disallows such ready distinctions, replacing every dualistic "or" with an "and."

[43] Paula Perlman, "Acting the She-Bear for Artemis," *Arethusa* 22 (1989), 111. Artemis Kourotrophos is "She of the Child-Bed."

[44] Zaidman, "Pandora's Daughters and Rituals in Grecian Cities," 342–43. See also Lilly Kahil, "Mythological Repertoire of Brauron," in *Ancient Greek Art and Iconography*, ed. Warren G. Moon, 231–44. Duerr disputes the notion that only young girls were among those initiated (*Dreamtime*, 163, n. 12), but the source upon which he bases his objection seems to have been superseded by subsequent scholarship.

[45] See, for example, Lewis Richard Farnell, *The Cults of the Greek States*, vol. 2, 435.

[46] Burkert, *Greek Religion*, quoted by Perlman, "Acting the She-Bear for Artemis," 121 n. 45. See also *Homo Necans*, 63–65.

[47] Perlman, "Acting the She-Bear for Artemis," 120–21. Greek natural science held that bear cubs were born formless and their mother literally "licked them into shape."

[48] Zaidman, "Pandora's Daughters," 344.

[49] In her reminiscence of adopting Artemis as a role model in the fourth grade (just the age of the *arktoi*), Sarah Carner writes: "I remember a picture of her in the woods, with green and brown clothes on (like Robin Hood) and a big bow and arrow." Just so are cultural images collapsed into one another. I remember dress-

ing up in my cowgirl outfit with Dale Evans six-shooters and pretending to be Annie Oakley. One might reasonably imagine that the festival at Brauron, serious as its message may have been from an adult point of view, had a playful "dress-up" dimension to it as well, at least for the young girls involved. A similar sort of initiation ritual in the modern world is the Roman Catholic First Communion ceremony, in which little girls dress up in white party dresses and veils: little "brides" of Christ simultaneously play-acting their future bridal stroll down the aisle, the religious ritual also reflecting assumptions about the girls' prescribed social roles.

[50] Graves, *The Greek Myths*, vol. 2, 383.

[51] Zaidman, "Pandora's Daughters," 343. They were also a way of putting Artemis under patriarchal control, to the extent that her rituals came to symbolize the transition from "wild" girl to married woman.

[52] Lilian Portefaix, "Religio-ecological Aspects of Ancient Greek Religion from the Point of View of Woman: A Tentative Approach," *Temenos* 21 (1985), 146. As both Butler and Anderson make clear, boar-hunting was the most highly esteemed form of hunting in the ancient world. Portefaix comments that the myth of the Calydonian boar "may be the archetypal myth of group hunting in Greek mythology" (146); it continued its fascination for later Roman poets. See, e.g., Anderson, *Hunting in the Ancient World*, 90–91.

[53] Portefaix, "Religio-ecological Aspects of Greek Religion," 147. It is, of course, by no means certain that the forbidden fruit of *Genesis* 3 was an apple. But in light of the present discussion, it is worth recalling that "paradise" may well have represented to the ancients a hunting-ground (see chapter 3, note 9), and when Adam and Eve are banished from Eden, her punishments include pain in childbearing and submission to her husband.

[54] The cult of Dionysus is known chiefly through Euripides' *The Bacchae*. The frenzied maenads were sometimes compared to Artemis' nymphs, especially in their strict exclusion of males from their company. Portefaix (147) sees in Euripides' portrayal of them "a picture of a technically very primitive hunting culture" and "a paradisal life." On Dionysus as a women's god and as the god of living nature, see especially Karl Kerenyi, *Dionysos: The Archetypal Image of Indestructible Life*, and Otto, *Dionysus: Myth and Cult*.

[55] Portefaix, "Religio-ecological Aspects of Ancient Greek Religion," 149. Portefaix relates the demand for ecological balance to the necessity of controlling human, and specifically female, populations. She thus sees female infanticide in the background of Artemis' midwifery: an inference supported by the story of Atalanta's exposure on the mountainside.

[56] Martin Nilsson, *A History of Greek Religion*, 49.

[57] Downing, *The Goddess*, 167.

[58] Gerda Lerner, *The Creation of Feminist Consciousness*, 282.

[59] Elinor Gadon, *The Once and Future Goddess*, ix.

[60] See Riane Eisler, *The Chalice and the Blade: Our History, Our Future* and *The Partnership Way*; Merlin Stone, *When God Was a Woman* and *Ancient Mirrors of Womanhood: Our Goddess and Heroine Heritage*; Gloria Feman Orenstein, *The Reflowering of the Goddess*; Buffie Johnson, *Lady of the Beasts: Ancient Images of the Goddess and Her Sacred Animals*; Monica Sjoo and Barbara Mor, *The Great Cosmic Mother: Rediscovering the Religion of the Earth*; Starhawk, *The Spiral*

Dance: A Rebirth of the Ancient Religion of the Great Goddess and *Dreaming the Dark: Magic, Sex and Politics*; Marija Gimbutas, *Goddesses and Gods of Old Europe*, *The Language of the Goddess*, and *The Civilization of the Goddess*.

61 For an overview of the ways in which these various social and intellectual trends intersect in practice, see Cynthia Eller, *Living in the Lap of the Goddess: The Feminist Spirituality Movement in America*. The Gaia hypothesis—which draws its name from the Greek goddess of primordial earth—is a complex theory of evolution, in which species and their environment evolve as a single life system, with the largest living organism being Gaia, or earth itself. See James Lovelock, *The Ages of Gaia: A Biography of our Living Earth*.

62 See, for example, Janet Biehl's trenchant attack on goddess spirituality in *Rethinking Ecofeminist Politics*, chaps. 3 and 4. See also Kathy Ferguson's discussion of "cosmic feminism" in *The Man Question: Visions of Subjectivity in Feminist Theory*, Chapter 4.

63 Orenstein, *The Reflowering of the Goddess*, xix. Italics in original.

64 Eisler, *The Chalice and the Blade*, 73.

65 Gadon, *The Once and Future Goddess*, xiii.

66 Eisler, "The Gaia Tradition and the Partnership Future. An Ecofeminist Manifesto," in Diamond and Orenstein, *Reweaving the World*, 23.

67 Eisler, "The Gaia Tradition," 27. Eisler's essay in this ecofeminist anthology is immediately followed by Sally Abbott's "The Origins of God in the Blood of the Lamb" (see chapter 3).

68 The quotation, from the *New York Times*, appears on the cover of the paperback edition of *The Language of the Goddess*.

69 Eller, *Living in the Lap of the Goddess*, 161. In her satirical novel *Hunters and Gatherers*, Francine Prose effectively captures not only the naiveté of this matriarchal myth, but more especially the social and psychological consequences of trying to organize one's life in accord with it.

70 Eisler, *The Chalice and the Blade*, 44–45.

71 The term is Eisler's: "*Gy* derives from the Greek root word *gyne*, or 'woman.' *An* derives from *andros*, or 'man.' The letter *l* between the two has a double meaning. In English it stands for the *linking* of both halves of humanity. . . . In Greek, it derives from the verb *lyein* or *lyo*, which in turn has a double meaning: to solve or resolve . . . and to dissolve or set free. . . . In this sense, the letter *l* stands for the resolution of our problems through the freeing of both halves of humanity from the stultifying and distorting rigidity of roles imposed by the domination hierarchies inherent in androcratic systems." *The Chalice and the Blade*, 105. Italics in original.

72 Eller, *Living in the Lap of the Goddess*, 161.

73 Such figures as the "Venuses" of Willendorf (c. 30,000–25,000 B.C.E.) and Lespugne (c. 23,000 B.C.E.) have become standard illustrations in texts about goddess spirituality and cosmic feminism. See Gimbutas' discussion of their significance as representations of the "Great Earth Mother" in *The Language of the Goddess*, 141–45.

74 Sarah M. Nelson, "Diversity of the Upper Paleolithic 'Venus' Figurines and Archeological Mythology," in Caroline B. Brettell and Carolyn F. Sargent, eds., *Gender in Cross-Cultural Perspective*, 51–58. For the phrase "Pleistocene pinup or centerfold girls" she cites Chester H. Chard, *Man in Prehistory*.

[75] Margaret Ehrenberg points out that personified gods and goddesses like those of ancient Greece and Rome arise from socially stratified conditions in which the hierarchical "pecking order" has become important. This would imply that the emergence of personified deities in the Neolithic reflects the process of social and gender stratification that is already under way. *Women in Prehistory*, 74. Note that it is in this period that burial sites first begin to reflect such stratification (see chapter 1, note 94).

[76] Ruth E. Tringham, "Households with Faces: the Challenge of Gender in Prehistoric Architectural Remains," in Joan M. Gero and Margaret W. Conkey, eds., *Engendering Archaeology*, 96, 115–16.

[77] See especially J. J. Bachofen, *Myth, Religion and Mother-Right*; Robert Briffault, *The Mothers*; Erich Neumann, *The Great Mother*; Robert Graves, *The White Goddess*. An excellent overview of the content of these and other theories of ancient matriarchy, and their implications for feminist consciousness, remains Adrienne Rich's discussion in *Of Woman Born: Motherhood as Experience and Institution*, chap. 4, "The Primacy of the Mother."

[78] Stella Georgoudi, "Creating a Myth of Matriarchy," in Pantel, *A History of Women: From Ancient Goddesses to Christian Saints*, 463. Regarding her use of the term "gynecocratic": The Greeks of the classical period attributed gynaecocracy, "the rule of women," to non-Greek ("barbarian") cultures; see, e.g., Herakleides' statement, "The Lycians are all pirates. They have no written laws, only customs, and have long since been under the rule of women." Simon Pembroke notes that "gynaecocracy was more an evaluative than a descriptive term. The word is not attested before the fourth century B.C., but we possess one authoritative definition, which was made by Aristotle. Gynaecocracy is 'women getting out of hand.'" See Simon Pembroke, "Women in Charge: The Function of Alternatives in Early Greek Tradition and the Ancient Idea of Matriarchy," *Journal of the Warburg and Courtauld Institutes* 30 (1967), 1–35. The quotation cited is on page 20.

[79] Kleinbaum, *The War Against the Amazons*, 1. Kleinbaum points out that the Amazons were products of a male imagination ill at ease with the idea of female destructive power. She goes on to remark that a survey of three thousand years of art and literature depicting the conquest of the Amazon as an "act of transcendance," reveals that "in the characteristically human, and even commendable pursuit of excellence, men have often been marvelously silly" (3).

[80] Kathleen M. Sands, *Escape From Paradise: Evil and Tragedy in Feminist Theology*, 41.

[81] Downing, *Women's Mysteries*, 32. In her critique of Eisler, Ferguson remarks an additional problem in this demonization of male violence: the "racial implications of centering 'our globe' in Europe, while designating non-white peoples as those who 'swarm,'" *The Man Question*, 112. Eller similarly discusses the strain of flagrant anti-Semitism implicit in Eisler's and others' tales of "shrewd" and "semicivilized" Hebrew warrior-priests. *Living in the Lap of the Goddess*, 165–66.

One further problem with the "Kurgan invaders" theory is the question of how these patriarchs *themselves* became patriarchal—as feminist theologian Rosemary Ruether put it, in response to cosmic ecofeminist Charlene Spretnak, "How did the bad guys get bad?" See Sands, *Escape From Paradise*, 84 and 190 n. 36. Historian Elizabeth Fox Genovese had raised the same question in her review of

Eisler's *The Chalice and the Blade* for the *New York Times Book Review*. See also Rosemary Radford Ruether, *Gaia and God: An Ecofeminist Theology of Earth Healing*, chaps. 6 and 7.

82 Sands, *Escape From Paradise*, 54.

83 Charlene Spretnak, *Lost Goddesses of Early Greece*, 77–81. Italics in original.

84 In her rather sketchy introductory notes (75–76), Spretnak implies that Artemis, "Goddess of untamed nature," only became the patron of hunters late in the Homeric period—against the evidence in the *Iliad* that her identity as huntress was not only long-established, but her primary quality, from the Homeric point of view. The classicist Portefaix is surely on sounder ground in seeing in Artemis's attributes and mythology traces of an archaic hunting society.

85 *Homeric Hymn* #27, "To Artemis," 1.1.6–9. *The Homeric Hymns*, trans. Apostolos N. Athanassakis, 65. In this hymn, after the day's hunting, Artemis joins the Muses and the Graces to dance at Delphi. Athanassakis assigns this hymn a fairly early date, possibly before the fifth century B.C.E.

86 See, for example, Sjoo and Mor, *The Great Cosmic Mother*, 183–84, 208–9; Spretnak, *Lost Goddesses*, 82–83.

87 As Christine Downing has reminded me, Hecate is in this regard anything but a "minor" goddess; see Downing's *Journey Through Menopause*. However, as Downing makes clear in that book, and Duerr even clearer in *Dreamtime*, Hecate's "witchiness" is nothing like the relatively benign and romanticized image of Hecate as found in cosmic feminism.

88 See Gadon, *The Once and Future Goddess*, 191; Stone, *Ancient Mirrors of Womanhood*, 381–84; also Starhawk, *Dreaming the Dark*, 82–83. Starhawk is unusual among cosmic feminists in that she takes a fairly positive view of hunting. She sees it as a male activity, however, and thereby evades the full implications of Artemis as a hunter. See her comments about the "Dying God" and hunting in *Dreaming the Dark*, 88, and *The Spiral Dance: A Rebirth of the Ancient Religion of the Great Goddess*, 113.

89 Jean Shinoda Bolen, *Goddesses in Everywoman: A New Psychology of Women*, 50, 49.

90 Bolen, *Goddesses in Everywoman*, 51–52.

91 See the discussion in Bolen, *Goddesses in Everywoman*, 46–54. The last quotation is a citation by Bolen to China Galland, *Women in the Wilderness*.

92 Orenstein, *The Reflowering of the Goddess*, 31. ("Nagual" is a shamanic term for the "numinous" or "sacred" or "spiritual" realm. For a discussion of this "dreamtime," which both draws upon the extensive anthropological literature about it and avoids the mature romanticism of goddess spirituality, see Duerr, *Dreamtime*, chaps. 6 and 7.) Orenstein's comment about the consciousness of "primal peoples" reflects a trend in ecofeminist spirituality noted by Eller: "a general romanticism . . . toward 'primal peoples,' or 'Third World peoples,' who are felt, despite all their cultural and religious differences, to share spiritual insights that are undisclosed to First World peoples." *Living in the Lap of the Goddess*, 77.

93 Regarding Artemis as "the Wolfish One": "In the months before Artemis's birth her mother, seeking to hide from Hera, moves through the world as a wolf; Artemis herself, we are told, was born in that hour before dawn when only the wolves

can see." Downing, *The Goddess*, 185 n. 5. Wolfish Artemis demands sacrifice: When Orestes was driven mad by the Furies for killing his mother, the Troezenians attempted to bring him to his senses using water from a sacred spring and blood from victims sacrificed for the purpose at the Temple of Wolfish Artemis in Troezen. Graves, *The Greek Myths*, vol. 2, 66.

94 Orenstein, *Reflowering of the Goddess*, 136–37. The idea of reversal as a fundamental principle of feminist theory and method derives from the theory of Mary Daly; see especially her *Gyn/Ecology*. Daly's critical insight in this regard is sound, and important, when it comes to patriarchally rooted myths about women and nature. However, reversal becomes a highly problematic critical move when it is only employed selectively, as is the case in cosmic feminism, and in such a way as to fly in the face not only of myth, but of empirical reality.

95 Clarissa Pinkola Estes, *Women Who Run with the Wolves: Myths and Stories of the Wild Woman Archetype*, xiii, 461. A similar tendency marks Annis Pratt's discussion of "the Artemis continuum," and her analysis of the bear as Artemisian animal par excellence, in pt. 3 of *Dancing With Goddesses: Archetypes, Poetry, and Empowerment*, "Where the Wild Things Are."

96 Ginette Paris, *Pagan Meditations: The Worlds of Aphrodite, Artemis, and Hestia*, trans. Gwendolyn Moore, 120–21. The question of human sacrifice in Neolithic settlements proves something of an embarrassment to cosmic feminists. In an early report of James Mellaart's work at Çatal Hüyük, Ann Barstow asserts that "neolithic female cults did not depend on sacrifice, either human or animal. . . . Evidence for goddess cults which demanded carnal sacrifice comes, in fact, from later times." "The Uses of Archeology for Women's History: James Mellaart's Work on the Neolithic Goddess at Çatal Hüyük," *Feminist Studies* 4:3 (October 1978), 10. However, Gimbutas herself had discerned evidence of infant sacrifice at some Neolithic sites, and subsequent research at Knossos—second only to Çatal Hüyük, in importance for goddess spirituality—has revealed what looks to be indisputable evidence of infant and child sacrifice there. See Biehl's well-documented discussion, *Rethinking Ecofeminist Politics*, 32–39.

97 Snyder, "The Rediscovery of Turtle Island," 456. Italics in original.

CHAPTER 6

1 See Snyder, "The Rediscovery of Turtle Island," 456.

2 Conkey, "Contexts of Action, Contexts for Power: Material Culture and Gender in the Magdalenian," *Engendering Archaeology*, 85.

3 Four novels in the "Earth's Children" series have appeared to date: *The Clan of the Cave Bear* (1980), *The Valley of Horses* (1982), *The Mammoth Hunters* (1985), and *The Plains of Passage* (1990).

4 Jean M. Auel, *The Clan of the Cave Bear*, 263–64.

5 *The Plains of Passage* was number one on the *New York Times* best-seller list the day it was released.

6 Auel, *Clan of the Cave Bear*, 162.

7 Gimbutas, *Goddesses and Gods of Old Europe*, 138. It is in this context that Gimbutas argues that Artemis—who came to Greece from elsewhere, and is known to have very archaic roots—is a direct descendent of the Paleolithic Earth Mother. One need not buy into the idea that such a universal goddess existed to accept that

as a nature goddess, the Lady of the Beasts is rooted in a hunter-gatherer worldview that preceded the agrarian revolution of the Neolithic, and that in their earliest form, nature goddesses would have been comprised of the light and dark aspects that were later split off into other divinities.

8 Auel, *The Valley of Horses*, 97.

9 Elizabeth Marshall Thomas, *The Animal Wife*, 106.

10 Snyder, "The Etiquette of Freedom," *The Practice of the Wild*, 19.

11 This image is reproduced in Johnson, *Lady of the Beasts*, 19. Johnson suggests that the egg-shaped ostrich "may be an alternate form" of the goddess.

12 Harrison, *Mother Earth Father Sky*, 71. For assistance and information about what the beliefs and practices of Paleolithic Bering Sea peoples might have been like, Harrison consulted anthropologist William S. Laughlin.

13 As ethnographer Richard Nelson, who has devoted the past thirty years to documenting the hunting techniques and rituals of Eskimo cultures, remarks: "Much of human experience over the past several million years lies beyond our grasp. Probably no society has been so deeply alienated as ours from the community of nature, has viewed the natural world from a greater distance of mind, has lapsed into a murkier comprehension of its connections with the sustaining environment. Because of this, we have great difficulty understanding our rootedness to earth, our affinities with nonhuman life." "Understanding Eskimo Science," *Audubon* (September/October 1993), 102. In a related discussion, Snyder writes: "The archaic religion is to kill god and eat him. Or her. The shimmering food-chain, the food-web, is the scary, beautiful condition of the biosphere. Subsistence people live without excuses. The blood is on your own hands as you divide the liver from the gallbladder. You have watched the color fade on the glimmer of the trout. A subsistence economy is a sacramental economy because it has faced up to one of the critical problems of life and death: the taking of life for food. . . . Our distance from the source of our food enables us to be superficially more comfortable, and distinctly more ignorant." "Survival and Sacrament," 184.

14 Working groups at the conference isolated the following as the chief barriers to women's participation in outdoor activities like hunting and fishing: the image of sport as portrayed by the anti-hunting movement, the expense and/or availability of suitable equipment, and social pressure from peers (significant others, friends, family members) who regard hunting as a male activity. Other barriers reported by a majority of working groups included lack of female role models, being raised in a nonhunting family, the fact that the "slob" or "Rambo" image of some hunters is a "turnoff," and lack of information about hunting. Significantly, factors like fear of guns, female vanity, and the isolation of being the only female in a hunting party were not regarded as important barriers. See Christine L. Thomas and Tammy Peterson, eds., conference proceedings, "Breaking Down the Barriers to Participation of Women in Angling and Hunting" (August 12, 1990; University of Wisconsin-Stevens Point), 11.

15 Thomas, "They Became Outdoors Women," *Deer & Deer Hunting* (June 1992), 50–51.

16 Workshops are coordinated through state departments of natural resources. Some states host annual workshops, and several states offer multiple workshops each year.

[17] On the structure and content of "Becoming an Outdoors-Woman" workshops and the philosophy behind them, see Thomas, "They Became Outdoors-Women"; also Thomas and Peterson, "Becoming an Outdoors-Woman," *Women in Natural Resources*, vol. 15, (3); and Lueck, "Women in the Outdoors," *Bowhunter* (June/July 1993). For an insider's view of the participants' experiences, see Suzanne Schlosberg, "A Hunting She Will Go," *Women's Sports and Fitness* (March 1996); and Stange, "Women in the Woods," *Sports Afield* (June 1995). I have attended four workshops as a participant (in Oregon and Texas, in 1993; in South Dakota and New York, in 1994); and in 1995 and 1996 as an instructor (of outdoor ethics, .22 caliber, and large-bore riflery) at the South Dakota workshop.

[18] Nor is "Becoming an Outdoors-Woman" the only such program; following its lead, organizations like Safari Clubs International and the National Wildlife Federation are also staging workshops for women and girls.

[19] Representative groups include Tomboy, Inc. in Oregon; Wilderness Women, Inc. in Colorado; the National Association for Outdoor Women in Georgia; Woodswomen, Women in the Wilderness, and Women for Fishing, Hunting and Wildlife, all in Minnesota; and OutdoorWomen of South Dakota, which is publishing a national newsletter, *OutdoorWomen of America*, and aims to become a national organization. The Women's Shooting Sports Foundation, based in Houston, Tex., is to date the largest of the women's hunting and shooting organizations. Founded in 1993, WSSF recorded nearly 900 members in its first year. By 1996 membership had more than doubled, to nearly 1,900. Of these members, only about 200 were from Texas.

[20] In 1994 the National Wildlife Federation responded to this increased participation by sponsoring two national conferences (one in Nevada, the other in Vermont) on "Taking Leadership Action: Women and the Environment." Since 1990 the National Rifle Association has maintained an office of Women's Issues and Information which, although its primary emphasis has been on self-defense issues, also compiles resource lists for women hunters.

[21] Sharon Begley, "Let's Talk Turkey," *Newsweek* (October 30, 1995), 71–72. Their reasons ranged from nature-appreciation and the desire for outdoor exercise, to demonstration of skill, to wanting to be involved with putting food on the table, to "getting away from it all." These, several studies have suggested, are the same sorts of reasons commonly cited by men, although women are more likely than men to rank nature-appreciation and companionship with friends and family as high priorities, and less likely than men to cite factors like utilizing hunting skills, taking trophies, and escape from routine.

[22] "Many women disparage the stuff-it-and-mount-it school of hunting. They make a point—in fact, almost a religion—of using any animal they kill. 'This is not about trophy hunting,' says [Laurie Lee]Dovey. Suzy Smith gets her kill turned into elk steaks and burgers and sausage; she tans the hide for gloves or chaps. Jennifer Sells, an Iowa game warden, says, 'I feel more of a connection with my dinner if I hunt it rather than buy it at the store.' And virtually all the women ask how critics dare denounce hunters when every nonvegetarian gets meat by having others do the killing." Begley, "Let's Talk Turkey," 72.

[23] See Jackson, "The Characteristics and Formative Experiences of Female Deer Hunters."

[24] Thomas, "They Became Outdoors Women," 51.

[25] The obvious reference here is to Carol Gilligan's theories, in *In a Different Voice* and her subsequent writings.

26 According to figures released by the National Shooting Sports Foundation in February 1995, between 1988 and 1993 the number of women hunting with firearms increased 23 percent, with 2.5 million women hunting in 1993. Determining the precise number of female hunters nationwide is complicated by the fact that fifteen states do not specify gender on hunting licenses. For representative discussions see, in addition to the *Newsweek* article cited above, Craig Holt, "Taking Aim at the Outdoor Life"; Peter Finn, "More Women Feel the Pull of Male Hunting Tradition"; "Women's Participation in the Shooting Sports: Upward Trend Continues," (National Shooting Sports Foundation Information Service, February 1995); and Alan Farnham, "A Bang That's Worth Ten Billion Bucks."

27 Michelle Leigh Smith, "Club of Legal Huntresses Kills to Network," *The National Law Journal* (Monday, April 25, 1994), A10. The club's name derives from the first kill recorded by a member—a particularly effective shot executed by business attorney Vanessa Gilmore, who at the time the article was written had just been nominated for a federal judgeship.

28 DeGuerin first achieved national notoriety as David Koresh's attorney.

29 Obvious analogies come to mind here, of other conventional masculine objections to women's encroaching on their professional turf: the opening of previously all-male clubs, for example, or the admission of women sports writers and reporters into men's locker rooms. But what was evidently particularly irksome to the men in Houston was that—as has happened with some professional women who declined admission to all-male clubs, preferring clubs of their own—these hunting trips were all-female affairs.

30 The article also describes a women's event their male colleagues approved of, "a Wicket & Racquet Garden Classic at Houston Country Club for all of the female clients. . . . Silver trays, white linens, mimosas and fresh flowers on every table. It looks like a scene out of 'The Great Gatsby.'" The men, the article goes on to say, would often schedule their golf rounds to end early enough so that they could watch this "outdoorsy athletic event for all female clients."

31 Jackson, "The Characteristics and Formative Experiences of Female Deer Hunters," 20.

32 Kheel, for example, writes in her recent critique of hunting, "Although there are some women who hunt and some who have glorified it as well, the vast majority of hunters are still men." She then proceeds to discuss hunting as a totally male activity. See her "License to Kill: An Ecofeminist Critique of Hunters' Discourse." In the same volume, Maria Comninou's article, "Speech, Pornography, and Hunting," raises—only to drop—the question of what hunting might mean for women. Adams, as the major proponent of the contemporary "Woman the Gatherer" school, simply ignores the existence of women hunters in her discussion of hunting in *Neither Man Nor Beast*.

33 Letter dated December 22, 1995. The letter goes on to accuse government agencies of playing "social engineer" and to assert that "outdoors persons of the future" will be "non-consumptive enjoyers of nature." Prescott's views in this regard have been widely quoted in the press.

34 Comninou, "Speech, Pornography, and Hunting," 141. This is Comninou's *sole* reference to women's hunting, an astonishing fact given that her subject is the relation of hunting to rape and pornography.

35 Some classics of this literature—to suggest only a few examples—are Beryl Markham, *West With the Night*; Isak Dinesen, *Out of Africa*; Grace Seton Thompson, *A*

Woman Tenderfoot; Eleanor Pruitt Stewart, *Letters on an Elk Hunt by a Woman Homesteader*; Osa Johnson, *I Married Adventure* and *Four Years in Paradise*; Mary Jobe Akeley, *Carl Akeley's Africa*; and Gretchen Cron, *The Roaring Veldt*. Vera Norwood discusses several women hunters in *Made From This Earth*; her discussion is very valuable, though it is underwritten by an antihunting bias that tends to blind Norwood to what hunting may have meant to many of these women, beyond their having "internalized male values."

Among representative examples of contemporary women's outdoor writing, all of which focus on the themes of why or how women hunt, see: Yvonne M. Rauch, "More Than the Kill," *Sports Afield* (September 1987); Kathleen O'Neal Gear, "Viva La Difference!" *Outdoor Life* (December 1986), and "The Most Dynamic Hunting Duo," *Outdoor Life* (November 1988); Eileen Clarke, "On Your Own," *Field & Stream* (April 1988); Kathy Etling, "Women Afield," *American Hunter* (January 1992); Stange, "Women Afield: The Invisible Hunters," *Sports Afield* (January 1994) and "Women in the Woods," *Sports Afield* (June 1995); Susan Ewing, "To Each Her Own," *Gray's Sporting Journal* (September 1994) and "Chasing Antelope With Annie Oakley," *Sports Afield* (November 1995); Frances Hamerstrom, *Is She Coming Too? Memoirs of a Lady Hunter* and *My Double Life: Memoirs of a Naturalist*; and "WSSF Members: Why We Hunt," *Open Sights: Official Publication of the Women's Shooting Sports Foundation* (Fall 1995). *Bugle!* the bimonthly publication of the Rocky Mountain Elk Foundation, has a "women in the Field" feature, by women hunters, in each issue.

See also the articles by Thomas, Petersen, and Lueck, cited in note 17, for detailed descriptions of the reasons BOW workshop participants typically cite for their interest in hunting, none of which readily conform to gender stereotypes.

[36] Her alliterative typology is actually sixfold, but in this essay she dispenses with discussion of the hired, hungry, and hostile hunters. The idea of typologizing hunters is, of course, not original with Kheel. She herself cites Adams's (rather murky) distinction between "aggressive" and "relational" hunting in *Neither Man nor Beast*. However, neither Kheel nor Adams references Kellert's widely cited typological essay, "Attitudes and Characteristics of Hunters and Anti-Hunters and Related Policy Suggestions." Given her supposed familiarity with literature for which Kellert's study is a standard resource, it is inconceivable that Kheel is unaware of Kellert's work. The only way to account for this omission is that, as we have already seen, Kellert's work supports the contention that hunters are, in fact, not only more knowledgeable about animals and the natural environment, but that they care more about them than nonhunters as well.

[37] "License to Kill," 88.

[38] In which case, of course, it is hard to see why *any* women would hunt in the first place.

[39] "License to Kill," 110. The quotation is from Shepard's essay "A Post-Historic Primitivism."

[40] "License to Kill," 107–8. The passage from Shepard is from his essay "Toward a Post-Historic Primitivism."

[41] See Chapter 4 in this book.

[42] Terry Tempest Williams, "Deerskin," 84. Italics in original.

[43] Albert Yendes, "Contrary to Popular Opinion," *Petersen's Hunting* (March 1993), 34.

[44] I am talking about real aggression here, not mere "assertiveness," the polite term generally invoked for women, as opposed to male "blood and guts" aggression.

[45] The term "earthcare" is Carolyn Merchant's; sensitive to the issue I am raising here, Merchant has recently argued against engendering nature, and by extension against privileging women's role as caretakers of nature. See her *Earthcare: Women and the Environment*. Regarding the idea of an "ethic of care," see (in addition to Merchant) Karen Warren, "The Power and the Promise of Ecological Feminism," and Jim Cheney, "Eco-Feminism and Deep Ecology." Radical eco-feminists like Greta Gaard, Carol Adams, and Marti Kheel also invoke the idea, but—as Cheney points out (142–43)—the animal liberationist variation on the theme tends to be a form of "moral extensionism" that admits certain nonhumans into the "moral club" at the expense of others.

Bibliography

ADAMS, CAROL J. *Neither Man Nor Beast: Feminism & The Defense of Animals.* New York: Continuum, 1994.

——— *The Sexual Politics of Meat: A Feminist-Vegetarian Critical Theory.* New York: Continuum, 1990.

ADAMS, CAROL J., AND JOSEPHINE DONOVAN, eds. *Animals and Women: Feminist Theoretical Explorations.* Durham and London: Duke University Press, 1995.

AKELEY, MARY JOBE. *Carl Akeley's Africa.* New York: Blue Ribbon Books, 1929.

ALBANESE, CATHERINE L. *Nature Religion in America: From the Algonkian Indians to the New Age.* Chicago. University of Chicago Press, 1990.

AMORY, CLEVELAND. "Now if I Ruled the World . . . ," *Sierra* (May/June 1992), 136–37.

ANDERSON, J. K. *Hunting in the Ancient World.* Berkeley: University of California Press, 1985.

The Animals' Agenda (March 1991).

ARDREY, ROBERT. *African Genesis.* London: Atheneum, 1961.

——— "The Basic Drive—for Territory," *Life* (September 1966).

——— *The Hunting Hypothesis: A Personal Conclusion Concerning the Evolutionary Nature of Man.* New York: Atheneum, 1976.

——— "Man—The Territorial Animal," *Life* (October 1966), 50–59.

ATHANASSAKIS, APOSTOLOS N., trans. *The Homeric Hymns.* Baltimore and London: Johns Hopkins University Press, 1976.

ATWOOD, MARGARET. *Surfacing.* New York: Fawcett, 1987.

AUEL, JEAN M. *The Clan of the Cave Bear.* New York: Bantam Books, 1981.

——— *The Plains of Passage.* New York: Crown Publishers, 1990.

——— *The Valley of Horses.* New York: Crown Publishers, 1982.

BACHOFEN, ROBERT. *Myth, Religion and Mother-Right,* trans. Ralph Manheim. Princeton: Princeton University Press, 1967.

BARBER, ELIZABETH WAYLAND. *Women's Work: The First Twenty Thousand Years.* New York: W. W. Norton and Company, 1994.

BARSTOW, ANN. "The Uses of Archeology for Women's History: James Mellaart's Work on the Neolithic Goddess at Çatal Huyuk." *Feminist Studies* 4:3 (October 1978), 7–18.

BAUMAN, BATYA. *Feminists for Animal Rights (FAR) Newsletter* (Winter-Spring 1990), 7.

BEGLEY, SHARON. "Let's Talk Turkey." *Newsweek* (October 30, 1995), 71–72.

BIEHL, JANET. *Rethinking Ecofeminist Politics.* Boston: South End Press, 1991.

BINFORD, LEWIS R. *Bones: Ancient Men and Modern Myths.* New York: Academic Press, 1981.

BLEIER, RUTH. *Science and Gender.* New York: Pergamon Press, 1984.

BLODGETT-FORD, SAYOKO. "Do Battered Women Have a Right to Bear Arms?" *Yale Law and Policy Review* 11 (1993), 509–60.

BLY, ROBERT. *Iron John: A Book About Men.* Reading, Mass.: Addison-Wesley, 1990.

BOLEN, JEAN SHINODA. *Goddesses in Everywoman: A New Psychology of Women.* New York: Harper Colophon, 1984.

BRETTELL, CAROLINE, AND CAROLYN F. SARGENT, eds. *Gender in Cross-Cultural Perspective.* Englewood Cliffs, N.J.: Prentice Hall, 1993.

BRIFFAULT, ROBERT. *The Mothers.* New York: Grosset & Dunlap, 1963.

BUCHWALD, EMILIE, PAULA R. FLETCHER AND MARTHA ROTH, eds. *Transforming a Rape Culture* New York: Milkweed Editions, 1993.

BUNN, HENRY T. AND ELLEN M. KROLL. "Systematic Butchery by Plio-Pleistocene Hominids at Olduvai Gorge, Tanzania," *Current Anthropology* (December 1986), 431–452.

BURKERT, WALTER. *Homo Necans: The Anthropology of Ancient Greek Sacrificial Ritual and Myth.* Trans. Peter Bing. Berkeley: University of California Press, 1983.

BUTLER, A. J. *Sport in Classic Times.* Los Altos, Calif.: William Kaufman, Inc., 1975.

CALDER, NIGEL. *Eden Was No Garden: An Enquiry into the Environment of Man.* New York: Holt, Rinehart and Winston, 1967.

CALLICOTT, J. BAIRD. *In Defense of the Land Ethic: Essays in Environmental Philosophy.* Albany, N.Y.: State University of New York Press, 1989.

CAMERON, KENNETH, M. "Rogue Male," *Sporting Classics* XII:1 (January/February 1993), 30–38.

CAMPBELL, ANNE. *Men, Women and Aggression.* New York: Basic Books, 1993.

CAPPS, WALTER H., ed. *Seeing With A Native Eye: Essays in Native American Religion.* San Francisco: Harper and Row, 1976.

CARAS, ROGER. *The Custer Wolf.* New York: Henry Holt and Company, 1979.

CARSON, GERALD. *Men, Beasts and Gods.* New York: Charles Scribners Sons, 1972.

CARTMILL, MATT. *A View to a Death in the Morning: Hunting and Nature Through History.* Cambridge, Mass.: Harvard University Press, 1993.

CAUSEY, ANN S. "On the Morality of Hunting," *Environmental Ethics* 11 (Winter 1989), 327–43.

CHARD, CHESTER S. *Man in Prehistory.* New York: McGraw-Hill, 1975.

CHASE, ALSTON. *Playing God in Yellowstone: The Destruction of America's First National Park.* New York: Harcourt Brace and Company, 1987.

CHENEY, JIM. "Eco-Feminism and Deep Ecology," *Environmental Ethics* 9 (Summer 1987), 115–46.

CHIDESTER, DAVID. *Patterns of Power: Religion and Politics in American Culture.* Englewood Cliffs, N.J.: Prentice Hall, 1988.

CLARKE, EILEEN. "On Your Own," *Field & Stream* (April 1988), 35–37.

COLLARD, ANDRÉE AND JOYCE CONTRUCCI. *Rape of the Wild: Man's Violence Against Animals and the Earth.* Bloomington and Indianapolis: Indiana University Press, 1989.

COMMONER, BARRY. *The Closing Circle.* New York: Alfred A. Knopf, 1971.

CRON, GRETCHEN. *The Roaring Veldt.* New York: G. P. Putnam's Sons, 1930.

DAHLBERG, FRANCES, ed. *Women The Gatherer.* New Haven: Yale Universtiy Press, 1981.

DALY, MARY. *Gyn/Ecology: The Metaethics of Radical Feminism.* Boston: Beacon Press, 1978, 1990.

———— *Outercourse: The Bedazzling Voyage.* San Francisco: HarperCollins, 1992.

DECKER, D. J., J. ENCK AND T. L. BROWN. "The Future of Hunting—Will We Pass On the Heritage?" A paper presented at the Second Annual Governor's Symposium on North America's Hunting Heritage. Pierre, South Dakota, August 24–26, 1993.

DIAMOND, IRENE AND GLORIA FEMAN ORENSTEIN, eds. *Reweaving the World: The Emergence of Ecofeminism.* San Francisco: Sierra Club Books, 1990.

DINESEN, ISAK. *Out of Africa.* New York: Modern Library, 1952.

DIZARD, JAN E. *Going Wild: Hunting, Animal Rights and the Contested Meaning of Nature.* Amherst: University of Massachusetts Press, 1994.

DOWNING, CHRISTINE. *The Goddess. Mythological Images of the Feminine.* New York. The Crossroad Publishing Company, 1981.

———— *Journey Through Menopause.* New York. The Crossroad Publishing Company, 1987.

———— *Women's Mysteries: Toward a Poetics of Gender.* New York: The Crossroad Publishing Company, 1991.

duBOIS, PAGE. *Centaurs and Amazons: Women and the Prehistory of the Great Chain of Being.* Ann Arbor: University of Michigan Press, 1982.

DUBOS, RENE. *Man Adapting.* New Haven and London: Yale University Press, 1965.

DUERR, HANS PETER. *Dreamtime: Concerning the Boundary between Wilderness and Civilization.* Trans. Felicitas Goodman. Oxford and New York: Basil Blackwell, 1985.

DUNLAP, THOMAS R. *Saving America's Wildlife*. Princeton: Princeton University Press, 1988.

EHRENBERG, MARGARET. *Women in Prehistory*. Norman and London: University of Oklahoma Press, 1989.

EISLER, RIANE. *The Chalice and the Blade: Our History, Our Future*. San Francisco: Harper and Row, 1987.

———— *The Partnership Way: New Tools for Living*. San Francisco: Harper and Row, 1990.

———— *Prehistory and the Beginning of Civilization*. New York: Harper and Row, 1963.

ELLER, CYNTHIA. *Living in the Lap of the Goddess: The Feminist Spirituality Movement in America*. New York: Crossroad, 1993.

ESTES, CLARISSA PINKOLA. *Women Who Run With the Wolves: Myths and Stories of the Wild Woman Archetype*. New York: Ballantine Books, 1992.

ETLING, KATHY. "Women Afield," *American Hunter* (January, 1992), 30–33, 66–67.

EVERS, LARRY AND FELIPE S. MOLINA. *Yaqui Deer Songs/Masi Bwikam*. Tucson: University of Arizona Press, 1987.

EWING, SUSAN. "Chasing Antelope With Annie Oakley," *Sports Afield* (November, 1995), 114, 104–5.

———— "To Each Her Own," *Gray's Sporting Journal* (September, 1994).

FARIA, MIGUEL A., M.D. "Second Opinion: Women, Guns and the Medical Literature—A Raging Debate," *Women & Guns*, (October, 1994)14–17, 52–53.

FARNELL, LEWIS RICHARD. *The Cult of the Greek States*. Vol. 2. Chicago: Aegean Press, 1971.

FARNHAM, ALAN. "A Bang That's Worth Ten Billion Bucks," *Fortune* (March 9, 1992), 80–86.

FERGUSON, KATHY E. *The Man Question: Visions of Subjectivity in Feminist Theory*. Berkeley: University of California Press, 1993.

FINN, PETER. "More Women Feel the Pull of Male Hunting Tradition," *Washington Post* (January 24, 1996), D1-D2.

FLADER, SUSAN L. *Thinking Like a Mountain: Aldo Leopold and the Evolution of an Ecological Attitude toward Deer, Wolves and Forests*. Lincoln and London: University of Nebraska Press, 1978.

FREY, RODNEY. *The World of the Crow Indians: As Driftwood Lodges*. Norman and London: University of Oklahoma Press, 1987.

GAARD, GRETA, ed. *Ecofeminism: Women, Animals, Nature*. Philadelphia: Temple University Press, 1993.

GADON, ELINOR. *The Once and Future Goddess*. San Francisco: Harper and Row, 1989.

GALLAND, CHINA. *Women in the Wilderness*. New York: Harper and Row, 1980.

GEAR, KATHLEEN O'NEAL. "The Most Dynamic Hunting Duo," *Outdoor Life* (November 1988), 93–94, 114–18.

———— "Viva La Difference!" *Outdoor Life* (December 1986), 52–54.

GERO, JOAN M. AND MARGARET CONKEY, eds. *Engendering Archaeology: Women and Prehistory*. Oxford: Basil Blackwell, 1991.

GILLIGAN, CAROL. *In a Different Voice*. Cambridge and London: Harvard University Press, 1982.

GIMBUTAS, MARIJA. *Goddesses and Gods of Old Europe*. Berkeley: University of California Press, 1982.

———— *The Civilization of the Goddess*. San Francisco: HarperSanFrancisco, 1991.

———— *The Language of the Goddess*. San Francisco: HarperCollins, 1989.

CRAVES, ROBERT. *The Greek Myths*. Baltimore: Penguin Books, 1955.

———— *The White Goddess*. New York: Farrar, Straus and Giroux, 1948.

GRAY, ELIZABETH DODSON. *Green Paradise Lost*. Wellesley, Mass.: Roundtable Press, 1981.

———— "Nature as an Act of Imagination," *Woman of Power* 9 (Spring 1988), 18–21.

GRIFFIN, SUSAN. *Woman and Nature: The Roaring Inside Her*. New York: Harper Colophon Books, 1978.

HALL, HEIDI. "Never Give Up," *Turkey Hunting* (Spring 1994), 66–68.

HARAWAY, DONNA. *Primate Visions: Gender, Race and Nature in the World of Modern Science*. New York: Routledge, 1989.

HARRISON, SUE. *Mother Earth Father Sky*. New York: Avon Books, 1991.

HARROD, HOWARD. "Is There a Native American Environmental Ethic?" *The Spire 14*. Vanderbilt University and Oberlin Graduate School of Theology, 1991.

———— *Renewing the World: Plains Indian Religion and Morality*. Tempe, Arizona: University Press, 1987.

HEBERLEIN, T. A. "Changing Attitudes and Funding for Wildlife: Preserving the Sport Hunter," *Wildlife Society Bulletin* 19 (1991), 528–34.

HEMINGWAY, ERNEST. *Green Hills of Africa*. New York: Charles Scribner's Sons, 1953.

HOFFMANN, MERLE. "Do Feminists Need to Liberate Animals, Too?" *On The Issues* (Spring 1995), 18–21, 54–56.

HOLT, CRAIG. "Taking Aim at the Outdoor Life." *The Herald-Sun*, Durham, North Carolina (March 5, 1995), D11.

HOUSTON, PAM, ed. *Women on Hunting*. Hopewell, NJ: The Ecco Press, 1995.

HRDY, SARAH BLAFFER. *The Woman That Never Evolved*. Cambridge, Mass.: Harvard University Press, 1981.

INGOLD, TIM. *The Appropriation of Nature: Essays of Human Ecology and Social Relations*. Iowa City: University of Iowa Press, 1987.

——— *Evolution and Social Life*. New York: Cambridge University Press, 1986.

ISAAC, GLYNN. "The Food-Sharing Behavior of Protohominids," *Scientific American* (April 1976), 90–108.

JACKSON, ROBERT M. "The Characteristics and Formative Experiences of Female Deer Hunters," *Women in Natural Resources* 9:3, 17–21.

JAPENGA, ANN. "Would I Be Safer With a Gun?" *Health* (March/April 1994), 52–63.

JOHANSON, DONALD AND MAITLAND EDEY. *Lucy: The Beginning of Humankind*. New York: Simon and Schuster, 1981.

JOHANSON, DONALD, LENORA JOHANSON AND BLAKE EDGAR. *Ancestors: In Search of Human Origins*. New York: Villard Books, 1994.

JOHANSON, DONALD AND JAMES SHREEVE. *Lucy's Child: The Discovery of a Human Ancestor*. New York: William Morrow and Company, 1989.

JOHNSON, BUFFIE. *Lady of the Beasts: Ancient Images of the Goddess and Her Sacred Animals*. San Francisco: Harper and Row, 1981.

JOHNSON, OSA. *I Married Adventure*. Philadelphia: J. B. Lippincott Company, 1940.

——— *Four Years in Paradise*. Garden City, New York: Halcyon House, 1944.

JONES, ANN. "Living With Guns, Playing With Fire." *Ms.* (May/June 1994), 38–43.

Journal of the American Academy of Religion. Special Thematic Issue on "Religion and Food." Vol. LXIII: 3 (Fall 1995).

KATES, DON B., JR. *Guns, Murders and the Constitution: A Realistic Assessment of Gun Control*. Policy Briefing, Pacific Institute for Public Policy: February, 1990.

———, ed. *Restricting Handguns: The Liberal Skeptics Speak Out*. Croton-on-Hudson, N.Y.: North River Press, 1979.

——— "The Value of Civilian Handgun Possession as a Deterrent to Crime or a Defense Against Crime," *American Journal of Criminal Law* (Winter 1991), 113–167.

KAYE, ROGER. "Saving Geese, Saving Himself," *National Wildlife* (June/July 1995), 38–42.

KELLERMANN, A., AND D. REAY, "Protection or Peril? An Analysis of Firearms-Related Deaths in the Home," *New England Journal of Medicine* (1986), 1557–60.

KELLERMANN, A., AND J. MERCY. "Men, Women and Murder: Gender-Specific Differences in Rates of Fatal Violence and Victimization," *Journal of Trauma* (1992), 1–5.

KELLERMANN, A., ET AL. "Gun Ownership as a Risk Factor for Homicide in the Home," *New England Journal of Medicine* (1993), 1084–91.

——— "Suicide in the Home in Relationship to Gun Ownership," *New England Journal of Medicine* (1992), 467–72.

KELLERT, STEPHEN. "Attitudes and Characteristics of Hunters and Anti-Hunters and Related Policy Suggestions." A working paper presented to the Fish and Wildlife Service, US Department of the Interior (November 4, 1976).

——— *The Value of Life: Biological Diversity and Human Society.* Washington, DC: Island Press/Shearwater Books, 1996.

KELLERT, STEPHEN AND JOYCE K. BERRY. "Attitudes, Knowledge, and Behaviors Toward Wildlife as Affected by Gender," *Wildlife Society Bulletin* 15:3 (1987), 363–71.

KERENYI, KARL. *Dionysus: The Archetypal Image of Indestructible Life*, trans. Ralph Manheim. Princeton: Princeton University Press, 1976.

KERASOTE, TED. *Bloodties: Nature, Culture, and the Hunt.* New York: Random House, 1993.

KENT, SUSAN ed. *Farmers as Hunters: The Implications of Sedentism.* Cambridge University Press, 1989.

KLEINBAUM, ABBY WETTAN. *The War Against the Amazons.* New York: New Press/McGraw-Hill Book Company, 1983.

KOLODNY, ANNETTE. *The Land Before Her: Fantasy and Experience of the American Frontiers, 1630–1860.* Chapel Hill and London. The University of North Carolina Press, 1984.

——— *The Lay of the Land: Metaphor as Experience and History in American Life and Letters.* Chapel Hill: University of North Carolina Press, 1975

KOPEL, DAVID B., ed. *Guns: Who Should Have Them?* Amherst, N.Y.: Prometheus Books, 1995.

——— *The Samurai, The Mountie, and The Cowboy.* Amherst, N.Y.: Prometheus Books, 1992.

KRUTCH, JOSEPH WOOD. *The Great Chain of Life.* Boston: Houghton Mifflin, 1956.

LaBASTILLE, ANNE. *Women and Wilderness.* San Francisco: Sierra Club Books, 1980.

LA VALETTE, MARY DE. "Sanctus," reprinted in *Feminists for Animal Rights Newsletter* (Winter-Spring 1990), 12.

LEAKEY, RICHARD, E. AND ROGER LEWIN. *People of the Lake: Mankind and Its Beginnings.* New York: Doubleday, 1978.

LEE, RICHARD AND IRVEN DeVORE, eds. *Man the Hunter.* Chicago: Aldine Publishing Company, 1968.

LERNER, GERDA. *The Creation of Feminist Consciousness.* New York: Oxford University Press, 1993.

———— *The Creation of Patriarchy*. New York: Oxford University Press, 1986.

LEOPOLD, ALDO. *A Sand County Almanac*. New York: Ballatine Books, 1970.

LINTON, RALPH. *The Tree of Culture*. New York: Alfred A Knopf, 1955.

LOVELOCK, JAMES. *The Ages of Gaia: A Biography of our Living Earth* . New York: Bantam Books, 1988.

LUECK, DIANE HUMPHREY. "Women in the Outdoors," *Bowhunter* (June/July 1993), 47–49, 10.

MARKHAM, BERYL. *West With the Night*. San Francisco: North Point Press, 1983.

MERCHANT, CAROLYN. *The Death Of Nature: Women, Ecology and Scientific Revolution*. San Francisco: Harper and Row, 1980.

———— *Earthcare: Women and the Environment*. New York: Routledge, 1995.

———— *Ecological Revolutions: Nature, Gender and Science in New England*. Chapel Hill and London: University of North Carolina Press, 1989.

METZGER, BRUCE AND MICHAEL COOGAN, eds. *The Oxford Companion to the Bible*. New York: Oxford University Press, 1993.

MITCHELL, JOHN G. *The Hunt*. New York: Alfred Knopf, 1980.

MOON, WARREN G. *Ancient Greek Art and Iconography*. Madison: University of Wisconsin Press, 1983.

MORRIS, DESMOND. *The Animal Contract*. New York: Warner Books, 1990.

———— *The Naked Ape*. New York: McGraw-Hill, 1967.

MOWAT, FARLEY. *Never Cry Wolf*. New York: Bantam Books, 1979.

MURDOCK, GEORGE P. *Social Structure*. New York: The Free Press, 1949.

NASH, RODERICK FRAZIER. *The Rights of Nature: A History of Environmental Ethics*. Madison: University of Wisconsin Press, 1989.

NELSON, RICHARD. "Understanding Eskimo Science," *Audubon* (September/October 1993), 102–9.

NEUMANN, ERICH. *The Great Mother*. Trans. Ralph Manheim. Princeton: Princeton University Press, Bollingen Series XLVII, 1963.

NEWKIRK, INGRID AND C. BURNETT. "Animal Rights and the Feminist Connection," *Woman of Power* 9 (Spring 1988).

NILSSON, MARTIN. *A History of Greek Religion*. New York: W. W. Norton, 1964.

NORWOOD, VERA. *Made From This Earth: American Women and Nature*. Chapel Hill and London: University of North Carolina Press, 1993.

OELSCHLAEGER, MAX. *The Idea of Wilderness: From Prehistory to the Age of Ecology*. New Haven and London: Yale University Press, 1991.

————, ed. *The Wilderness Condition.* San Francisco: Sierra Club Books, 1992.

O'LEARY, J. T. ET AL., eds. *Proceedings: Natural Outdoor Recreation Trends Symposium III.* Lafayette, Ind.: Purdue University Department of Forestry and Natural Resources, 1990.

ORENSTEIN, GLORIA FEMAN. *The Reflowering of the Goddess.* New York: Pergamon Press, 1990.

OTTO, WALTER. *Dionysus: Myth and Cult.* Bloomington: Indiana University Press, 1995.

———— *The Homeric Gods: The Spiritual Significance of Greek Religion.* Trans. Moses Hadas. New York: Pantheon Books, 1954.

OUTDOOR RECREATION COMMISSION. *Hunting in the United States: Its Present and Future Role.* Washington, DC: US Government Printing Office, 1962.

PANTEL, PAULINE SCHMITT, ed. *A History of Women in the West: Volume I, From Ancient Goddesses to Christian Saints.* Cambridge, Mass.: The Belknap Press of Harvard University Press, 1992.

PARIS, GINETTE. *Pagan Meditations: The Worlds of Aphrodite, Artemis, and Hestia.* Trans. Gwendolyn Moore Dallas: Spring Publications, 1986.

PEMBROKE, SIMON. "Women in Charge: The Function of Alternatives in Early Greek Tradition and the Ancient Idea of Matriarchy," *Journal of the Warburg and Courtauld Institutes* 30 (1967).

PERLMAN, PAULA. "Acting the She-Bear for Artemis," *Arethusa* 22 (1989), 111–30.

PHILLIPS, JOHN A. *Eve: The History of an Idea.* San Francisco: Harper and Row, 1984.

PLANT, JUDITH, ed. *Healing the Wounds: The Promise of Ecofeminism.* Philadelphia: New Society Publishers, 1989.

PORTEFAIX, LILIAN. "Religio-ecological Aspects of Ancient Greek Religion from the Point of View of Woman; a Tentative Approach," *Temenos* 21 (1985), 144–51.

PORTER, ROY. *A Social History of Madness.* London: Weidenfeld and Nicholson, 1987.

PRATT, ANNIS. *Dancing With Goddesses: Archetypes, Poetry, and Empowerment.* Bloomington and Indianapolis: Indiana University Press, 1994.

PROSE, FRANCINE. *Hunters and Gatherers.* New York: Farrar, Straus and Giroux, 1995.

RAUCH,YVONNE M. "More Than the Kill," *Sports Afield* (September 1987), 154, 136.

REIGER, GEORGE. "Instinct and Reality," *Field and Stream* (September 1991), 12–15.

REITER, RAYNA R. ed. *Toward an Anthropology of Women.* New York: Monthly Review Press, 1975.

RENSBERGER, BOYCE. *The Cult of the Wild*. Garden City, New York: Anchor Press/Doubleday, 1977.

RICH, ADRIENNE. *Of Woman Born: Motherhood as Experience and Institution*. New York: W.W. Norton and Company, 1976.

RITVO, HARRIET. *The Animal Estate: The English and Other Creatures in the Victorian Age*. Cambridge, Mass.: Harvard University Press, 1987.

ROSALDO, MICHELLE. "The Use and Abuse of Anthropology: Reflections on Feminism and Cross-cultural Understanding," *Signs: Journal of Women in Culture and Society* 5:3 (1980), 389–417.

ROSALDO, MICHELLE ZIMBALIST, AND LOUISE LAMPHERE, eds. *Woman, Culture, and Society*. Pala Alto: Stanford University Press, 1974.

ROSE, H. J. *A Handbook of Greek Mythology*. New York: E.P. Dutton and Company, 1950.

RUETHER, ROSEMARY RADFORD. *Gaia and God: An Ecofeminist Theology of Earth Healing*. San Francisco: HarperCollins, 1992.

RUTHSTROM, ELLYN. "Feeling the Power of Nature," an interview with Carol B. Christ. *Woman of Power* 9 (Spring 1988), 22–24.

SACKS, KAREN. *Sisters and Wives: The Past and Future of Sexual Equality*. Westport, Conn.: Greenwood Press, 1979.

SANDAY, PEGGY REEVES. *Female Power and Male Dominance: On the Origins of Sexual Inequality*. Cambridge and New York: Cambridge University Press, 1981.

SANDS, KATHLEEN M. *Escape From Paradise: Evil and Tragedy in Feminist Theology*. Minneapolis: Fortress Press, 1994.

SCHAMA, SIMON. *Landscape and Memory*. New York: Alfred A. Knopf, 1995.

SCHIEBINGER, LONDA. *Nature's Body: Gender in the Making of Modern Science*. Boston: Beacon Press, 1993.

SCHLOSBERG, SUZANNE. "A Hunting She Will Go," *Women's Sports and Fitness* (March 1996), 55–57.

SCRIBNER, CHARLES, JR., ed. *The Enduring Hemingway*. New York: Scribner's and Sons, 1974.

SEED, JOHN, et al. *Thinking Like A Mountain: Towards a Council of All Beings*. Philadelphia: New Society Publishers, 1988.

SESSIONS, GEORGE, ed., *Deep Ecology for the Twenty-First Century*. Boston: Shambhala, 1995.

SETON, GRACE THOMPSON. *A Woman Tenderfoot*. New York: Doubleday, Page and Company, 1900.

SHEPARD, PAUL. *Nature and Madness*. San Francisco: Sierra Club Books, 1982.

———— *The Tender Carnivore and the Sacred Game*. New York: Charles Scribner's Sons, 1973.

———— "A Theory of the Value of Hunting," *Transactions of the Twenty-Fourth North American Wildlife Conference*. Washington, DC: American Wildlife Institute, 1959, 504–12.

SHIPMAN, PAT. "The Ancestor That Wasn't," *The Sciences* (March–April 1985), 43–48.

———— "Scavenger Hunt," *Natural History*, (April 1984), 20–27.

SINGER, PETER. *Animal Liberation*. New York: A New York Review Book, distributed by Random House, 1990.

SJOO, MONICA AND BARBARA MOR. *The Great Cosmic Mother: Rediscovering the Religion of the Earth*. San Francisco: HarperCollins, 1989.

SLOTKIN, RICHARD. *Gunfighter Nation: The Myth of the Frontier in Twentieth Century America*, New York: Atheneum, 1992.

SMITH, MICHELLE LEIGH. "Club of Legal Huntresses Kill to Network." *The National Law Review* (April 25, 1994), A10.

SNYDER, GARY. "Cultivating Wildness," *Audubon* (May–June 1995), 64–71.

———— *The Practice of the Wild*. New York: North Point Press/Farrar, Straus and Giroux, 1990.

SPIEGEL, MARJORIE. *The Dreaded Comparison: Human & Animal Slavery*. New York: Times Mirror Books, 1989.

SPRETNAK, CHARLENE. *Lost Goddesses of Early Greece*. Boston: Beacon Press, 1978.

STANGE, MARY ZEISS. "Arms and the Woman: A Feminist Reappraisal," In David Kopel, ed. *Guns: Who Should Have Them?* Amherst, N.Y.: Prometheus Books, 1995.

———— "Women Afield: The Invisible Hunters," *Sports Afield* (January 1994), 98–99.

———— "Women in the Woods," *Sports Afield* (June 1995), 100–3.

STARHAWK. *Dreaming the Dark*. Boston: Beacon Press, 1982.

———— *The Spiral Dance: A Rebirth of the Ancient Religion of the Great Goddess*. Boston: Beacon Press, 1989.

STEWART, ELEANOR PRUITT. *Letters on an Elk Hunt by a Woman Homesteader*. Lincoln and London: University of Nebraska Press, 1979.

SUTER, EDGAR A., M.D. "Guns in the Medical Literature—A Failure of Peer Review," *The Journal of the Medical Association of Georgia* (March, 1994), 133–48.

SWAN, JAMES A. *In Defense of Hunting*. San Francisco: HarperCollins, 1995.

TABET, PAOLA. "Hands, Tools, Weapons," *Feminist Issues* (Fall 1982), 3–62.

TAKSEL, REBECCA. "Feminists in the Making: Women Activists in the Animal Rights Movement," *Feminists for Animal Rights (FAR) Newsletter* (Fall–Winter 1991–1992), 4–5.

TANNER, NANCY AND ADRIENNE ZIHLMAN. "Women in Evolution. Part I: Innovation and Selection in Human Origins," *Signs: Journal of Women in Culture and Society* 1:3 (1976), 585–608.

THOMAS, CHRISTINE L. "They Became Outdoors Women," *Deer & Deer Hunting* (June 1992), 49–54.

THOMAS, CHRISTINE L. AND TAMMY A. PETERSON, "Becoming an Outdoors-Woman," *Women in Natural Resources* 15:3, 16–21.

———, eds. Conference Proceedings: "Breaking Down the Barriers to Participation of Women in Angling and Hunting." University of Wisconsin-Stevens Point, August 12, 1990.

THOMAS, ELIZABETH MARSHALL. *The Animal Wife*. Boston: Houghton Mifflin Company, 1990.

——— *Reindeer Moon*. New York: Pocket Books, 1991.

TIGER, LIONEL. *Men in Groups*. New York: Random House, 1971.

VERNANT, JEAN PIERRE. *Myth and Thought Among the Greeks*. London: Routledge and Kegan Paul, 1983.

WARREN, KAREN. "The Power and the Promise of Ecological Feminism," *Environmental Ethics* 23 (Summer 1990), 125–46.

"What Do Men Really Want? Now They Have a Movement of Their Own." *Newsweek* (June 24, 1991), 46–53.

WOLF, NAOMI. *Fire With Fire*. New York: Random House, 1993.

"Women's Participation in the Shooting Sports: Upward Trend Continues." National Shooting Sports Foundation Information Service (February 1995).

"WSSF Members: Why We Hunt." *Open Sights: Official Publication of the Women's Shooting Sports Foundation* (Fall 1995), 1–6.

YENDES, ALBERT. "Contrary to Popular Opinion," *Petersen's Hunting* (March 1993), 33–34.

ZIHLMAN, ADRIENNE. "Women in Evolution. Part II: Subsistence and Social Organizations among Early Hominids," *Signs: Journal of Women in Culture and Society* 4:1 (1978), 4–20.

Index

243

Library of Congress Cataloging-in-Publication Data

Stange, Mary Zeiss.
Woman the hunter / Mary Zeiss Stange.
p. cm.
Includes bibliographical references and index.
ISBN 0-8070-4638-8
1. Hunting—Philosophy.   2. Hunting—Moral and ethical aspects.
3. Women hunters.   4. Feminism.   I. Title.
SK14.S88   1997
306.3'64—dc20   96-39045